Postcolonialism and Religions

Series Editors
Joseph Duggan
Postcolonial Networks
San Francisco
California, USA

J. Jayakiran Sebastian
United Lutheran Seminary
Philadelphia
Pennsylvania, USA

The Postcolonialism and Religions series by its very name bridges the secular with the sacred through hybrid, interstitial, and contrapuntal inquiries. The series features the scholarship of indigenous scholars working at the intersections of postcolonial theories, theologies, and religions. The editors welcome authors around the world in an effort to move beyond and interrogate a historical North American and Euro-centric postcolonial studies disciplinary dominance. The series seeks to foster subaltern voices especially from Africa, Asia, Central and South America, and the liquid continent.

More information about this series at
http://www.springer.com/series/14535

Bernon Lee

Marginal(ized) Prospects through Biblical Ritual and Law

Lections from the Threshold

Bernon Lee
Bethel University
St. Paul, Minnesota, USA

Postcolonialism and Religions
ISBN 978-3-319-55094-7   ISBN 978-3-319-55095-4 (eBook)
DOI 10.1007/978-3-319-55095-4

Library of Congress Control Number: 2017939731

© The Editor(s) (if applicable) and The Author(s) 2017
This work is subject to copyright. All rights are solely and exclusively licensed by the Publisher, whether the whole or part of the material is concerned, specifically the rights of translation, reprinting, reuse of illustrations, recitation, broadcasting, reproduction on microfilms or in any other physical way, and transmission or information storage and retrieval, electronic adaptation, computer software, or by similar or dissimilar methodology now known or hereafter developed.
The use of general descriptive names, registered names, trademarks, service marks, etc. in this publication does not imply, even in the absence of a specific statement, that such names are exempt from the relevant protective laws and regulations and therefore free for general use.
The publisher, the authors and the editors are safe to assume that the advice and information in this book are believed to be true and accurate at the date of publication. Neither the publisher nor the authors or the editors give a warranty, express or implied, with respect to the material contained herein or for any errors or omissions that may have been made. The publisher remains neutral with regard to jurisdictional claims in published maps and institutional affiliations.

Cover illustration © ameya Natu / FOAP

Printed on acid-free paper

This Palgrave Macmillan imprint is published by Springer Nature
The registered company is Springer International Publishing AG
The registered company address is: Gewerbestrasse 11, 6330 Cham, Switzerland

For Connie, Zechariah, and Mattya

Acknowledgments

This book began in the course of a major revision of a dissertation submitted to the Toronto School of Theology at the University of Toronto. In plodding along, I realized that my emerging vision for that work was leading to *another* book altogether—a (sometimes) happy circumstance not uncommon for writers, I'm told. And so I released for publication the dissertation with revisions of a more modest scale, and embarked with earnest on my new quest. My fascination with biblical prescription and the theoretical speculations of Wolfgang Iser are the two tethers to the earlier project. Then came a later shift in direction that almost prompted the genesis of a *third* work. I am happy to report that, this time, a desire to escape the charge of inveterate irresolution prevailed, and I persisted in the project in one piece. The fresh insight, if indeed insightful, would just have to wait. A shot of good sense in good time, one might say.

Through the twists of the road, many have aided in the book's precarious development. Earlier versions of its chapters were aired at various meetings of the Society of Biblical Literature (SBL). The Asian and Asian American Hermeneutics Section of the 2013 meeting of the society in Baltimore, Maryland, heard parts of Chapter 5, as did the Asian Perspectives in Biblical Studies, Theology, and Religious Studies group gathered in St. Paul, Minnesota, for the Upper Mid-West Region meeting of the same society in the following year. Peers coming together at the Postcolonial Studies and Biblical Studies Section of the society's national meeting in San Diego, California (November 2014), responded to what is now a portion of the fourth chapter. I am grateful for the queries and suggestions at these venues that have stimulated my thinking and pressed me toward clarity and precision in the execution of my task.

Chapter 2 is an updated and expanded form of "'Face to Face': Moses as Prophet in Exodus 11:1-12:28" in the volume *Prophets, Prophecy, and Ancient Israelite Historiography* (Eisenbrauns, 2013). I am grateful for the editorial ministrations of Mark Boda and Lissa Wray Beal in bringing that essay to completion. Thanks are due, also, to Jim Eisenbraun for the permission to reuse this material in the current volume.

In Baltimore, at the SBL meeting of 2013, I had the pleasure and the good fortune of meeting J. Jayakiran Sebastian. Kiran, as coeditor of the Postcolonialism and Religions Series (of Palgrave Macmillan) with Joseph Duggan (the founding editor of the series and the guiding hand behind the reconciling ministry of Postcolonial Networks), encouraged me to explore publication through the series. Together, their felicitations and facilitations have buoyed the spirits of this neophyte writer. Thank you, Joe and Kiran!

At times the technical aspects of getting a manuscript in order were daunting. The cheery, patient, and prompt guidance of, first, Alexis Nelson and, then, Amy Invernizzi saved me from several missteps.

No sustained writing engagement, of course, is possible without time tucked away in libraries and behind closed doors. For this I am thankful to the College of Arts and Sciences at Bethel University for three terms of leave from teaching and faculty governance—two January terms in 2013 and 2017, and the Spring semester of 2015. The college, also, was generous in the offer of a Faculty Development Grant in 2013, as was the Bethel University National Alumni Association with a Faculty Grant in the same year.

Angela Shannon, Scott Winter, Thomas Becknell, and Gary Long read portions of the manuscript. Jione Havea, Corrine Carvalho, and Mark Brett read the work in its entirety. Their critical prodding has sharpened the final product. Its remaining flaws, of course, are my responsibility.

My family has been most gracious in putting up with my suspended attention at the dining table and elsewhere. My wife Connie's sustained humor and compassion, as always, were a balm through bouts of uncertainty in the undertaking. Zechariah and Mattya, our children, offered gibes of good nature through spells of misplaced, not to mention audible, rumination: 'Mum, Daddy's whispering again!' I cherish these times. Connie, Zechariah, and Mattya, our life together is the measure of my joy, and I ask your pardon for the days I've been less able to see that. I dedicate this book to you.

Contents

1. Introduction: A Prologue to *Wandering* — 1
2. Staying In: The Moses-God Exchanges on the Passover — 25
3. On Sacred Heads and Sullied Wombs: Bouncing Between Leviticus and Numbers — 55
4. On Bad Sex and Bad Seed: Doubting Deuteronomy — 107
5. Coming Home: Through the Doors of Ephraim and Egypt — 155
6. Epilogue: Scenes from Afar — 211

Index — 217

List of Abbreviations

AHw   Wolfram Von Soden, ed. *Akkadisches Handwörterbuch*. 3 vols. Wiesbaden: Otto Harrassowitz, 1965–1981.
BDB   Francis Brown, S.R. Driver and Charles A. Briggs. *A Hebrew and English Lexicon of the Old Testament*. Oxford: Oxford University Press, 1907.
CAD   Leo Oppenheim et al., ed. *The Assyrian Dictionary of the Oriental Institute of the University of Chicago*. Chicago: The Oriental Institute of the University of Chicago, 1956–2006.
DCH   David J.A. Clines, ed. *Dictionary of Classical Hebrew*. 9 vols. Sheffield: Sheffield Phoenix Press, 1993–2014.
HALOT   Ludwig Koehler, Walter Baumgartner, M.E.J. Richardson and Johann Jakob Stamm, ed. *The Hebrew and Aramaic Lexicon of the Old Testament*, trans. M.E.J. Richardson. 5 vols. Leiden: Brill, 1994–2000.
NRSV   New Revised Standard Version
TDOT   G. Johannes Botterweck et al., ed. *Theological Dictionary of the Old Testament*, trans. J.T. Willis, G.W. Bromiley and D.E. Green. 15 vols. Grand Rapids, MI: Eerdmans, 1974–2006.
TWOT   R. Laird Harris, Gleason L. Archer, Jr. and Bruce K. Waltke, ed. *Theological Wordbook of the Old Testament*. 2 vols. Chicago: Moody, 1980.

A Note on Transliteration and Translation

In the interest of ameliorating the experience of the nonspecialist reader, I have kept citations of texts in Hebrew (and other Semitic tongues) to a minimum. There are times, however, when lexicographical details or points of grammar are relevant to the argument at hand. Then, I have confined myself to referring to the transliterated values of the consonantal text, almost exclusively. In transliteration, I have followed the standard systematized practices of the Society of Biblical Literature's Handbook of Style (see Sections 5.1.1.1–2 of the second edition).

All texts in the ancient languages are accompanied by translations in English. With few exceptions (and then only for the sake of precision in making a point), I have stuck with the translations of the New Revised Standard Version (NRSV).

CHAPTER 1

Introduction: A Prologue to *Wandering*

Cheryl Anderson's introductory anecdote to her volume on the interpretation of biblical law resonates with me.[1] She tells of a student's encounter with the diminutive and harsh biblical vision on slaves and women, an in-class orchestrated engagement designed to drive home the need for an equitable spirit of emancipation in biblical interpretation. Anderson's ploy, in this instance, backfires. The lexical odyssey through scenes of rape, pillage, and violence against slaves and other powerless groups only arouses the student's defensive ire. Apparently, her membership in a historically oppressed group—the student was an African American female in the United States—barely puts a dent in her Christian zeal to find unambiguous authority in the words of the Holy Scriptures. Her religious commitments trump any suggestion that the oppressively discriminatory tune to the text is anything less than consonant with the judicious, even compassionate, auspices of a sovereign deity. 'This is the Word of God,' the student ejaculates. 'If it says slavery is okay, slavery is okay.' Even rape, by this student's estimation, must not be as offensive as it seems! The same defensive, even pugnacious, habits of mind inhabit my classroom. My bodacious attempts to inject a modicum of disturbance in the minds of my students to arouse a taste for critical engagement are shorn of their subversive tones and the texts, ever so gently, fall in tune with the steady, placid tempo of a narrative of divine 'justice and compassion' playing and replaying in the minds of my interlocutors. The rough bits of the story are but manifestations of the deity's 'tough love.' Evidently, Anderson's assessment of such readings hits the mark. Readers imbibe of the ethos of their formative communities, discerning well the perspectives to ignore and—I would add—those to embrace.[2] There seems a stolid resilience to the orientation of a reader in acts of interpretation, a stalwart directionality *in spite* of the texts. Seemingly dissonant elements of the canon, if encountered, are re-visioned and set in line with the dominant (and domineering) ideological imagination of the community. No word strays from the paradigm. What seems to me a delectably ambivalent work—and here I betray my propensities—dons a monochromatic hue. Texts, then, are pliable and amenable to an ascribed angle of vision.

What Is This Book About?

At the most abstract level, this book argues for a stance to reading that is ubiquitous, commonplace. 'Wandering' in the title to the introduction has reference to Wolfgang Iser's 'wandering viewpoint.' The phrase encodes a wilfulness to reading which is at the heart of this study and Anderson's anecdote.[3] It denotes the active, evolving ideational consciousness so essential to computations of 'meaning' in reading. The wandering viewpoint plies the spaces between texts. It rests in that fecund liminal space between reader and text. Restless, it moves in various and unpredictable directions, choosing from a range of strategies in posing connections between texts. The wandering viewpoint, like that of my students and Anderson's (I presume), is selective in its views to the text. It embraces some, dismisses others, and keeps even more in suspended abeyance, always flirting with fresh possibilities with emerging data in a dynamic continuum. The putative connections across a work, often aided by malleable lexical and grammatical features in texts, color the perception of the parts, marshaling the tropes that lend a sense of conformity to the projected 'whole.' But all constructs of meaning and their attendant strategies are vulnerable—certainly, the irritation of Anderson's student bespeaks an awareness of such—and subject to ongoing revision. Reflective readers, though willful, remain mindful (if grudgingly) of their conditioned and tentative positions. An air of reticence affects the wandering viewpoint's surveillance, even as it asserts its predilection for blindness to alternative viewpoints. The viewpoint wonders in wandering. This playful, prejudicial, yet mutating disposition of readers, I argue, is essential to interpretation.

This very stance governs the interpretation of select portions of (mostly) ritual and law in the Hebrew Bible. But 'wandering' (back to the title of this introductory chapter)—the term is apropos given the methodological positioning—denotes *also* the context for Mosaic legislation: Israel's sojourning between Egypt and the divinely sanctioned homeland. The reference to the locus (the 'threshold' of Israelite homes in Egypt) of the Passover sacrifice in the subtitle to the volume, the event at the beginning of Israel's journey, has the same function. The Pentateuch is home to the four passages of prescribed ritual and law that are of interest to this study: roughly, Exodus 11–13, Leviticus 21–22, Numbers 5–6, and Deuteronomy 22–24. A single selection of narrative from the prophetic corpus (Judg 19)—the sole digression from biblical law in the Pentateuch—enters the mix for its interaction (my imputed connection) with the tropes and the topoi of the aforementioned texts. This book—cumulative to my introductory statement so far—brings an active readerly imagination to tracing a network of rites and rituals regarding election, sacred personages, pristine spaces, offerings, vows, and sexual/marital protocols. The wandering viewpoint bounces between the guarded uterus and the hazard-free interior spaces of Israel's homes, between the pure precincts of Israel's camp and the sanctity of the Levites, between the immaculate form of sacrificial donations and the exclusionary logic to the constitution of the assembly. Relentlessly, the spectral spectrum of the associative imaginary covers also the virulent hazards to the esteemed entities: the malevolent nocturnal energies of Egypt and Gibeah, scabs and damaged testicles, profane diners, 'whoring' daughters, human excrement, bastard races, assertive wives, and decaying bodies. The legislative curbs survey all things unseemly (not to mention contagious) and beyond ancient Israel's moral, cultic, and aesthetic taste. This brief study, therefore, attends to the articulation of a matrix of dichotomies germane to laws that underwrite the conception of Israelite identity and to the genesis of equivalences—the points of perceivable similarity—under the auspices of a binary optic that straddles these texts.

My wrestling with law and ritual, in course, is imbricated within a hermeneutic of decolonization. Specific emancipative positions of reading come into focus. Of interest are strains gathered under the penumbra of postcolonial theory, feminist criticism, and Asian American hermeneutics. The adopted construct of an 'active ideational consciousness' to the interrogation of ritual and law, to put it another way, is cathected by the proclivities of and the attendant methodologies inherent to these intellectual stances. The counter-hegemonic ethos (of the specified species) animates the readerly disposition that meets the laws and rituals of our particular texts. Called into question is the facile assimilation of the analogical imaginary to the segregationist optic of gendered and racialized hierarchies that inhabit these texts. The suppressed infelicities in the invented schemes of the wandering viewpoint—the metonymic transfers of the associative sensibility—return to haunt fence-building identity formations across the canonized discourses in view. Can eugenics, genealogical purity, secure moral character? Might the entrenched binarisms to a narrative sustain a dominant assessment of a character's moral disposition? The vaunted assemblage of tropes across texts, then, becomes the path for a deconstructive valence in the interest of Majority World feminist critique and Asian American biblical interpretation. The work is, at last, an intertextual scrutiny of the recessed spaces and prized entities in legal discourse *through* the lens(es) of counter-imperialistic interpretive modes.

In sum, I cultivate and articulate a hermeneutic of reticence in forging connections between clusters of prescriptive discourse on exclusive entities and spaces, in moving toward engagements with postcolonial studies, feminist criticism, and Asian American hermeneutics.

But Why (these Texts of) Law and Ritual? Why a Decolonizing Hermeneutic?

It is fitting that a book privileging readerly inclination and whim should proffer a tale of a writer-reader's journey in the way of an apology for the scope of the project. My initiation into academe had aroused in me a taste for reading biblical ritual and law.[4] A stolen hour spent perusing various passages of such generic variety is not uncommon. On more than one such occasion, my interest was piqued by the *sensation* of familiarity in making my way through the hodgepodge collection of prescriptions to Numbers 5–6. This, in itself, is not remarkable. It is well known that the various bodies of law in the Bible recycle subject matter in their course and that the biblical corpus is the effect of a process of literary growth and editorial accretion. Much ink, indeed, is spilt in deciphering the direction of literary influence across the Pentateuch's bodies of legal promulgation. The detection of inner-biblical commentary and allusion, what Daniel Boyarin terms, in addressing the phenomenon of midrash, the 'voiceless subservience' to an 'anterior text' with a 'slightly altered meaning' that 'both continues and breaches the tradition,' is *de rigueur* in Hebrew Bible studies.[5] The sensation of a tour through a house of mirrors in reading biblical law is to be expected. What stood out to me, on the particular occasion in question, was the invocation of a *cluster* of topoi, a consecutive series of laws guarding sacred and exclusive entities, lodged in my memory. More specifically, the prescriptions of Numbers 5–6 regarding sacred donations, sexual impropriety, corpse contagion, sacred anatomies, and vows mimic, *mutatis mutandis,* the menu of concerns germane to the prescriptive corpus of Leviticus 21–22. The link seemed that much stronger for the near identical delineations of the Nazirite and priestly sacred forms (compare Lev 21:10–12 and Num 6:6–8). The strong resemblance across a distance impelled me—I'm not the first—to closer inspection.[6] At the time I was concerned less with the significance of the intertextual link—that came later—than with the quality of the experience aroused by the *sensation* of familiarity; the sheer elation in stumbling upon a (not so) subtle echo of a previous iteration and the affect it had on me. The analogical imagination to biblical law—an argument of Mary Douglas—came to the fore in my apperception of a metonymic logic to the construal of the exclusive elements and spaces across the texts.[7] Legal reasoning in this vein is relational. The rationale for one prescription is its resemblance to another. Correlation is systemic and its movements are a hermeneutical habit inhabiting the whole. Immersed in the Douglasesque view to law and ritual, I proceeded to read across these texts with an eye to the genesis of meaning(s) in a given text infected by traces of others in my memory. My being, it seemed to me, was baptized in the experience, one that birthed a strain of readerly productivity I could faint resist. I was consumed less by the 'veracity' of the intratextual nexus than by the consciousness of a new consciousness and its lust for detecting ever more literary resonances. A hunger was born, and it proceeded to interrogate, to devour, the (then) seemingly similar bevy of topical vignettes of Deuteronomy 22–24. At about the same time, I became intrigued by the idea of the gruesome story of the rape of the Levite's wife in Judges 19 as a troubling seconding of the tale of Israel's deliverance (in Exod 11–12)—the construction of an intertextual connection aided by the similar fixation on 'doorways' and the binary vision to the construal of the spaces on either side. The story of Israel's deliverance in Exodus would prove the link to the larger project on the elected passages of Leviticus, Numbers, and Deuteronomy. The point of contact is the context for the series of rulings of Numbers 5–6: the election and the installation of the Levites and its prescriptive rhetoric of a correspondence to the divine election of

Israel in the Exodus story (Num 8:16–19). As God laid claim to Egypt's and Israel's firstborns, so God takes the Levites for the sanctuary. Numbers (1–9), by my view, proves the lynchpin that holds the complex of ritual, law, and storytelling together.

The details of the (imagined) literary correspondences and the significances they set off are the stuff of this book. Many pages shall be devoted to fleshing out the minutiae of the analogical vision between the texts. The initial spark that fires the work, though, is my absorption with the reader's spectral perturbation in the experience of *déjà vu* in a phrase, a proposition, a trope, the assonance of an earlier thought. The salient aspect to my memory of that experience is the ephemeral quality to the schematic construct of the imaginary that would straddle the distance between texts. It seems, here, that phantasmagoria reigns. As compelling the associations seem, the feeling of a seamless, flawless fit is elusive, fleeting. The contrived juxtapositions reveal *likenesses*, nothing more, nothing less. Close inspection brings to light gaps in the associative logic. The reader's ideation teeters between assurance—the low-hanging fruit of a totalizing framework—and the despair of a haphazard chaos. Will the correspondence hold? This book, concisely stated, attempts a description of this sense and sensibility in encounters with law and ritual. The project turns on projections of *meaning* and their failures, the satisfaction of the semblance of unity and the frustration of diffusion.

But I must not get too far into the details of the project at this point. There will be time for that. I mean to provide here only an account of how I came upon the endeavor and to underscore the serendipitous nature of the way to the texts of interest. A consequence of this last fact is that the study does not exhaust the texts of the Hebrew Bible in connection with the subject matter in discussion. These are the passages that presented themselves to my imagination in the course of my encounters. Certainly, a treatment of all texts with bearing on the thematic matter of the choice passages is beyond the realm of possibility for a little book as this.

Happenstance is not insignificant too in the choosing of a decolonizing optic. The matter of 'positioning' in the interpretive task is central to my argument. The situated perspective(s) of the reader is the fecund locus for the genesis of fresh trajectories in the experience of texts. My situated perspective is a sensibility formed in post-colonial Singapore. Born of southern Chinese extract and raised in the environment (then invisible to me) of a Confucian(ist) ethos, I attended a school founded by Western missionaries of the Methodist Church. On Founder's Day, we'd sing of the 'dauntless hero' who came 'from western shores' to found here 'a Beacon of Truth and Light.' Its brilliance would draw many sons from 'India's strand,' 'China's shores,' and 'the Land of Rising Sun.' The fervent desire to the tune is that 'our hearts, our hopes, our aims are one.' That 'heart' was one nurtured on a steady diet of a romanticized vision toward Western norms and ideals. The school's traditions, in capturing the cultural diversity to the region under the broad umbrella of an Anglo-Scottish mold, arguably, repeated the patterns and practices of English colonialism. While inclusive of the Malay, Indian, and Chinese strands of the conglomerate culture of the island state, there was—if only to my imagination—an unspoken, but clarion, summon to the sensibility of an Anglo-European ethos that superintended the diversity. The winds of colonialism—a decade after England's departure—filled the sails of school spirit, its appeal heightened, perhaps, by the absence of the protean manifestations of British colonial arrogance and segregationist policy. The lure of the Occident seemed ubiquitous. Unquestionably—certainly, I never posed the question—the path to Albion's shores was the way of progress, and many a pilgrim took the high road to Britain's fine schools of tertiary education. My imagination cast in such context rendered *mimicry*—Homi Bhabha's articulation of that 'complex strategy of reform, regulation and discipline, which "appropriates" the Other as it visualizes power'—a felicitous path.[8] The cultural hybridity that attends mimicry is 'a process of splitting as the condition of subjection,' a 'discrimination between a mother culture and its bastards, the self and its doubles.'[9] Moreover, the cultural orientation 'disavowed is not repressed but repeated as something *different*—a mutation, a hybrid.'

My heart is cleft. It is the site of contestation, a place where cultural vectors envision and re-vision one another. Here, the familiar warmness of a Southeast Asian inflection of Chinese culture coincides with the unmistakable traces of Anglophilia. The aftermath of English colonialism and the persistence of Anglo-American hegemony are never far from my imagination. They stoke a fascination for power differentials in articulations of culture, for the persistence of the construction of hybrid identities in communities of diaspora, for the contestations of subordinated groups in metropolitan spaces. The jaundiced and ambivalent subaltern mien is mine. Mine is the sense of a life lived under strange, yet familiar, social mores of distant origin, received darkly through translation. True to the fundament of the project—reading as a subjective affair—I read from where I sit, through my lenses, chosen and imposed. This volume (perhaps, unfortunately so for the reader) is about me as much as it is of the aforementioned subject interests.

METHODOLOGICAL CONSIDERATIONS

My thinking on interpretation is shot through with traces of Roland Barthes, Mikhail Bakhtin, and Wolfgang Iser. Iser, in particular, informs and expresses well my instincts in the practice of reading. I am not the first to see the relevance of Iser's theorizing for biblical interpretation, and I am confident that I shan't be the last.[10] This book is not intended to be a comprehensive demonstration of Iser's theories in a reading of biblical law. An exhaustive description of his theoretical apparatus, then, is unnecessary. My purpose at this juncture is something of a confession. It is the circumscription of the disingenuous notion that a *tabula rasa* on matters theoretical precedes my analysis. I offer, merely, a brief account of salient points—the parts most relevant to my deliberations—in Iser's learned description and assessment of the mechanics of reading as a disclosure of the methodological sinews to my project.

Reading, by Iser's insistence, is an affective affair.[11] The experience stands in the liminal space between text and reader, betwixt the verbal and the ideational dimension to the experience. The phenotypical traits of texts—its grammatical formations and lexical features—guide interpretation; but the activity of the reader, with her attendant proclivities, remains an operation in the virtual space *above* the text. Reading is an aesthetic—and 'ecstatic' to the text!—experience. Indeed, for Iser, to speak of an aesthetic to reading 'is an embarrassment to referential language, for it designates a gap in the defining qualities of language rather than a definition.'[12] Reading is the reader's closure of those gaps. It is a *response* to the verbal text, a succession of inferences by which 'meaning'—the illusion of an aesthetic object that hovers just over the text—is the accomplishment *through* texts. A corollary to the foregoing proposition is the eschewal of a singular, pristine aesthetic object to the interpreter's quest. Interpretation is not an excavation of texts in the quest for a singular gem buried in verbal tissue. It is, rather, a production in the liminal space between texts and between text and reader. The interpreter's task in these interstitial gaps, therefore, 'should be to elucidate the *potential meanings* of a text, and not restrict herself to just one.'[13]

In other words, the passage from 'potential' to meaning(s) is an act of translation.[14] It is the reader's navigation of the chasm between the subject matter of a text and her elected framework(s) and register(s): the exigencies of the community, the 'viewpoints and the assumptions that provide the angle from which the subject matter is approached.'[15] The work comes to life, so it seems, buoyed by the readerly animus. The complexity to the endeavor, in fact, is a 'diversifying' of 'the framework into which the subject matter is transposed.' The registers, or the frameworks,

> not only change but are fine-tuned in each act of interpretation. Such reciprocity indicates that interpretation takes place within historical situations that we cannot get out of. Whenever we translate something into something else, the register is nothing but the bootstraps by which we pull ourselves up toward comprehension.[16]

Cast in such terms reading is more a performance and less an explanation. The feat is a reciprocal, mutual agitation of text and reader in which the shifting interests of the reader's contemporary interests are integral.[17] As the situation changes, the register morphs. The reader's disposition, her or his affective states, is inseparable from interpretation.

This subjective dynamism to the translation project is essential to the reader's process through the work. The vehicle for the oscillation betwixt the verbal and the aesthetic *through* a work, in Iser's parlance, is the 'wandering viewpoint.'

The 'Wandering Viewpoint' and the Dynamics of Reading

Iser's postulation of a 'wandering viewpoint' through texts is his alternative to the classical construct of a subject-object relationship to interpretation. 'Meaning,' the constituted aesthetic object in a reader's imagination, is not a static given in the work, but is, rather, a chameleonic entity born of a series of consecutive perspectives: the reader's fumbling for an elusive object in phases.[18] Apperception is a procession of views, readerly productions in turn; none of which are properly representative of the aesthetic object. The configuration at every turn is but 'a *pars pro toto* fulfillment of the text.'[19] The lust for a consistent pattern reveals always 'other impulses which cannot be immediately integrated or will even resist final integration.'[20] A sensation of partial vacuity attends the imagination at every phase.[21] This evolving viewpoint sits at the point of intersection between retention and pretension. Governed by this very logic, the components to a paragraph—sentences—are a microcosm for the infrastructure of the larger work. Iser's view is that the correlate to a sentence

> prefigures a particular horizon, but is immediately transformed into the background for the next correlate and must therefore be modified. Since each sentence correlate aims at things to come, the prefigured horizon will offer a view which—however concrete it may be—must contain indeterminacies, and so arouse expectations as to the manner in which these are to be resolved.[22]

Always transcended by the object, the wandering viewpoint traverses a tension that necessitates continuous acts of synthesis bridging freshly concocted perspectives with one's past. Elements in view stimulate the recall of past perspectives, which are modified in light of fresh data. The modified views pass, then, into retention in the anticipation of fresh turns of plot. Flux is the stuff of reading, and the wandering viewpoint is the moving locus of the reading subject.

There is, of course, a skittish disposition to the wandering viewpoint. Neither confined to a singular perspective nor to the strict sequential order of the work, readers respond to stimuli in summoning contrived perspectives of varying distance from their present place in the work. This movement of the wandering viewpoint between perspectives is bidirectional.[23] While the lexical flow throws earlier views into relief, the reader's retrogressive glance may reverse the view, recalling a previous perspective with the 'present' as backdrop. The backward looping wandering viewpoint is, in this manner, quite capable of shifting the spotlight in retrieving a perspective for *reconsi*deration. Influence is a two-way street. The perspectives embedded in memory remain available for second and third readings in accordance with the whims of readers. And a second reading, so Iser emphasizes, 'will never have the same effect as the first, for the simple reason that the originally assembled meaning is bound to influence the second reading.'[24] Second glances are modifications of first ones, not original productions but belated projections of consistency. The reader's wandering viewpoint enacts a reciprocal modification that is potentially subversive of any point of view in the unfolding work. Posterity by lexical order is not necessarily privileged.

The operative assumption to Iser's view on interpretation is the ineluctable drive for consistency across the correlates to a work. At heart is a propensity for 'consistency-building' that forms the platform of a wandering viewpoint's interrogation of works at the convergence of memory and expectation.[25] The incessant activity of moderation germane to the composition of perspectives—the postulation of equivalences between units of text at the numerous phases of perceived perspicuity—is the prerogative of the reader, albeit a response to signals in texts. The reader's conception of consonance, of a grand gestalt across an otherwise unwieldy series of literary segments, is 'a product of the interaction between text and reader, and, being so, cannot be *exclusively traced back either to the written text or to the disposition of the reader*.'[26] The interpretive task, by Iser's insistence, is dialectical. The text-ward movement in the dialectic is the reader's endowment of 'the linguistic signs with their significance' through the concatenated series of postulated designs to the work.[27] The subjective input flows into the given framework of the text, 'as if the schema were a hollow form into which the reader is invited to pour *his own* knowledge.'[28] So crucial is consistency-building to reading that Iser hazards the guess that a reader would set down a book where no semblance of coherence is forthcoming.[29] Comprehension is but a coerced coherence. The operation is not unlike the pleasure of finding patterns in the stars of the night sky.[30]

Star gazing, of course, entertains one pattern at a time; so too consistency-building. The consequent foreclosure of alternative interpretive rubrics to the polyvalent text is the flipside to the selectivity of the wandering viewpoint in readerly productions. The business of gestalt forming necessitates, nothing less, 'selections in favor of specific connections.'[31] Such determinations of equivalence are *also* acts of exclusion. The narrowing view to the text is but the reader's investment in the signifiers of the text. Text and reader, reader and text, are enmeshed. This discriminatory aspect to interpretation is not beyond the ken of readers ensnarled in the task. The import of Iser's observations on this point warrants scrutiny.

> Through gestalt forming, we actually participate in the text, and this means that we are caught up in the very thing we are producing... This entanglement brings out another quality of illusion, different from that which we considered in our discussion of consistency-building. There the illusory factor was that gestalten represented totalities in which possible connections

between signs had been sufficiently reduced for the gestalt to be closed. Here illusion means our own projections which are our share in gestalten which we produce and in which we are entangled. This entanglement, however, is never total, because the gestalten remain at least potentially under attack from those possibilities which they have excluded but dragged along in their wake. Indeed, the latent disturbance of the reader's involvement produces a specific form of tension that leaves him suspended, as it were, between total entanglement and latent detachment. The result is a dialectic—brought about by the reader himself—between illusion-forming and illusion-breaking... The conflict can only be resolved by the emergence of a third dimension, which comes into being through the reader's continual oscillation between involvement and observation. It is in this way that the reader experiences the text as a living event. The event links together all the contrary strands of the gestalten, and it takes on its essential openness by making manifest those possibilities which have been excluded by the selection process and which now exert their influence on these closed gestalten.[32]

The illusory gaze of Iser's reader is a vulnerable optic to texts fraught with pitfalls. The works traversed are filled with indices to other angles on the text, constant temptations to alternative strategies in the computation of meaning. Insight is at once willed certainty and frail construct, the site of dogmatic tenacity and interpretive anxiety. (Recall here the vulnerable decidedness of Cheryl Anderson's student.) This entanglement of the reader in the text, I think, bears elaboration. The mechanics of the wandering perspective come to light in a focused consideration of the triggers of a reader's ideation: the text's stimuli to consistency-building.

Of Stimulants, Gaps, and Blanks

The primary locus of readerly productivity is the 'blank' in the text. The term 'designates a vacancy in the overall system of the text, the filling of which brings about an interaction of textual patterns.'[33] It is an indeterminacy of the relationship between perceived segments of text. The completion of the nexus, the filling of the blank, thus calls for an act of combination. By this view, the drive for connection *is* the wandering viewpoint's quest for consistency. Blanks, to put it another way, are disturbances to consistency-building—blockages to the reader's productivity in ideation—in that they 'break up the connectability of the schemata.'[34] The work's blanks, if the fruit of authorial or editorial intent, are structured irritations and challenges for the ruthlessly harmonizing logic of comprehension. But for Iser they can hardly be considered shortcomings in the interpretive enterprise. Blanks, for him, are spurs to imagination, goads to explore the myriad possibilities in reading. They summon the mind's mobilization of a range of strategies for completion.

The perception of blanks proliferates at the points of abrupt transition in works: stark shifts in literary genre, ruptures in chronology, the inception a novel topos, and the conveyance of readers to fresh sites stocked with new characters.[35] Numbers 5 is a case in point. The passage, at a glance, is a patchwork of disparate rulings on a range of issues: campsite purity (1–4), restitution for the breach of trust (5–10), and a case of suspected adultery (11–31). The chapter as a whole is an abrupt departure from the enumeration of the Levites (Num 4:1–49). What have these things to do with each other? The enigma is an affront to consistency-building.

The same assiduous attention pertains to other obstacles to consistency. Unmotivated actions in a tale, unexplained departures from perceived norms, and contradictions to a reader's understanding of plot all provoke similar responses from the ideational faculties of the wandering viewpoint.[36] The gaps to a work's edifice undermine readers' projections of a gestalt and arouse 'feelings of exasperation.'[37] The incongruities, for any one of the reasons stated, elicit conjecture—the marshaling of signifiers into patterns congruent with projected gestalten. Blanks and gaps, together, are the missing links in the quest for a consistent story.

Where obstructions to consistency-building persist readers stave off surrender, by Frank Kermode's assessment, in the belief in 'the existence of other satisfactions, deeper and more difficult.'[38] The disappointment of 'conventional expectations' is but the promise of profundity. Granting that the existence of dissonant elements may signal a quest for verisimilitude—mimicking the randomness of life—Kermode's proposition, nevertheless, assumes modern criticism's abhorrence for incidental details in literary works.[39] The absence of consistency is but the invitation *to look harder*. Surely, an obscure detail somewhere, explicit or implicit, holds the key to a seamless fabula. The logic to storytelling demands a plausible solution to the conundrum. Kermode's reader, clearly, possesses the Iserian lector's penchant for consistency.

But what is the source for the wandering viewpoint's projections of order? For Iser, it is the *repertoire*. Its stock is 'all the familiar territory within the text': works within the referential system of the text; the work's historical and social norms; indeed, 'the whole culture from which the text has emerged.'[40] Foremost, perhaps, is the range of literary patterns to the work, the constructs of order within a work and its generic norms.[41] In the narratives of the Pentateuch, we might consider, for example, the familiar cadences of the courtship tales or the repeated deceptive maneuvers of the patriarchs in passing a wife off as a sister. Access to the repertoire is the reader's privilege and prerogative. The reading subject—Roland Barthes puts it well—approaches the text 'already itself a plurality of other texts, of codes which are infinite, or more precisely, lost (whose origin is lost).'[42] The text may be the playground where 'multiple writings, proceedings from several cultures' enter 'into dialogue, into parody, into contestation.'[43] But, Barthes insists that the collation of this multiplicity is not the labor of the author, but the reader: 'that *someone* who holds collected into one and the same field all of the traces from which writing is constituted.'[44] Such allusions are grist for interpretive strategies that set the familiar to the unfamiliar, the *strangeness* of a work before the reader. In this back-and-fro between text and reader, the elements of the repertoire

> are continually backgrounded or foregrounded with a resultant strategic overmagnification, trivialization, or even annihilation of the illusion. This defamiliarization of what the reader thought he recognized is bound to create a tension that will intensify his expectations as well as his distrust of those expectations.[45]

The determination of 'fit' or 'misfit'—not to mention the significance to that determination—is part and parcel of the strategy the reader brings to the construct of a relationship between the work and an element of the repertoire. The reader's labor is tireless, exceeding the bounds of a work's system of explicit allusion. In this qualified sense, readers *invent*.

With its repertoire and a general deference to the sequential progression of a work, the wandering viewpoint produces thematic equivalences in the seams to a work, where blanks present themselves to a reader's perception.[46] The blank stimulates the production of a perspective to combine the segments of text into a seemingly seamless whole. The stability to the image—a conjuring of a holistic aesthetic object to the work—seems in place until a subsequent filling of a blank is required. Then, the first image or perspective must be modified to accommodate the imputed semantic import of the emergent segment of text. The new, modified, image unfolds even as the previous one recedes into the horizon. Reading, so perceived, is an accretion of 'discarded' perspectives forming an ever-expanding literary horizon. The stock of 'meanings' multiplies. Each eschewed image forms the *basis* for a reaction in the production of novel views—Iser terms this the 'second-degree image' in relation to the foregoing perspective. The series of blanks, essentially, orchestrate a sequenced collision of perspectives that plays to the imagination of the reader. The expulsion, or re-visioning, of the old forces us 'to imagine something in the offered or invoked knowledge which would have appeared unimaginable as long as our habitual frame of reference prevailed.'[47] Reading, it seems, is incessantly masturbatory and resolutely excessive beyond the compass and the order of the marks on the page. Ideation cooks up fresh insights—novel angles on a tale—in re-visioning old ones. The reader's way is one of continual repentance. In the wake of the reader's dramatic imaginary is strewn a trail of abandoned images.

These evacuated images—the consequence of the necessary focus on a singular perspective at given moments in reading—are, in Iser's parlance, the 'vacancies' of readerly productions in the wandering viewpoint.[48] Their assignment to the periphery of a reader's awareness, however, is no guarantee of dormancy. Standing within the referential field of the wandering viewpoint, these remembered views remain candidates for resumption in cases where subsequent data suggest renewed relevance in pursuing the aesthetic object. The wandering viewpoint's recall of perspectives past, in such a scenario, may effect a renewal of the readerly vision that is retrogressive. The regressive gaze here may revaluate a 'discarded' perspective. As such, the quest for consonance exceeds the strict order of the text. The reader's 'past' may invade her 'present.' Old schemes that lost their luster are rehashed with the emergence of fresh data. The revision, in these instances, is undertaken with the perspectives of an earlier reading *and* that of the reader's present location in the work as background. The move is nothing short of an interweaving of the new with the old, a juxtaposition of perspectives aroused by texts separated by distance.[49] It is a wandering perspective's freedom to loop backward where lexical and thematic signs induce it to do so. The blank, in such instances, straddles a distance. This 'switching and reciprocal conditioning of our viewpoints,' a mixing of streams of insight, is the stuff of the numerous pauses in reading.[50] It is the arrest of the imagination born of a (often vague) memory of a sense past, a vantage point forgotten in course. Not infrequently, the recovered sensibility becomes the spur to a reader's astonishment at the breadth of transformation elicited by a work.

A Reasonably Broad Account of Readers Responding

To the degree that the concatenation of novel vistas forces an incessant turning of the wandering viewpoint, readers cultivate an awareness of their productivity in the process. The dynamic aesthetic experience sharpens the sense that grasping a work comes in increments, the formulations of sense against an ever regressive horizon. The inevitable result, for Iser, is the reader's objectification of the process. The self-conscious reader comes to occupy a 'strange, halfway position,' participating *and* watching that participation.[51] Every impediment to the readerly ideation of an aesthetic object shatters the imputed scheme, inducing the imagination to reconfigure the arrangement of the parts of the tale. Friedrich Schleiermacher knew this well. The hallmark of his hermeneutics, Iser reminds us, is a duality that arises out of the space—never filled—between the 'strange word' and comprehension.[52] In this liminal gap, 'understanding' is a phantom, its operations of determination and exclusion *inevitably* short of the mark. Indetermination is the only determination in the valiant quests of interpretation. The laborious—if engrossing—quality to the reader's labors cannot but foster a distrust of a totalizing optic. The repeated compulsion to forego a correlative gestalt breeds a disposition on reading as a grasping for a well-nigh unimaginable object just beyond the 'habitual frame of reference.'[53] Forever transcendent, the prospect of possession—of finality in interpretation—feeds a frustration and a growing sense that consistency-building is but the genesis of illusions, the experience of a series of tentative satisfactions withdrawn in the face of the unfamiliar at the turn of a page.[54] 'Meaning' is an event indeterminately deferred. The hermeneutical stance is one of reticence. This 'frustration' to reading, of course, is also its pleasure.

My take on reading, in sum, assumes the position of Iser's reader. My presumption (perhaps faulty) is that his description of the experience is sufficiently complex to warrant contemplation *and* common enough to circumscribe the charge of idiosyncrasy. The propensities, even the whims, of readers are integral players in the genesis of meaning in encounters with texts. While following the inclination at times to interrogate a work out of order, the wandering viewpoint largely defers to the broad progression of the discourse. At numerous points in the flow, the schematic imaginary endeavors to fit the perceived parts of a work within imputed frames—drawing from the repertoire of literary patterns, themes, and tropes from known generic categories—in responding to absences (gaps and blanks) in the discursive/narratorial continuum. The persistently revisionary stance to the task leaves a growing trail of vacated perspectives in its wake, prompting a cognizance of the tentative, conditioned nature to interpretation.

(A Touch) Off the Beaten Path

It cannot escape the notice of the biblical scholar that this project departs from the mainstream of biblical law studies. The astute tracings of the direction of influence, for example, in Deuteronomy's adaptive augmentations of its literary forebears so central to the admirable and painstaking labors of Bernard Levinson and Jeffrey Stackert, for example, do not characterize my task.[55] Quite beyond the compass of my quest also are postulations of provenance for the incremental movements in the development of the pentateuchal corpus whose deposits constitute the literary and theological complexity of the text. Missing from this study, then, are the methodological refinements of Reinhard Achenbach's perceptions of fourth-century priestly and theocratic leanings in Numbers.[56] Outside the compass of this book also are the lines of religious-historical inquiry that lead Israel Knohl to specify a late eighth-century, post-Ahaz Jerusalem context for the Holiness School's inclusiveness amid an insistence on the distinction of the Aaronide priesthood.[57] Notwithstanding these disclaimers, it would be a gross overstatement to proclaim a stark disruption to the established modes of modern critical inquiry in the scrutiny of biblical law. I am the beneficiary, evidently, of the erudite critical observations that have discerned the subtle turns of phrase and the ideological/theological deviations that inspire the isolation of sources and interpolations, a laying bare of the multi-vocality to the texts I survey. The inventive extensions of the semantic penumbra of prescriptions by allusion and the incoherencies engendered by these inventive productions—matters of grave interest in the scholarly works just named—are the heart of my endeavor. Harmony as a quality *of the text* is not my argument. Meir Sternberg's construal of the literary artifice—the object of a pointed critique by Bernard Levinson—as 'a compositional unity, the product of the artistic control of its author,' is not the point of departure for the present task.[58] It's quite the opposite. The unfolding sacred fabula is aporetic, its consistency fleeting and quite beyond the grasp of a reader. My reader is the patient of a multilateral assault, a soul pulled apart in diverse directions, a heart consistently embroiled in a flirtation with myriad perspectives. Finality vis-à-vis the view on a text—the fruit of a teleologically tailored series of reactions of authorial or editorial articulation—is quite beyond the grasp(ing) of the interpreter of my figuration.

No. The difference to my project is its dogged commitment to tracing the astonishment, the incredulity, and the bewilderment of an imaginary with a penchant for *making* the text 'work.' This study is ahistorical to the extent that it contemplates the relationship of time to eisegesis and interpretation only in the flux of the plot and the wandering viewpoint's striving—the very essence of its 'wandering'—*within* that lexical flow. My inquiries stop short of the satisfaction that comes with the postulation of sources, the isolation of monological iterations within a pluri-vocal composite whole. Such recourse to a degree of compartmentalization is not the way of my conceived lectors. Their gaze, rather, is one haunted by the prospect of consistency without ever arriving at its projected destination, wherever that may be. Always (at least a little) perplexed, it remains inveigled in the cacophony of the canonical composition(s), suspended in a desultory haze. Yet, it persists. In this specified sense, my stance on the interpretive task is synchronic. I stand with Ben Sira in his view to Israel's story (a vision underlined in his grandson's prologue) as one trained on the Torah-Prophets sequence (Sir 44:1–49:16) in the plenitude of its rhetorical diffusion. I walk in the way of the revisionist logic of Josephus's rewriting of an epic tale *already* known, its dissonance *already* set in a sequence demanding (projections of) thematic comportment, but never yielding such. Our task is the making-sense of a sense-eluding story set in the storying strictures of an already storied story.[59] Where political-historical-social factors intersect with the project, these occur *after* the canonical text—not at the stages of its genesis—in the intricate negotiations of the communities that receive the text, conceptualizing its significance. The undertaking concerns the (possible) responses of readers, specifically, imaginaries soused in and aroused by the potent potables of feminist rhetoric and after-colonialism. Such are my obsessions.

OF THINGS TO COME

The course through the guarded spaces and the esteemed entities of Hebrew ritual and law begins with God's rescue of Israel from Egypt. In the focus of the next chapter is the tendentious nature of interpretation through a close reading of the God-Moses exchange in the story of the

Passover (Exod 11–13). Interlocution in this pastiche of law and ritual is the site of entrenched, (deeply) interested interpretations of the other's words. Perversion seems the rule to comprehension. The selectivity essential to Iser's construct of the 'wandering viewpoint' lives and breathes in the vested hearings of another's utterance. Moses and God model for the reader the tunneled vision germane to reading/hearing. The foundational import to this chapter consists also in its laying down of the beginnings of a binary logic in defining Israel's exclusive (and excluded) categories. From the prescriptions for Egypt's separation to the celebration of that excommunication from divine favor in the institution of firstfruits/firstling offerings, the emergent dichotomies—Israel-Egypt, inside-outside, security-hazard—enact a paradigm for subsequent acts of interpretation and the transference of abstracted conceptions of abjection (in subsequent chapters).

Chapter 3 takes the now emergent logic of separation into the intertextual exchange between Leviticus 21–22 and Numbers 5–6. The Passover of Exodus 11–13, however, remains in the background through the broader context of Numbers 5–6: the election of the Levites (Num 3–4, 8) that turns on the logic of the prescribed firstfruits offerings of Exodus 13 as an inflection of God's bloody claim to the firstborns. An analogical vision is brought to a reading of legislative segments across the texts (Lev 21–22 and Num 5–6). Sacred personages, cultic donations, promises (vows), and sexual propriety (the priest's prospective wife, his daughter [Lev 21], and the test for adultery [Num 5]) assume a thematic resemblance in a reader's surveillance. The dominant agenda of this chapter is the mapping of an intertextual correlative calculus to the bridging of legislation across varying distances in the (ongoing) invention of sacred/guarded categories. At points, the chapter turns to elicit the reader's imagination to entertain possible implications for reading individual instructions in light of the panoply of legislation in relief. Where fresh vistas open up, I pursue, in varying degrees, the consequences of emergent trajectories. Consistently, the productivity of readers in interpretation and speculation remains in view. The reader's generative vision, in the course of the chapter, uncovers the tropes and the methods—the building blocks—of Israel's identity formation. The stage, then, is set for the emancipative gaze of the following chapters that will question the hermeneutical gestures to the now evident correlative logic of biblical prescription.

Chapter 4 brings the specific energies and interests of Majority World liberal feminist criticism to consider the expanding conception of pristine spaces. The literary topoi to Deuteronomy 22–24—sexual impropriety, Israel and the 'other,' campsite purity, sacred offerings, and vows—are familiar as is the dichotomous vision to the conception of exclusive categories. The chapter, in marking the inception of a decolonizing agenda, takes a turn toward deconstruction in contesting the binary constructs to the delimitation of Israel's boundaries. In this chapter, I commence with the disclosure of inconsistencies in Israel's exclusion of specified ethnicities from its assembly. The emergent ethos of suspicion carries over, then, into a negative evaluation of Israel's construct of gender in the surrounding legislation on the protocols of sex and marriage. The disarming of the racialized and gendered tenets to the promulgations parallels the liberating tactics at the productive intersection of postcolonial studies and feminist interpretation. Reading Deuteronomy 22–24—quite beyond the fecund intertextual exchange characteristic of the study thus far—is an imbrication of biblical law interpretation in the rhetorical tissue of counter-hegemony discourse: the confused energies of misogyny and racism at this point are the brands of imperialism of interest.

Chapter 5 is the sole foray beyond the Pentateuch/Torah. It charts a return to the beginning of the book in regarding the sordid tale of rape and murder in Judges 19 as a tenebrous reflection of the Passover narrative and ritual (Exod 11–13). As common in the volume, the gamut of prescribed distinctions germane to the Manichean sensibilities of the preceding laws forms the horizon to the interpretive project. Anti-imperialism, too, persists in this chapter. The interpretive registers of the text-reader relay are those of Asian American biblical interpretation with a dash of Homi Bhabha's determination of 'ambivalence' and 'hybridity' in the subaltern imagination. In the spaces between Exodus and Judges, the wandering viewpoint—inflected through Jean Jacques Rousseau's retelling of the Judges story—problematizes the distinction between aggressor and victim. The view to the disturbing story finds no one innocent, no unalloyed motive in the turns to the tale. The cruelly exclusionary animus touches all players in the drama, and a simple and simplistic reading of Israel's deliverance and the butchering of the Levite's woman—indeed, of all the acts of boundary discernment in between—seems now implausible, perhaps impossible. The same ambivalence, I argue, blocks a clean distinction between hegemonic ambition and subaltern resistance in Asian American negotiations of the US racial and political landscape. The storyteller, through a Bhabhan lens, would seem to caution against a naive assumption of purity in motive to subaltern contestations of metropolitan invective. Asian America, resolute in cause, must proceed with care, ever mindful of its own propensities for waywardness.

My wandering through texts and interpretations ends with a reflection on things from my formative years that have shaped my views. This self-disclosure in the final chapter seems appropriate in a volume with quite a lot to do with the prejudicial proclivities of a reader.

My view to law and ritual, at the last, is a marriage of a multi-visional hermeneutic of reticence and the disturbing (and disturbed) adversarial valencies of counter-imperialism. The blanket of instability covers texts and readers, the conceived positions of the latter almost as shaky as the construed virtues and vices of the former. I sit, therefore, in the contested spaces between texts and the factions that consume them. The excruciating pleasure of reading is my lot. I go now to my task.

Notes

1. Cheryl B. Anderson, *Ancient Laws and Contemporary Controversies: The Need for Inclusive Biblical Interpretation* (Oxford and New York: Oxford University Press, 2009), 3–4.
2. Ibid., 4–5.
3. Wolfgang Iser, *The Act of Reading: A Theory of Aesthetic Response* (Baltimore and London: The Johns Hopkins University Press, 1978), 107–34. The specifics of Iser's theory of reading most relevant to my thesis shall be matter for attention later in this chapter.
4. In reference is my slightly revised dissertation *Between Law and Narrative: The Method and Function of Abstraction* (Gorgias Biblical Studies 51; Piscataway, NJ: Gorgias, 2010).
5. Daniel Boyarin, *Intertextuality and the Reading of Midrash* (Bloomington and Indianapolis: Indiana University Press, 1990), 24. The last two statements in quotes are from Boyarin's citation of an essay by Stefan Morawski on the use of quotation.
6. Among others, see Jacob Milgrom, *Numbers* (New York: Jewish Publication Society, 1990), 355. The correspondence was noted, already, in rabbinic commentary (see Sifre[Numbers] to Num 6:6–8, and Numbers Rabbah 10:11).
7. Mary Douglas, *Leviticus as Literature* (Oxford and New York: Oxford University Press, 1999), 13–40.
8. Homi K. Bhabha, *The Location of Culture* (London and New York: Routledge, 1994), 122.
9. Ibid., 159.
10. See, for example, Angela R. Roskop, *The Wilderness Itineraries: Genre, Geography, and the Growth of Torah* (History, Archaeology, and Culture of the Levant 3; Winona Lake, IN: Eisenbrauns, 2011), 14–49; William K.

Gilders, *Blood Ritual in the Hebrew Bible: Meaning and Power* (Baltimore, MD: The Johns Hopkins University Press, 2004), 10–11.
11. Iser, *The Act of Reading*, 21–22; idem., 'The Reading Process: A Phenomenological Approach,' in *Reader-Response Criticism: From Formalism to Post-Structuralism* (ed., Jane P. Tompkins; Baltimore and London: The Johns Hopkins University Press, 1980), 50–51.
12. Iser, *The Act of Reading*, 21.
13. Ibid., 22. My emphasis.
14. Wolfgang Iser, *The Range of Interpretation* (New York: Columbia University Press, 2000), 5–7.
15. Ibid., 6.
16. Ibid., 6.
17. Ibid., 6–7, 20–21, 31–32.
18. Iser, *The Act of Reading*, 108–18.
19. Iser, 'The Reading Process,' 60.
20. Ibid., 60.
21. Iser, *The Act of Reading*, 109.
22. Ibid., 111.
23. Ibid., 115–16.
24. Ibid., 149.
25. Ibid., 118; Iser, 'The Reading Process,' 58–60.
26. Iser, *The Act of Reading*, 119. My emphasis.
27. Ibid., 121.
28. Ibid., 143. Emphasis is mine.
29. Iser, 'The Reading Process,' 59.
30. Ibid., 57.
31. Iser, *The Act of Reading*, 126. Iser's analysis of Friedrich Schleiermacher's hermeneutics makes the same point (*The Range of Interpretation*, 48–49).
32. Iser, *The Act of Reading*, 127–28.
33. Ibid., 182.
34. Ibid., 186.
35. Ibid., 184, 195–96.
36. Ibid., 167–69. Where 'blanks' and 'gaps' are distinct categories here, Iser combines both under the latter term with general reference to *all* indeterminacies of the lexical order: see, for example, 'The Reading Process,' 54–57; *The Range of Interpretation*, 24.
37. Iser, 'The Reading Process,' 55.
38. Frank Kermode, *The Genesis of Secrecy: On the Interpretation of Narrative* (Cambridge and London: Harvard University Press, 1979), 7.
39. Ibid., 9, 51–52.
40. Iser, *The Act of Reading*, 69.
41. Iser, 'The Reading Process,' 62–63.

42. Roland Barthes, *S/Z: An Essay* (trans. Richard Miller; New York: Hill and Wang, 1974), 10.
43. Roland Barthes, *The Rustle of Language* (trans. Richard Howard; New York: Hill and Wang, 1986), 54.
44. Ibid., 54. Emphasis in original.
45. Ibid., 63.
46. Iser, *The Act of Reading*, 186–89.
47. Ibid., 189.
48. Ibid., 198.
49. Ibid., 184, 197–98.
50. Ibid., 201.
51. Ibid., 134, 189.
52. Iser, *The Range of Interpretation*, 47–48.
53. Iser, *The Act of Reading*, 189.
54. Iser, 'The Reading Process,' 63.
55. Bernard M. Levinson, *Deuteronomy and the Hermeneutics of Legal Innovation* (Oxford and New York: Oxford University Press, 1998); Jeffrey Stackert, *Rewriting the Torah: Literary Revision in Deuteronomy and the Holiness Legislation* (Forschungen zum Alten Testament 52; Tübingen: Mohr Siebeck, 2007).
56. Reinhard Achenbach, 'The Pentateuch, the Prophets, and the Torah in the Fifth and Fourth Centuries B.C.E.,' in *Judah and the Judeans in the Fourth Century B.C.E.* (ed. Oded Lipschits, Gary N. Knoppers and Rainer Albertz; Winona Lake, IN: Eisenbrauns, 2007), 257, 260–61.
57. Israel Knohl, *The Sanctuary of Silence: The Priestly Torah and the Holiness School* (Minneapolis: Fortress, 1995), 180–86, 204–212.
58. Bernard M. Levinson, 'The Right Chorale: From the Poetics to the Hermeneutics of the Hebrew Bible,' in *'Not in Heaven': Coherence and Complexity in Biblical Narrative* (ed. Jason P. Rosenblatt and Joseph C. Sitterson, Jr.; Bloomington and Indianapolis: Indiana University Press, 1991), 132.
59. *Jewish Antiquities*, 1–5.

References

Achenbach, Reinhard. 2007. 'The Pentateuch, the Prophets, and the Torah in the Fifth and Fourth Centuries B.C.E.' In *Judah and the Judeans in the Fourth Century B.C.E.*, ed. Oded Lipschits, Gary N. Knoppers and Rainer Albertz. Winona Lake, IN: Eisenbrauns.

Anderson, Cheryl B. 2009. *Ancient Laws and Contemporary Controversies: The Need for Inclusive Biblical Interpretation*. Oxford and New York: Oxford University Press.

Barthes, Roland. 1974. *S/Z: An Essay*, trans. Richard Miller. New York: Hill and Wang.
Barthes, Roland. 1986. *The Rustle of Language*, trans. Richard Howard. New York: Hill and Wang.
Bhabha, Homi K. 1994. *The Location of Culture*. London and New York: Routledge.
Boyarin, Daniel. 1990. *Intertextuality and the Reading of Midrash*. Bloomington and Indianapolis: Indiana University Press.
Douglas, Mary. 1999. *Leviticus as Literature*. Oxford and New York: Oxford University Press.
Gilders, William K. 2004. *Blood Ritual in the Hebrew Bible: Meaning and Power*. Baltimore, MD: The Johns Hopkins University Press.
Iser, Wolfgang. 1978. *The Act of Reading: A Theory of Aesthetic Response*. Baltimore and London: The Johns Hopkins University Press.
Iser, Wolfgang. 1980. 'The Reading Process: A Phenomenological Approach.' In *Reader-Response Criticism: From Formalism to Post-Structuralism*, ed. Jane P. Tompkins. Baltimore and London: The Johns Hopkins University Press.
Iser, Wolfgang. 2000. *The Range of Interpretation*. New York: Columbia University Press.
Kermode, Frank. 1979. *The Genesis of Secrecy: On the Interpretation of Narrative*. Cambridge and London: Harvard University Press.
Knohl, Israel. 1995. *The Sanctuary of Silence: The Priestly Torah and the Holiness School*. Minneapolis: Fortress.
Lee, Bernon. 2010. *Between Law and Narrative: The Method and Function of Abstraction*. Gorgias Biblical Studies 51; Piscataway, NJ: Gorgias.
Levinson, Bernard M. 1991. 'The Right Chorale: From the Poetics to the Hermeneutics of the Hebrew Bible.' In *'Not in Heaven': Coherence and Complexity in Biblical Narrative*, ed. Jason P. Rosenblatt and Joseph C. Sitterson, Jr. Bloomington and Indianapolis: Indiana University Press.
Levinson, Bernard M. 1998. *Deuteronomy and the Hermeneutics of Legal Innovation*. Oxford and New York: Oxford University Press.
Milgrom, Jacob. 1990. *Numbers*. New York: Jewish Publication Society.
Roskop, Angela R. 2011. *The Wilderness Itineraries: Genre, Geography, and the Growth of Torah*. History, Archaeology, and Culture of the Levant 3; Winona Lake, IN: Eisenbrauns.
Stackert, Jeffrey. 2007. *Rewriting the Torah: Literary Revision in Deuteronomy and the Holiness Legislation*. Forschungen zum Alten Testament 52; Tübingen: Mohr Siebeck.

CHAPTER 2

Staying In: The Moses-God Exchanges on the Passover

Recent research in the literature of the Second Temple period has shown the figure of Moses a spirit of innovation in the interpretation of ancient traditions. By association with the prophet *par excellence*, the affinity of the scribal establishment for religious renewal through interpretation finds legitimacy.[1] In Moses, the prophetic imagination draws inspiration for engaging divine communiqués, prophetic and legal, as enshrined in texts of prestige from days of yore.[2] This sensibility, by the reckoning of James Watts and Marc Zvi Brettler, goes back to the Pentateuch, to its texture of the subtle discretions of Moses in legal promulgation. In its perusal, a tension, sometimes stark, opens up between prophet and God.[3]

Tracing this prophetic temperament in the parts of the multi-vocalic text is the broad concern of this chapter. Listening for the fine distinctions in rhetorical flourish, for the points of dissonance in the flow, is my object. The goal, given the connection of the legendary figure to literary creativity, is to unravel the complexities of scribal artistry ensconced in ancient texts. The laying bare of said artistry, of course, has been the stuff of literary-historical reconstruction, the fastidious labor of biblical scholars untangling the compositional layers to a conglomerate text.[4] Such diachronic interests, however, are not mine. The sequence of literary influence between the parts in the growth of the text through time is quite beyond the scope of this chapter. I am concerned, rather, with the *dissonance* of the text—the spur to the postulation of a compromised composite text—as it stands. I am engrossed by the subtle turns of thought germane to the reader's progress through the text, the set of experiences effected in no small measure by the perspectival plurality that is the detritus of editorial manipulation, the literary creativity of the imputed Mosaic disposition. The minute calculations of Iser's 'wandering viewpoint' in its genesis of illusions, the construal of aesthetic objects in the crevices *between* iterations, are foremost in my mind. I am, at last, engrossed with the *idea* of a Mosaic interface with divine authority and the sacred word in the unfolding drama of the fictive discourses of a (biblical) narrative. The cacophony of discrepant tones, the play of perspectives in computations of Israelite identity, religious, racial, political— all germane to the tensions and the contentions of the interactions between divinity and prophet—is my pleasure. In this sense, keeping with the interests of Watts and Brettler, the invention and the maintenance of a 'Mosaic ethos' in snippets of biblical literature take front stage.

The phenomenon in focus is ubiquitous in the biblical corpus. What text, specifically, falls in view in this brief chapter? And how does it connect with the broader interests of the book?

THE LOCUS OF INQUIRY AND ITS SIGNIFICANCE IN THE BROADER PROJECT

Of specific interest is the rally of orations shuttling between God and Moses in spelling out the procedures of the Passover. Through several speeches, Exodus 11:1–13:16 prescribes a series of rites leading to Israel's happy (for Israel) expulsion from Egypt. The distinct orientation to each act of speech and its interaction with those preceding are in focus. The study proceeds in six parts: Exodus 11:1–10; 12:1–13; 12:14–20; 12:21–28; 12:43–49; and 13:1–16. My argument is that each interlocutor picks up the language, imagery, and concepts of the other in extending the nuances of previous speeches in novel directions.[5] Such departures from previous rhetorical direction often take the form of conceptions absent in, or marginal to, preceding utterances, promoting these novel arguments as concerns central to the discourse at hand. Within this rich network of exchange, the prophet may become, at times, an affront to divine communication, while remaining the face of God to the people. The voice of God exhibits similar tendencies in relation to the prophet's speech. The result is a portrayal of the prophet in Moses consistent with a dialogical approach to prophetic practice, one cherished and enshrined in the ideals of ancient Israelite scribal practice up through the period of the Second Temple.[6]

The dialogical sensibility to every iteration, of course, inhabits the intertextual negotiations across the Pentateuch and beyond within the compass of the broader project. The patterns of mutual engagement germane to the Moses-God speeches, in other words, are a microcosm of the dialectic between the parts of the broader corpus of interest in this study. The paths of the 'wandering viewpoint,' to return to Iser's favored phrase, is the very tissue of the rhetorical turns in what seems, at a glance, a clumsy patchwork of sources on this important event in Israel's historical and mythic memory.

The twists to the God-Moses duet are also significant for the larger project for their articulation of a basic binary vision—night and day, indoors and outdoors, Israelite and gentile. Our contemplation of Israel's protected things and spaces begins here with Israel's election and subsequent separation from Egypt. Exodus 11–13 is ground zero, so to speak, for our elaborate exposition of a complex network of esteemed categories across a segment of biblical law and ritual. Here, in Israel's Passover, the correlative imagination begins its work of forging a series of metonymies that will take us to the shocking story of severed limbs in the hills of Ephraim (Jud 19) and back again to Egypt. Here, in Israel's separation is the beginning of a logic for abjection that will resonate through the ages, well into the imperialistic discourses of later times. Our odyssey through ritual and law starts with Exodus 11:1–10.

Exodus 11:1–10: One Last Smiting for Egypt

A series of three speeches announces the intention of Israel's god to smite Egypt's firstborn children. The divine speeches initiating the despoilment of Egypt (Exod 11:1–3) and anticipating Pharaoh's intransigence (Exod 11:9–10) enclose the prophet's communication of divine intent (Exod 11:4–8).

Many scholars point to confusion in the chunks of speech, the effect of the conjunction of material from disparate literary sources. The deity's direction for Egypt's despoilment (Exod 11:1–3) is considered, usually, the work of the so-dubbed Elohistic source (E). This instruction to procure gifts from Israel's neighbors is an intrusion in the exchange between Moses and Pharaoh (Exod 11:4–8, by this scheme, picks up from Exod 10:29).[7] The interpolation—Exodus 11:1–3—adds a dash of irony: Pharaoh's steadfast refusal to grant the divine request (Exod 20:28) is juxtaposed with a forecast of the monarch's reversal of his own position (Exod 11:1–3). The impact of Pharaoh's hardened demeanor wanes beside the proleptic vision of the ruler's desperate plea for Israel's departure, with gifts to boot![8] 'Indeed,' God foresees, 'when he [Pharaoh] lets you go, he will *drive you away*' (Exod 11:1; my emphasis). The achievement of this colossal victory over Pharaoh, however, must wait: the Egyptian remains resolute for now.

The gloss of Exodus 11:1–3 has another effect. The direction for Moses to speak to Israel in Exodus 11:2a—'Tell the people...'—leads, quite naturally, to the expectation that the words from verse 4b onwards address Israel. Moses, in speaking here, represents the divine perspective ('Thus says the Lord...'). God, in Moses, speaks in the first person: 'About midnight *I* will go out through Egypt' (my emphasis). Israel, it seems, receives these words. Certainly, the designation of the addressee in the plural—'... so that you may know [plural] that the Lord makes a distinction...'—sustains this impression. Israel, collectively, is the object of the prophetic-divine address. But, of course, if the members of Pharaoh's court (mentioned later in v. 8) are included with the sovereign as addressees, the plural designation would be appropriate.[9] Surely, the absence of a designated addressee in the narrator's introduction to the prophet's speech (Exod 11:4a) might prompt us to entertain this possibility. Notwithstanding this consideration, the preponderance of the direction to speak to Israel in the preceding speech by God (Exod 11:1–3) fortifies the impression that Moses is doing just such—speaking to Israel—in the very next verse. In the flow of the story, this seems the preferable option. But the portrayal of Pharaoh's humbling, a touch later in the same speech (Exod 11:8–9), overturns this presumption: 'Then all these officials of *yours* [singular] shall come down to me' (v. 7; again, my emphasis). Pharaoh, singularly, is in reference by the second-person pronominal suffix.[10] The readerly construct of Israel as addressee unravels in the course of the prophet's speech of Exodus 11:4b–8. In the uncertainty, readers are compelled to reevaluate, retroactively, the object of the Mosaic address.

With the emergent clarity on the addressee (in Exod 11:8), Moses departs from a direct quotation of divine utterance. The pretense of divine speech (from vv. 4b to 7) ceases. Pharaoh's predicted harried dismissal of Moses (and Israel)—still Moses speaking—is followed by the prophet's proclamation 'I [Moses, not God] will leave.' Moses, now, speaks for himself. Divested of oracular function, the naked voice of the prophet emerges. This unmarked transition, if disconcerting, renders prophetic speech doublespeak. Mosaic enunciation through Exodus 11:4b–8 exemplifies prophetic voice as a conglomeration of divine tongue and prophetic gloss, a hybrid orientation through and through. Obscurity on this matter, perhaps, is apropos.

But the (orchestrated) sense of aural (dis)harmony does not obscure the fissures of the speech(es). The unmediated divine utterance of verses 1–3 remains juxtaposed to the following incipient prophetic representation of divine intent (vv. 4b–8). The Mosaic annunciation of impending deliverance is grossly emphatic of Israel's exception from God's destructive designs (v. 7). The divine speech on the same matter omits such emphasis, confining itself to securing Israel's material welfare at Egypt's expense (v. 2). God's intention in initiating such action relates to the enhancement of the prophet's stature (v. 3).

Succinctly stated, my point is this. The tapestry of speeches in Exodus 11:1–10 generates ambiguities regarding the identities of addressor and addressee. God speaks to Moses; Moses speaks for God to Israel (?); Moses speaks for himself to Pharaoh. The passage fosters the genesis of assumptions, which must suffer reevaluation in course. Who, exactly, is speaking to whom? The various indices of disparate sources become in the present composite text points of misdirection and redirection for readerly speculation as to the recipient of the speech. One effect of this literary artistry, if it be that, is the perceived *convergence* of the voices of the prophet and the deity. The rhetorical trajectories of the two speakers, however, maintain a touch of disparity. The prophet and God speak on similar subjects with different emphases; and the tension, if subtle, is tangible between the units of speech. If the accomplishment of Exodus 11:1–10 is to raise awareness of *both* the conflation and the distinction of the voices, it remains to be seen how these opposing tendencies will play out in subsequent speeches.

Exodus 12:1–13: Instructions for Israel's First Passover

In unmediated divine speech, next, comes instruction for the selection of a sacrificial beast, its preparation, and consumption (Exod 12:1–13). The prophetic voice is muted for now. The divine oration here, in tandem with a latter portion of the previous speech (Exod 11:4–10), forms a chiasm; the flow of the prescription turns in on itself:

A: Egypt shall be smitten (Exod 11:4–6)
B: Israel shall be set apart from the destruction (Exod 11:7–8)
X: Egypt shall remain resolute (Exod 11:9–10)
B': The Passover meal; the setting apart of Israel (Exod 12:1–11)
A': Egypt shall be smitten, but not Israel (Exod 12:12–13)

The pattern suggests a divine response (in Exod 12:1–13)—even a riposte—to elements in the closing lines of Moses's words in Exodus 11:1–10. A forecast of Pharaoh's staunch resistance is the turning point (X) in the chiasmus. This central feature, Pharaoh's stubbornness, is enclosed by divine resolution to shatter Egypt's resolve (A, A'). Caught between the contest of divine wills—Pharaoh and Israel's god—is Israel's safety and destiny, the very concern of Moses in Exodus 11:7–8 and God's rejoinder in 12:1–11 (B, B'). The deity's response unfolds a tactic for establishing Israel's distinction from Egypt, from destruction (Exod 12:1–11). Its contribution, with regard to Moses's earlier annunciation of Israel's deliverance (Exod 11:4–10), is an articulation of the manner by which Israel's security shall be achieved.

Beyond the framework of this patterning, other elements serve to advance the rhetoric of God's speech in Exodus 12:1–13.[11] The deity's statement is profuse with reference to consumption, 'eating' (*'kl*). In a short space, the term appears seven times (vv. 4b, 7b, 8a, 8b, 9a, 11a, 11b). The act is located within instructions prescribing the time (v. 8a), location (v. 7b) and manner for the consumption of the sacrificial portion (vv. 11a, 11b), its method of preparation (v. 9a), accompanying foods (v. 8b), and the number of participants at each meal (v. 4b). Also prominent in the passage are the multiple occurrences of 'house' (*byt*).[12] The clauses deploying the term display similar concerns to those with reference to eating: the number of participants in the slaughter and consumption of each animal (vv. 3b [both occurrences], 4a and 4b) and the location for its consumption (v. 7b). The case of verse 13b is unique for its focus on the blood of the beast as a marker of Israelite households, a matter also of concern in verse 7b. By and large, the clauses altogether using either term (or both terms) designate the procedural, temporal, and local boundaries governing the preparation and consumption of the meal.[13]

The clauses invoking the terms are part of a larger network of statements within the speech tracing the spatiotemporal boundaries of the Passover meal. The members of the household should partake of the sacred portion within the physical structure of the domicile (Exod 12:7b) and within the night of the 14th day of the first month (Exod 12:8a; compare Exod 12:6). As dawn marks the terminus of the temporal boundary (Exod 12:10), so the entranceway to every Israelite household—the doorposts (*hmmzwzwt*) and the lintel (*hmmšqwp*)—the spatial bounds for the meal (Exod 12:7). In keeping with protocols for sacred meals elsewhere (compare Exod 34:25; 29:34; Lev 7:15, 17; 8:32; 22:29–30; Deut 16:4), the prescriptions proscribe consumption beyond a designated place and time.[14] The Passover meal, by this conception, is an exclusive meal, taking place in a prescribed place and time. Not unlike the divine directions with reference to households and ingestion, the conceptions of sacred space and time will find new direction as the discourse unfolds further.

A restatement of the impending nocturnal act of destruction (Exod 12:12–13) stands at the close of the instructions for the Passover. Echoes of the prophet's initial announcement in Exodus 11:4–8 may be found in the divine speech at hand. The location of the terrifying visitation is located, once again, 'in the land of Egypt,' and designated as an event of the night (*bllylh hzzh*, 'on this night'). As in the communication of Moses (Exod 11:5), the object of destruction shall be 'the first-born in the land of Egypt' (*bkwr b'rs mṣrym*), 'human,' (*'dm*) and 'beast' (*bhmh*).[15] The Mosaic turns of phrase, so it seems, resonate with God. Absent in Exodus 12:12–13, however, is any extensive prospection regarding the humiliating capitulation of Pharaoh and his courtiers (Exod 11:8). Neither are there elaborate images of Egypt's suffering (Exod 11:6) and Israel's security (Exod 11:7). Instead, we find the inclusion of the Egyptian pantheon as an object of defeat (Exod 12:12b). Also extraneous to the forecast of Moses in Exodus 11:4–8 is the indication of the blood on the threshold as a sign (Exod 12:13a) and, of course, the extensive ritual that spawns that sign. But perhaps the most prominent rhetorical shift in the divine forecast of the destruction of the Egypt's offspring may be found in the series of first-person verbal forms emphasizing God as the agent of destruction: 'For *I will pass through* (*w'brty*) the land of Egypt that night, and *I will strike down* (*whkkyty*) every firstborn . . . *I will execute* (*'śh*) judgments . . . when *I see* (*wr'yty*) the blood, *I will pass* (*wpshty*) over you' (Exod 12:12–13).¹⁶ The sole direct designation of divine agency in the destruction in Exodus 11:4 ('I will go out'), in contrast, appears anemic.¹⁷

In sum, God's speech seconds the prophet's previous assurance of a distinction between Egypt and Israel (Exod 12:13; compare Exod 11:7). In light of Exodus 12:13, the prescriptions for the preparation of the Passover meal are an elaboration upon the method of this distinction, though not exclusively. The correspondence of Exodus 12:1–11 (B') to Exodus 11:7–8 (B) in the patterning of Exodus 11:1–12:13 would support such interpretation. In adopting Mosaic diction, God supersedes the prophet by foregrounding divine initiative in the undertaking. As the one forging Israel's (and Egypt's) fate, God authors and prescribes a course of action that will create in space and time a structure that will separate Israel from its captors.

Exodus 12:14–20: Instructions for the Festival of Unleavened Bread

The divine speech proceeds in Exodus 12:14–20 with instructions for the festival of unleavened bread. With the exclusion of Exodus 12:14, chiasmus—once again—governs this segment of speech:

A: Seven days (*šbʿt ymym*) you shall eat unleavened bread; on the first day you shall remove leaven from your houses, for whoever eats leavened bread (*ky klʾ kl ḥmṣ*) from the first day until the seventh day shall be cut off (*wnkrth hnnpš hhwʾ*) from Israel. (Exod 12:15)

B: *On the first day* you shall hold a solemn assembly, *and on the seventh day* a solemn assembly; no work shall be done on those days; only what everyone must eat, that alone may be prepared by you. (Exod 12:16; my emphasis).

X: You shall observe the festival of unleavened bread, for on this very day I brought your companies out of the land of Egypt: you shall observe this day throughout your generations as a perpetual ordinance. (Exod 12:17)

B': *In the first month from the evening of the fourteenth day until the evening of the twenty-first day*, you shall eat unleavened bread. (Exod 12:18; my emphasis)

A': For seven days (*šbʿt ymym*) no leaven shall be found in your houses; for whoever eats what is leavened (*ky klʾ kl mḥmṣh*) shall be cut off (*wnkrth hnnpš hhwʾ*) from the congregation of Israel, whether an alien or the native of the land. You shall eat nothing leavened; in all your settlements you shall eat unleavened bread. (Exod 12:19–20)

The assignment of the festival as a commemorative gesture to the impending deliverance of Israel (Exod 12:17) stands at the center of the chiasmus (X). This single statement forges the connection with the preceding prescriptions for the Passover meal.

Furthest removed from the center of the structure are similar injunctions against the consumption of leaven under penalty of excommunication (Exod 12:15 [A]; Exod 12:19–20 [A']).[18] The cluster of similar phrases across both units (see underlined text in A and A') reinforces the thematic correspondence between the units at this level (A, A').[19]

Two seemingly disparate subjects—two solemn gatherings at the extremities of the duration for the festival (Exod 12:16) and the avoidance of leaven (Exod 12:18)—take up residence one level removed from the center (B, B'). These units (B, B') share a preference for designations of a temporal duration that denote the beginning and the end of the period of time (see text in italics in B and B'). In contrast, the units of the outermost ring (A, A') deploy a single phrase ('seven days') to designate a duration without explicit indication of the boundaries (beginning and end) of that period. The fruit of the comparison between B and B', an effect of the resumptive pattern of the passage, is the recognition of an analogous relationship between abstinence from leaven (B') and cessation from labor (B). Associations with Genesis 2:2–3 and Exodus 20:8–11 through similar concerns with periods of seven days and cessation from labor reinforce the perception of abstinence from leaven as an exceptional activity within a specific time. The network of correspondences grows.

The reference to structures of inclusion (and exclusion) in the passage as a whole (Exod 12:14–20) is, of course, reminiscent of previous spatiotemporal constructions in Exodus 12:1–13. By this point, the respect for boundaries of time and space is familiar. Perhaps in this aspect the festival fosters remembrance of the Passover event, the central purpose behind the festival, and the point to the structure of the passage. What more can one say about connections with the preceding instructions for the Passover meal?

Beyond thematic similarities (to which I shall return) are similarities in vocabulary.[20] The repeated references to 'house' (*byt*) and 'eating' (*'kl*) in Exodus 12:1–13 appear again here in this segment of divine speech. In fact, Umberto Cassuto has noted that the seven-fold repetition of 'eating' in Exodus 12:1–13 is matched in Exodus 12:14–20.[21] Without exception, the object of consumption in the seven occurrences of the verb in Exodus 12:1–13 is a portion of the designated sacrificial beast (vv. 4b, 7b, 8a, 8b, 9a, 11a, 11b). This stands in contrast to the passage at hand. Here, in Exodus 12:14–20, the object of consumption, with the exception of the case in verse 17a, is the unleavened cakes (vv. 15a, 18a, 20b) or the proscribed article with leaven (vv. 15b, 19b, 20a). Not surprisingly, instructions for the festival of unleavened bread (Exod 12:14–20) contain numerous references to a baked item as the object of consumption. Exodus 12:14–20, in its constitution, substitutes unleavened cakes for the beast of the Passover meal as the direct object of consumption. But the recurrence of a series of clauses deploying the verb *'kl* begs comparison with Exodus 12:1–13, and comparison yields another similarity: temporal restrictions.

'House' shows up twice in the passage at hand (Exod 12:15a, 19a). Both occurrences of the noun are in statements calling for the removal of leaven from the home within prescribed periods ('on the first day'; 'for seven days') a concern of the outermost bracket (A, A') in the chiastic order of Exodus 12:14–20. As was the case in the instructions for the Passover meal, the prescriptions for the festival of unleavened bread involve the collocation of 'house' and 'eating' in a spatiotemporal scheme of exclusion. The point is this: the festival of unleavened bread is *like* the Passover meal, which is a type of Sabbath (by association with Gen 2:2–3 and Exod 20:8–11). The genesis of broad and abstract categories transcends the particularities of the individual rituals. The conjunction of the two appears seamless.[22]

To summarize the divine contributions in Exodus 12:1–20 as a whole, God is emphatic, even exclusive, in speaking about divine initiative in Israel's deliverance. In pursuing this initiative, God spells out a method for the distinction of Israel from Egypt, a matter also of concern for the prophet (Exod 11:4–8). This method involves both the Passover rite and the festival of unleavened bread. Broad similarities bring a sense of coherence to both rites. Essential to this resemblance is a spatiotemporal scheme that locates specified items beyond select boundaries. The correspondences across the various prescriptions in the speech are represented in the following table:

Activity	Spatial boundaries	Temporal boundaries	Excluded activities or things
Consumption of Passover sacrifice	In the house	During the night	Eating leftovers at dawn
Consumption of unleavened cakes	In the house	For seven days	Eating leaven (nonconforming member of community to be excommunicated)
Sabbath observance	None	On the first and seventh days in a seven-day period	Labor

Similarities in language pave the way for similar ideas, drawing lines of correspondence across separate rituals. The speech of God is beginning to look like a house of mirrors, multiplying rituals even as the speech reflects the interests of Moses. Now, what will the prophet say to all this?

Exodus 12:21–28: Instructions for the Passover, Once Again

The voice of Moses returns to instruct the people, again, on the sacrificial rite. The discourse follows the general outline witnessed, already, in the earlier speech of the deity: selection and slaughter of an animal (Exod 12:21b; see 12:3b–6), blood application (Exod 12:22; see 12:7), slaughter of Egyptian firstborn, escape of Israel from destruction (Exod 12:23; see 12:12–13).[23] Along with the familiar sequence of prescribed actions are words and phrases known from previous instructions for the event. The compliant Israelite 'takes' (*lqḥ*; v. 21b; compare vv. 3b, 5b) and 'slays' (*šḥṭ*; v. 21b; compare v. 6b) the choice animal. God 'passes through' (*'br*; v. 23a; compare v. 12a) the land; God 'sees' (*r'h*; v. 23a; compare v. 13a) and 'passes over' (*psḥ*; v. 23b; compare v. 13a), saving Jacob's descendants from 'destruction'/'the destroyer' (*hmmšḥyt*; v. 23b; compare 'to destroy' [*lmšḥyt*] in v. 13b). Again, there is talk of 'the doorpost' and 'the lintel' (*hmmzwzwt* and *hmmšqwp*, respectively; v. 22a; compare v. 7a) of the 'house' (*byt*; vv. 22b, 23b, 27a, 27b; compare vv. 3b, 4a, 4b, 7b, 13b, 15a, 19a) and of restrictions 'until dawn' (*'d-bqr*; v. 22b; compare v. 10). The images are familiar, and the action is predictable.

Beyond the familiar turns of phrase and sequence of action are the unique pursuits of the prophet's communication of divine instruction. Shorn of interest in the preparation and consumption of the sacrificial beast (see Exod 12:8–11; 'eating' does not show up in this speech), Moses expands upon instructions for the application of the blood of the sacrificial beast (Exod 12:22).[24] As with the festival of unleavened bread, the ritual of the Passover here becomes an object for future religious attention, and directions for informing posterity of the meaning of the rite ensue (Exod 12:24–28). The procedure is designated an 'ordinance' (*ḥq*; v. 24) for the first time.

The prophet, here, makes a contribution to the strictures of space and time established in previous communication. Every Israelite, in the final clause of Exodus 12:22, is cautioned against leaving the house prior to dawn. This untimely transgression of the threshold would bring the individual out into the realm of the destroyer, thus forfeiting the protection of the prescribed procedure. The temporal boundary of dawn is reminiscent of the requirement to confine consumption of the meal to the night by God's earlier instruction of Exodus 12:10: all leftovers, by that prescription, are to be disposed of by burning at dawn. The common phrase across both statements suggests a connection between the prescriptions in the grand scheme of things: the Israelite stepping outdoors in the night (Exod 12:22) matches the post-dawn Israelite diner (Exod 12:10). Both activities, in different ways, stand outside stipulated boundaries. Through Exodus 12:10, the transgressing Israelite of the deity's description in Exodus 12:22 joins the list of designated items excluded by the (still) growing spatiotemporal scheme of the broader literary context.

A second initiative of Moses's rehearsal of the procedure is to direct attention to the doorways of Israelite homes. The salience of the portal is a concomitant feature of the emphasis on the blood rite. The return to the subject of blood application in Exodus 12:22 is marked by the reprisal of 'the two doorposts' and 'the lintel' in reversed sequence (see for comparison Exod 12:7a).[25] Moses tarries at this point in the procedure, lingering upon details in the method of blood application (the immersion of the applicator in blood, touching it to parts of the threshold) and the requisite instruments for the task (a bundle of marjoram, a receptacle for the blood), all this extraneous to the preceding instructions of Exodus

12:1–13. The rigors of the rite fix the reader's imagination on the entrance to the house.²⁶ The choice of the ambivalent term *sp*, 'basin' or 'threshold,' is yet one more index to the point of transition between the outside and the inside of the home.²⁷ The prescriptions, as if readers would miss the first indication of the source of the blood (the 'basin'/ 'threshold'), return them to this selfsame fact in the very next sentence.

> Take a bunch of hyssop, dip it in *the blood that is in the basin* (*sp*), and touch the lintel and the two doorposts *with the blood that is in the basin* (*sp*). None of you shall go outside the door of your house until morning. (Exod 12:22; my emphasis)

The awkward flow to the lines makes for additional direction to the reader's gaze toward the threshold.

The choice of the phrase 'from the door of his house' (*mppth bytw*)²⁸ in the warning against wandering outdoors on the night of the Passover is surprising (Exod 12:22). The earlier reference to evacuation (of leaven) from the area within the house in Exodus 12:15a designates the space indoors by 'from your houses' (*mbbtykm*). A similar prepositional phrase in Exodus 12:22, 'from his house,' would hardly alter the sense of the clause. The expanded phrase of Exodus 12:22 ('from the door of his house'), of course, includes 'door': one more index to that central prop of the prophet's discourse. But there's more!

The prophet's reprisal of the smiting of the firstborn in Exodus 12:23, while following the same sequence of action in Exodus 12:12–13, elevates the prominence of the portal. This particular interest of the statement is evident in comparison with the corresponding material in the former unmediated words of God (Exod 12:13). See the words of God and prophet side by side.

When he sees the blood *on the lintel and the two doorposts*, the Lord will pass over *that door*. (Exod 12:23; emphasis added)	When I see the blood, I will pass *over you*. (Exod 12:13; emphasis added)

The prophet's prolixity is evident in juxtaposition to the economy of divine communication on this point. The distinctive components—the additional prepositional phrase and the substitution of 'that door' for 'you'—are in tune with the particular emphases to Moses's instructions elsewhere in the speech. The doorway, quite specifically, is foregrounded. But why would Moses follow this particular oratorical trajectory?

Here, again, reading between texts proves instructive. This time, by the Mosaic spin, the barring of death and destruction is in view. The boon to fastidious adherence to the prophet's directions, in the words of Moses, is that God 'will not allow *the destroyer to enter your houses* (*hmmšḥyt lb' 'l-btykm*) to strike you down' (Exod 12:23; emphasis is mine). The deity's coverage of that detail in a preceding statement is that 'no plague shall destroy you when I strike the land of Egypt' (Exod 12:13). Moses's depiction, quite beyond the fixation on the inert threshold, is notable for its addition of the destroyer's (averted) passage through the door (Exod 12:23). The slayer's nontransition matches the (proscribed) opposite movement of the household member (Exod 12:22b). No danger attains as long as the boundary is respected. The Israelites stay in; the avenging emissary stays out. The destroyer's 'consumption' remains outside; the Israelites eat indoors. There is, I am suggesting, a symmetry to Moses's unfolding of the forecasted event. The index to the threshold is effective of a spatial dichotomy—this is already evident from previous speeches—across which corresponding, parallel acts take place. The dark deeds of the destroyer beyond Israel's doors are a feasting of sorts, a double to Israel's hasty meal behind doors. Richard Friedman alludes to just such a perception to the scene in noting the propinquity—literal *and* semantic—between *šḥt*, the root behind 'the destroyer' (*hmmšḥyt*; Exod 12:23), and *šḥṭ* ('to slay'), the prescribed act on the Passover lamb (Exod 12:6b, 21b). The import to the pun is ironic: 'the Israelites are to slaughter (root *šḥṭ*) the lamb so as to keep out the destroyer (root *šḥt*).'²⁹ The sense of a balance—a slaughter on each side to the door—underscores an unlikely kinship to the victims across the portal. The ingestion of lamb on one side and the devouring of Egypt's young on the other are two acts of 'consumption' across two mutually exclusive realms. Moses, in a later commandment, will exploit the portmanteau image to depict one slaying as an exchange for another, a ransom to avert the slaughter of children behind Israel's doors. But for now the contribution to the spatiotemporal configuration is one of symmetry across exclusive zones. Nothing more. What happens inside is *like* what happens outside.

Summing up Moses's inflections on the directions at this point, the prophet declares the outdoor spaces out of bounds for Israel on the fated, fearful night. The recurrence of 'until morning' suggests this transgression is in the same category as that of eating leftovers from the Passover sacrifice and, by analogy, that of other proscribed activities within designated times (consuming leaven, working). By his emphasis on the blood rite, Moses implies an analogy between the destruction indoors and outdoors by imposing a reflective surface at the threshold, the boundary between parallel spaces. The mirror effect is reinforced by the phonetic resemblance across two verbal roots for destruction (*šḥṭ* and *šḥt*) and the clear delineation of the realm for each act of slaughter/consumption. This correspondence between the two spaces moves us a step closer to the perception that the slaughter of the Passover animal stands *in lieu* of the death of a child in the house.

Exodus 12:43–49: Excluded Parties from the Passover

The divine voice intervenes, again, to supplement the prophet's increasingly precise directions to Israel's elders. Post-plague, the discourse is oriented toward the annual ritual observance inspired by the deliverance. Gone is the focus on the apotropaic elements to the rite—the blood application on doors. The present discourse, rather, returns to the alimentary aspects to the rituals. Specifically, the speech constrains participation in the festive meal. The pattern to the instruction is the by-now-familiar variety of a palistrophe. Statements designating the ruling an 'ordinance for the passover' (*ḥqqt hppsḥ*; v. 43) and a 'law' (*twrh*; v. 49) envelope units specifying excluded and included non-Israelites (vv. 44–45, 48). The center strikes a note of unity to the rite (vv. 46–47): *one* house (*byt*), *one* unbroken beast, and *one* congregation (*ʿdh*). The emphatic solidarity to the law is underscored by its conjunction to the requirement that the animal is to be eaten with its bones intact (v. 46b).[30]

The turns of phrase are evocative, mostly of Moses's construct of a bizonal structure in his most recent unfolding of the final plague (12:21–28). The emphatic stipulation that the meal should take place 'in one house' and that no part of it should be conveyed out of doors (v. 46) is reminiscent of the stark boundary between the zones of danger and security (12:23) and of the strict caution against anyone in the house transgressing that boundary (12:22b). The designation of the rite as an 'ordinance for the passover' (*ḥqqt hppsḥ*)—a novel term for the procedure—dimly recalls Moses's phrase, 'a perpetual ordinance (*ḥq*) for you and your family' (12:24). The same nomenclature, however, also connects to the preceding divine instruction concerning the festival of unleavened bread (12:14, 17).

If the intimations of an overture to the Mosaic discourse of Exodus 12:21–27 are warranted, then the central turn in divine rhetoric here toward an exclusive solidarity to Israel makes its argument against the backdrop of the prophet's dual-zone construct of that speech. How is the invocation of the prophet's words productive for God's illocution here? In the light of Mosaic proclamation—and reaching further back to God's legislation of Exodus 12:1–20—the divine voice confirms (by reiteration) the place of the Passover meal indoors: the meal 'shall be eaten *in one house*' and no part of the animal is to leave the house (Exod 12:46; my emphasis). The statement, effectively, trades on the established spatiotemporal paradigm to the rites. But there is an increment to the divine statement here. There always is. With Egypt beyond Israel's doors, according to divine stipulation, are the uncircumcised. 'Foreigner' (*bn-nkr*; v.43b), in divine parlance here, is the 'alien' (*gr*), the 'slave who has been purchased' (*kl-ʿbr'ys mqnh-ksp*; v. 44), and the 'bound or hired servant' (*twšb wśkyr*; v. 45)[31] who is uncircumcised (v. 48b). With the Egyptians, untimely labor, leaven, and the negligent Israelite, these are parties external to the 'one house' where the meal is to take place. The list of outsiders grows.[32]

The import of the divine interdiction of Exodus 12:43–49, simply stated, is the manipulation of the spatial partitioning of previous legislation for the purpose of specifying 'Israel,' the privileged occupants of the safe zone.

Exodus 13:2–16: A (Mostly) Mosaic Summary

This final segment of discourse to my analysis consists of two speeches in quick succession. The major part is a lengthy expansion by Moses (vv. 3–16) of an initial divine prescription for offerings of firstlings (v. 2).

The structural outline to the combined instruction, according to Brevard Childs, captures well the intercalated quality of the discourse.[33] God's opening command for firstling offerings (v. 2) is picked up later in the prophet's instruction on specifics in this matter (vv. 11–16). In the intermediate space is a rehash of previous directions from the divine voice for the festive consumption of unleavened bread (vv. 3–10, especially vv. 6–10; compare Exod 12:14–20). The pattern to the speeches, thus, makes for an intermingling of legislation for the festive meal and the offering of firstfruits. There is a distinct symmetry to the two parts of the Mosaic speech (vv. 3–10, 11–16). The instructional sets cycle through forecasts of settlement in the land

(vv. 5 and 11), catechism (vv. 8 and 14–15) and the prescription of mnemonic aids, concrete or virtual (vv. 9 and 16).[34] The recall of Israel's deliverance, in both parts to the speech of Moses, makes reference to the divine 'strength of hand' (vv. 3 and 16). Indeed, the reminder of the spectacular display of force envelopes the two parts to the prophet's locution. There is, on the whole, here a sense of unity and order to the oration of Moses. The parts of the speech, on distinct instructional matter, touch on similar topoi.

Childs finds in this speech an echo to the pattern of the divine directions for the Passover sacrifice and the meal of unleavened cakes in Exodus 12:1–20.[35] The Mosaic seconding of that divine prescription here, therefore, sets up a joint ritualized commemoration of Israel's flight and God's providential protection over its offspring. A connection to the combined speeches of God and Moses in Exodus 12:14–20 and 21–27, however, seems more plausible to me. The overlap in content—the details to the consumption of unleavened cakes—between Exod 13:6-7 and 12:20 is obvious. But similarities forge, also, a nexus to a textual segment that includes the prophet's careful instructions for turning aside the rage of God's agent of death (Exod 12:21–27). The direction to catechism in Exodus 13:8, 14–15 is resonant of the prescription of Exodus 12:26–27. In both acts of speech, too, this component follows a projection of residence in Israel's own territory (Exod 13:11, 5; compare 12:25). The central placement of the qualification of the instructions as an 'ordinance' ($ḥq$) in Exodus 13:10 echoes the first time the term is used with reference to the Passover rite in Exodus 12:24—God picks up the word from Moses later in v. 43. The instructions of Exodus 13:3–16, therefore, forge ties with the mixed voices (God's and the prophet's) of Exodus 12:14–27. Moses's allusion to his earlier instruction at this juncture (Exod 12:21–27) is apropos, given the attempt to locate the rationale for God's claim to Israel's firstlings in the focused carnage of the awful night (Exod 13:15; compare 12:21–23). The divine claim persists beyond the Egyptian bloodbath.

Beyond the mimicry of Exodus 12:14–27, the prescriptions are evocative, vaguely, of God's initial revelation of Egypt's impending embarrassment in Exodus 11:1–3. The double reference to the agency of God's 'strength of hand' (Exod 13:3, 16) smacks of the sheer puissance—a tenor to the talk the narrator picks up in depicting Egypt's desperation (Exod 12:33–36)—that will force Pharaoh's hand to drive Israel out of Egypt with gifts in tow (Exod 11:1–2). The prophet's gesture here seems an acknowledgment of God's emphasis—the profusion of first-person forms in the deity's address—on the personal, divine attention to Israel's deliverance and Egypt's suffering (Exod 12:12–13). Things turn out as projected!

But what is Moses's spin in harnessing the hype of previous utterances? Absent, conspicuously, is the foregoing (Mosaic) statement's tunnel vision to the blood rite—the scrupulous attention to the lintel—and the barring of the night's murderous forces from Israelite homes (Exod 12:21–27). The danger has passed; the shift to *commemoration* and a meditation on significance is now in order. The restatement of the requirements to the feast of unleavened cakes locates the festive meal in the month of 'fresh ears' (Abib) and advocates catechistic instruction on the significance to the rite with mnemonics (Exod 13:8–9; compare 12:14–20). These are new. Perhaps the major thrust to the speech is the conjunction of the feast and the novel requirement for firstling offerings by the balance to the legislation—the common 'settlement-catechism-mnemonic sign' cycle to the bipartite prescription. This binding of the new to the old, of course, reprises the allusion to the next portion of the divine agenda of a previous statement—Israel's settlement in Canaan (Exod 12:25). But here in Exodus 13, that projection of a vital need of religious instruction for posterity spawns a new component: the offering of Israel's firstborns in remembrance of Egypt's fateful night.

It is in this matter that the genius of Mosaic manipulation in the rehearsal of prior stipulation shines through. The groundwork for the prescriptive inauguration of firstling offerings was laid in the preceding speech of Moses. The requirement for a substitute offering for firstborn donkeys and children (Exod 13:13) turns on the foundation that there was a claim on the lives of Israelite firstborns in the event that inspired the rite. The re-visioning prophetic gaze of Exodus 13, by inference, construes the slaying of the Passover beast as a *replacement slaying*, a slaughter at the door that obviates the need for further slaughter *indoors*. An apotropaic maneuver—the display of the beast's blood on the door to turn away the bloodthirsty divine emissary—assumes the function of a ransom. The makings of this logic, of course, are in place already in the inside/outside binary of the earlier framing of the slaughter. The obsessive focus on the threshold, on the limits to the maleficent intentions of the slayer, and the balance to the slaughter within and without the home (the šḥṭ/šḥt resonance on both sides of the threshold) are the building blocks that pave the path to the institution of firstling offerings. The strictures to the legislation codify, extend, and ritualize a broad claim to lives on both sides of the door and a logic of substitution already incipient in the night of Israel's release. The bearing of the tradition into the land is but an adumbration of a *modus operandi* of Israel's mythological heritage.

BETWEEN MOSES AND GOD: SOME THOUGHTS IN CONCLUSION

Our brisk canter through Exodus 11–13 bears up the broad-based understanding up through the Second Temple period that the (Mosaic) prophetic mantle represents a robust, sometimes contentious, but always creative, engagement with voices past, divine or otherwise. Mutual adaptation and modification is the rule in the God-Moses oral relay. The transforming view on the Passover rites in the ping-pong exchange, summarily stated, is as follows. The initial announcement of divine intent, a joint statement by prophet and divinity (Exod 11:1–10), has Moses shifting emphasis to Israel's exclusion from divine wrath (Exod 11:4–8) in a follow-up to God's unmediated forecast of the terminus to Egyptian control (Exod 11:1–3). Between readerly conjecture and reevaluation the realization dawns that an intercalation of divine and prophetic voices permeates the unit of speech. The next burst of direct divine communication (Exod 12:1–13)—as if to confirm this instinct in reading—carries with it the prophet's assurance to the people and his choice of terms; but alongside is God's indication of divine initiative behind Israel's deliverance. This emphatic rejoinder stands over and against the prophet's slight representation of that fact. The structures of exclusion germane to the prescribed procedure for the Passover meal—still God speaking—carry over into that of the festival of unleavened bread (Exod 12:14–20). The specifications of space, time, and the entities they exclude in each unique rite line up. A spatiotemporal rubric emerges. The prophet's distinct concerns, when his voice returns in Exodus 12:21–28, are to include the unwary Israelite who wanders outdoors in the list of excluded entities and to reenvision the slaughter of the Passover lamb as a counterpart to the killing of Egypt's young beyond the boundaries of Israelite homes. Shorn of any interest in the blood rite, God's prescriptive voice comes back in Exodus 12:43–49 to clarify Israel's identity by the exclusion of parties uncircumcised from the festive meal. This assertion is a focused attention to one side—indoors—of the incipient dichotomous spatiotemporal scheme of the preceding discourses. Finally, in Exodus 13:2–16, Moses's brilliant expansion of God's command for firstling offerings (v. 2) blends the themes of settlement, the festive meal, the dual-zone configuration to Egypt's terror, and Israel's deliverance. The foregoing construct of parallel actions across Israel's doorways becomes the constitutive image for the transformation of an apotropaic rite into one of substitution in the genesis of a new law.

The series of speeches is a concatenation of units deploying similar language, imagery, and concepts; each subsequent segment squeezes fresh significance from previous ones. Things of less import (e.g., divine agency in Israel's deliverance) or nonexistent in earlier speeches (e.g., the slain lamb in the house as counterpart to the slain offspring outside the house) find themselves central subjects in subsequent discourse. Through a network of analogies, the significance of concepts grows: new boundaries of time and space are added and the list of excluded entities/activities expands. One rite is fashioned in the image of another; one set of requirements for conformity resembles a previous one. A likeness of consonance emerges. The prophet speaks through the words of God, and God through the prophet's; words and the traces of previous meanings in those words are twisted in the mouth of each other in the genesis of fresh perspectives. In this manner, both prophetic and divine speech is *perverse*, a deviation from previous direction. But it is this perversion that animates the reader's imagination in revisiting familiar nuances in earlier utterances, tracing the points of aberration. Did Moses, in his announcement of divine intent in Exodus 11:4–8, anticipate the need for a sign to distinguish Israelite homes from others (Exod 12:13)? Does God's vision for the preparation and consumption of the Passover lamb (Exod 12:12–13) envision these actions as a likeness to the slaughter that will take place beyond the houses of the Israelites, as the prophet would suggest (Exod 12:22–23)? Did divine imagination in Exodus 13:2–3 foresee firstling offerings as substitute ritual slayings modeled on the Passover sacrifice (Exod 13:14–15)? Are there other ways of comprehension beyond the ones proposed? The contingency of each act of interpretation becomes stimulus for further speculation. Within the interstices of the dialectic between God and Moses, scribes—meticulous readers—find inspiration for fresh acts of interpretation and a basis for a recasting of prophetic vision and religious sensibility.

The interface between prophet and deity in this brief segment of the Pentateuch sets the tone for active readerly engagement in the rest of this study. This positioning of readers between utterances, of listening in the lull between bursts of diction, is a foretaste of our broader project. The echoes of themes, images, phrases, and, especially, of the dichotomous vision to Israel's self-understanding will persist. Of these we have not heard the last. Egypt will not be the sole disdained party to find itself outside Israel's protective doors.

Notes

1. See Eva Mroczek, 'Moses, David and Scribal Revelation: Preservation and Renewal in Second Temple Jewish Textual Traditions,' in *The Significance of Sinai: Traditions about Sinai and Divine Revelation in Judaism and Christianity* (ed. George J. Brooke, Hindy Najman and Loren T. Stuckenbruck; Leiden: Brill, 2008), 112. Mroczek's argument proceeds with reference to Jub. 1:5–7, 1:26–2:1. For a similar perspective, see Hindy Najman, 'Interpretation as Primordial Writing: Jubilees and Its Authority Conferring Strategies,' *Journal for the Study of Judaism* 30 (1999): 406–08; idem., *Seconding Sinai: The Development of Mosaic Discourse in Second Temple Judaism* (Leiden: Brill, 2003), 12–25.
2. For Moses as a paradigm for the eschatological prophet in the Dead Sea Scrolls, see George J. Brooke, 'Moving Mountains: From Sinai to Jerusalem,' in *The Significance of Sinai: Traditions about Sinai and Divine Revelation in Judaism and Christianity* (ed. George J. Brooke, Hindy Najman and Loren T. Stuckenbruck; Leiden: Brill, 2008), 81–84; Marcus Tso, 'The Giving of the Torah at Sinai and the Ethics of the Qumran Community,' in *The Significance of Sinai: Traditions about Sinai and Divine Revelation in Judaism and Christianity* (ed. George J. Brooke, Hindy Najman and Loren T. Stuckenbruck; Leiden: Brill, 2008), 123. Brooke's comments stem from an analysis of portions from 4Q174 (Florilegium), 4Q175 (Testimonia), and 4Q177 (Catena^a). Elsewhere, Brooke explores the prophetic imagination in rewritten prophetic texts at Qumran ('Prophecy and Prophets in the Dead Sea Scrolls: Looking Backwards and Forwards,' in *Prophets, Prophecy, and Prophetic Texts in Second Temple Judaism* [ed. Michael H. Floyd and Robert D. Haak; Library of Hebrew Bible/Old Testament Studies 427; New York: T & T Clark, 2006], 151–65; see especially 154–56). According to Brooke, the profuse deployment of biblical prophetic texts coupled with the absence of any argument for legitimacy, as seen in Pseudo-Ezekiel^{a-d} (4Q385, 4Q385b, 4Q386, 4Q388) and the Jeremiah Apocrypha (A-C^{a-f}) (4Q383, 4Q384, 4Q385a, 4Q387, 4Q387a, 4Q388a, 4Q389, 4Q389a, 4Q390), betrays the assumption of a prophetic function by the authors of such texts. These writers, in spelling out for their contexts meanings incipient in and inherent to earlier prophetic visions, were no less engaged in prophecy.

3. James W. Watts, 'The Legal Characterization of Moses in the Rhetoric of the Pentateuch,' *Journal of Biblical Literature* 117 (1998): 418–22; Marc Zvi Brettler, '"Fire, Cloud and Deep Darkness" (Deuteronomy 5:22): Deuteronomy's Recasting of Revelation,' in *The Significance of Sinai: Traditions about Sinai and Divine Revelation in Judaism and Christianity* (ed. George J. Brooke, Hindy Najman and Loren T. Stuckenbruck; Leiden: Brill, 2008), 22–27. Watts and Brettler stand at the end of a long line of scholars investigating the legal innovations in the book of Deuteronomy. Watts, in particular, pursues a distinction between the roles of Moses as prophet and scribe; acts of interpretation and innovation belong, properly, in the latter role. This boundary, in my analysis, is porous.
4. As mentioned in the chapter of introduction, such goals, often of penultimate import, are ubiquitous in Hebrew Bible studies. See, for example, the recent thorough analysis of the Pentateuch's dissonance on prophecy by Jeffrey Stackert, *A Prophet Like Moses: Prophecy, Law, and Israelite Religion* (Oxford and New York: Oxford University Press, 2014).
5. While my analysis shall note the speaker for each segment of speech, I shall consider direct quotations of divine speech within the speeches of the prophet to belong to the perspective of the prophet. This approach is useful, especially, when distinctions in the prophet's communication of divine instruction occur in comparison with a preceding speech by God on the same subject: the distance between the two voices becomes evident.
6. As the choice of terms here betrays, Mikhail Bakhtin's conception of 'polyphony' in the novel inspires my thoughts on this matter. All utterances, by this conception, are multi-voiced, a conglomeration reflecting the religious, socioeconomic, ideological, and other variations representative of other voices in dialogical tension within a work. For a demonstration of Bakhtin's approach in reading Dostoevsky's novels, see Mikhail Bakhtin, *Problems of Dostoevsky's Poetics* (trans. Caryl Emerson; Theory and History of Literature 8; Minneapolis: University of Minnesota Press, 1984). For a comprehensive and systematic introduction to the often complex thinking of Bakhtin, see Michael Holquist, *Dialogism: Bakhtin and his World* (London: Routledge, 1990); Sue Vice, *Introducing Bakhtin* (New York: Manchester University Press, 1997). For a concise overview and application in biblical studies, see Barbara Green, *Mikhail Bakhtin and Biblical Scholarship: An Introduction* (Semeia Studies 38; Atlanta: Society of Biblical Literature, 2000).
7. Among others, A. H. McNeile, *The Book of Exodus* (London: Methuen, 1908), 60; B. D. Eerdmans, *Das Buch Exodus* (Giessen: Alfred Töpelmann, 1910), 29; S.R. Driver, *The Book of Exodus* (Cambridge: Cambridge University Press, 1953), 84; Brevard S. Childs, *The Book of Exodus: A Critical Theological Commentary* (Old Testament Library;

Louisville: Westminster, 1974), 160–62. The portion of Exodus 11:4–8 is thought to derive from the Yahwistic source (J). For a concise overview of literary problems in Exodus 11:1–10, see Martin Noth, *Exodus* (trans. J.S. Bowden; Old Testament Library; Philadelphia: Westminster, 1962), 92–93; John I. Durham, *Exodus* (Word Biblical Commentary 3; Waco: Word, 1987), 146–47. For a concise outline of the rationale(s) for the identification of the sources of the Pentateuch, their idiosyncratic traits and the twists and turns in the discussion, see Joseph Blenkinsopp, *The Pentateuch: An Introduction to the First Five Books of the Bible* (The Anchor Bible Reference Library; New York and London: Doubleday, 1992), 4–12; Jean-Louis Ska, *Introduction to Reading the Pentateuch* (trans. Sr. Pascale Dominique; Winona Lake: Eisenbrauns, 2006), 131–61. A robust defense and revision of the Documentary Hypothesis with extensive demonstration of its cogency is Joel S. Baden, *The Composition of the Pentateuch: Renewing the Documentary Hypothesis* (The Anchor Bible Reference Library; New Haven and London: Yale University Press, 2012).

8. Childs, *The Book of Exodus*, 161–62. For an argument along similar lines, see Waldemar Janzen, *Exodus* (Waterloo: Herald, 2000), 134; Terence Fretheim, *Exodus* (Louisville: John Knox, 1991), 131.
9. On this perspective, see Cornelis Houtman, *Exodus* (trans. Sierd Woudstra; 4 vols.; Kampen: Kok, 1993–2002), 2:134; William H. C. Propp, *Exodus 1– 18: A New Translation with Introduction and Commentary* (Anchor Bible 2; New Haven: Yale University Press, 1999), 344. Propp goes as far as to include the Israelites and readers as addressees.
10. Frederick V. Winnett, *The Mosaic Tradition* (Toronto: University of Toronto Press, 1949), 11–12, places Exodus 10:28–29 between Exodus 11:8a and 11:8b in an earlier version of the text. See also John Van Seters, *The Life of Moses: The Yahwist as Historian in Exodus-Numbers* (Louisville: Westminster, 1994), 108; Paul Heinisch, *Das Buch Exodus* (Bonn: Peter Hanstein, 1934), 95–96. For Winnett, the clauses of Exodus 10:28–29 were removed to the present location by the Priestly (P) author in order to mark a conclusion to the story of the plagues at the end of chapter 10. Subsequently, Exodus 11:9–10 was composed to set the inauguration of the Passover within the context of a final (tenth) plague.
11. Most scholars find P's handiwork in the passage: among others, Noth, *Exodus*, 94; Childs, *The Book of Exodus*, 184; Propp, *Exodus 1–18*, 379–80. Childs and Propp offer concise outlines of the distinctive characteristics of P's version of the ritual in comparison with the pre-P preoccupation with the blood rite (see Exod 12:21–23). See also McNeile, *The Book of Exodus*, 63.
12. The clauses of Exodus 12:1–13 attest to a semantic range in the use of the term 'house' (*byt*). While 'house' in vv. 3b (two times), 4a, and 4b refers to

members of a household, 'the houses' (*hbbtym*) in vv. 7b and 13a almost certainly designate the physical structures of the domiciles. Shimon Bar-On has noted the repeated use of the term and finds in the similar prominence of 'house' in Exodus 12:22–27a indication that Exodus 12:22–27a followed Exodus 12:7 at an earlier stage in the development of the text ('Zur Literarkritischen Analyse von Ex 12,21–27,' *Zeitschrift für die Alttestamentliche Wissenschaft* 107 [1995]: 23–25).

13. The senses to 'house' and 'eating' will narrow in Exodus 12:14–20.
14. The sacredness and elevated status to these rituals of consumption are the affects of such proscriptions. See, among others, J. B. Segal, *The Hebrew Passover from the Earliest Times to A.D. 70* (London: Oxford University Press, 1963), 207; Propp, *Exodus 1–18*, 396–97; Houtman, *Exodus*, 2:181. Roland de Vaux, *Les Sacrifices de l'Ancien Testament* (Paris: Gabalda, 1961), 12, links the restriction of consumption to the night and the disposal of leftovers at daybreak to nomadic practice, the imputed original context for the rite.
15. The designation of the object of destruction in Exodus 12:12 may be read as an abbreviation of the longer statement in Exodus 11:5, maintaining the categories (animal and human) of the preceding expression (Exod 11:5).
16. The emphasis on divine agency has been noted by several scholars: U. Cassuto, *A Commentary on the Book of Exodus* (trans. Israel Abrahams; Jerusalem: Magnes, 1967), 140; Childs, *The Book of Exodus*, 192; Van Seters, *The Life of Moses*, 116. Italicization in the text is my doing.
17. The preference for the abstract infinitival expression *lmšḥyt* ('to destroy') in Exodus 12:13b, instead of the personified agent of destruction, *hmmšḥyt* ('the destroyer'; see also 2 Sam 24:16; 1 Chr 21:12) in Exodus 12:23b, may indicate P's aversion to the idea of ministering angels (see Richard E. Friedman, *Who Wrote the Bible?* [New York: Summit], 191; Propp, *Exod –18*, 401–02). Priestly reservation in such matters, as it turns out, contributes to the rhetorical direction of the passage in emphasizing God as the agent of destruction. No other 'destroyer' (*hmmšḥyt*) exists in the speech of Exodus 12:1–13 to steal the show from Israel's national deity. However, H. G. May contends, with reference to Exodus 13:14, 15 and Deuteronomy 6:20, that Israel's god is often indistinguishable from the extraterrestrial agents of his will ('The Relation of the Passover to the Festival of Unleavened Cakes,' *Journal of Biblical Literature* 55 [1936]: 70). Reference to such beings, in his view, does not diminish divine participation. May's contention presents no problem to my argument here. The function of emphasis inherent to the selection of certain lexical or grammatical forms over others does not presume the absence of the object of amplification in a text under comparison. In fact, the opposite is the case. The proliferation of first-person verbs and the choice of the infinitive construct *lmšḥyt* embolden

a notion (divine initiative) already present in surrounding texts. Emphasis, in this capacity, draws attention to something present *already* in a work.
18. The progression of thought in both statements is identical: a call to abstain from leaven leading into a stipulated consequence for failure to do such.
19. Israel Knohl finds in Exodus 12:18–20 a structure that places the grave consequence of excommunication in focus (*The Sanctuary of Silence: The Priestly Torah and the Holiness School* [Minneapolis: Fortress, 1995], 21): command to eat unleavened bread (v. 18), prohibition of leaven (v. 19a), *consequence of excommunication* (v. 19b), prohibition of leaven (v. 20a), and command to eat unleavened bread (v. 20b). Combining the foci of both constructions in the passage (Knohl's and mine) leads to an understanding of Passover observance/remembrance as inclusion in the congregation of Israel, a state diametrically opposed to that of excommunication.
20. The postulation that the festival was a celebration of the harvest and only subsequently related to the Passover has been rehearsed elsewhere: J. Morgenstern, 'The Origins of Massoth and the Massoth Festival,' *American Journal of Theology* 21 (1917): 275–93; J. Pedersen, *Israel: Its Life and Culture* (2 vols.; London: Oxford University Press, 1940), 2:399–401; R. de Vaux, *Ancient Israel: Its Life and Institutions* (trans. John McHugh; London: Darton, Longman & Todd, 1961), 490–92. The details of that theory are not the concern of this study, but only the connections, albeit artificial and secondary, forged in the conjunction of Exodus 12:1–13 and 14–20, and the inconcinnities that remain for readers encountering the text.
21. Cassuto, *A Commentary on the Book of Exodus*, 140.
22. Even the chronological irregularities in the speech of Exodus 12:1–20 participates in bridging the two rites. One might ask: does 'this day' of Exodus 12:14a refer to the day of the Passover meal, the destruction, the departure (see Exod 12:17), or the inception of the festival of unleavened bread (Exod 12:18)? The list of activities straddles two days (14 and 15 Nisan). By formal and semantic resemblance, 'this day' echoes other temporal phrases in surrounding texts. Looking backward from Exodus 12:14a, 'this day' picks up 'this month' in Exodus 12:1a (the start of the year that commemorates the exodus) and 'on this night' of Exodus 12:8a, 12a (the night of the Passover meal and of the destruction, respectively). Looking ahead from Exodus 12:14a, 'this day' designates the day of Israel's departure (15 Nisan) in Exodus 12:17a, b, which the festival (its inception slated for 14 Nisan according to Exod 12:18) commemorates. The cluster of similar temporal expressions draws together the various activities of both days, underscoring the temporal confusion. Confusion, however, may be in order in a speech that seeks to con-fuse two rituals. Several commentators follow this trend when they suggest that 'this day' in Exodus 12:14a refers

to both days *loosely*: Childs, *Exodus*, 197; Durham, *Exodus*, 157–58; Knohl, *The Sanctuary of Silence*, 19–20. A similar fastidious attention to temporal delimitations, even if inaccurate, straddles both acts of ritual. The fusion of the start of both rites is also the accomplishment of Ezekiel 45:21, as Knohl points out, but in contrast to Leviticus 23:5–8 and Numbers 28:16–18.

23. George W. Coats, *Exodus 1–18* (Forms of the Old Testament Literature 2a; Grand Rapids: Eerdmans, 1999), 83.
24. The unique properties of Exodus 12:21–28 and the assignment of the bulk of it by many to a pre-Priestly (P) stratum have been flagged in an earlier part of this essay (see n. 15). While the narrow focus on the blood rite is unique to Exodus 12:21–23, the literary, lexical, and thematic links with P's prescriptions of Exodus 12:1–13 (some of which have been mentioned earlier) have led some to seek the origins of Exodus 12:21–28 in that source (see May, 'The Relation of the Passover,' 71–73; B.N. Wambacq, 'Les Origines de la *Pesah Israélite*,' *Biblica* 57 [1976]: 316–18; Coats, *Exodus 1–18*, 82–83; Van Seters, *The Life of Moses*, 115–16; Bar-On, 'Zur literarkritischen Analyse,' 22).
25. So noted by Bar-On, 'Zur literarkritischen Analyse,' 22 n. 25.
26. Several scholars have noted here the significance of the threshold as the transit space between the benign spaces of the house and the external environment populated by malevolent forces: Bernard M. Levinson, *Deuteronomy and the Hermeneutics of Legal Innovation* (Oxford: Oxford University Press, 1998), 58–59; Houtman, *Exodus*, 2:175–76; Propp, *Exodus 1–18*, 434–39. In Exodus 12:22, the administration of blood to ward off the onslaught of the 'destroyer' from outside the house seems superfluous in the light of Exodus 11:4–7 (see also Exod 4:24–26); there God recognizes Israelite homes without need for a sign. Propp finds a ritual similar to the Passover in the Muslim rite of *fidya*. The latter is an undertaking in times of danger (transition, disease, etc.) for the community. Blood from a slain beast is applied to various objects, including doorways, for the purpose of protecting those inside. Houtman observes similarities between the blood rite of the Passover and the Jewish practice of attaching scrolls of scriptural passages to doorposts (see Deut 6:5; 11:20), and also the Christian practice of installing crucifixes in the same location.
27. Both meanings are possible. The concept of a receptacle is appropriate to 2 Samuel 17:28, 2 Kings 12:14, and Jeremiah 52:19. 'Doorway' would suit the contexts of Judges 19:27, Isaiah 6:4, and Amos 9:1. The Aramaic versions prefer the idea of a receptacle, while the Septuagint and the Vulgate reference a doorway. Similarly, scholars are divided on this matter. In favor of 'threshold,' with the implication that the slaughter takes place by the entrance, are A. M. Honeyman ('Hebrew ףס "Basin, Goblet",' *Journal of Theological Studies* 37 [1936]: 59), Houtman (*Exod*, 2:193), and

Levinson (*Deuteronomy and the Hermeneutics of Legal Innovation*, 59). Others consider 'receptacle' a better fit: McNeile, *The Book of Exodus*, 72; Segal, *The Hebrew Passover*, 158 n. 1; Propp, *Exodus 1–18*, 408. This last option suits the degree of attention to the threshold in Exodus 12:21–24. The alternative ('receptacle'), however, would not subtract from my argument here. The image of a doorway would remain a possibility, a playful offering through the choice of the ambiguous term for readers who would perceive a connection with the broader literary context.

28. The efficiency of the NRSV here obscures the Hebrew in this case, omitting the very parenthetical phrase of distribution to which I allude. A more precise, but clumsy, translation is: 'You shall not go forth, *a man from the door of his house*, until dawn' (Exod 12:22).
29. Richard Friedman, *Commentary on the Torah* (San Francisco: Harper, 2001), 207. Of course, the implication of a vicarious function to the lamb's slaughter in Exodus 12:22–24 is but one interpretation of these verses. Other postulated meanings to the sacrifice and the blood manipulation, beyond an apotropaic function, include the related acts of purification (Segal, *The Hebrew Passover*, 157–62, 185–86; see Lev 14:2–9, Num 119:2–10, and Ezek 45:18–20) and reconciliation (Heinisch, *Das Buch Exodus*, 101–2).
30. This is the dominant reading of the significance to the requirement: for example, Propp, *Exodus 1–18*, 418; Houtman, *Exodus*, 2:208; Durham, *Exodus*, 173; McNeile, *The Book of Exodus*, 77. The proscription, of course, accords with the element of haste (see 12:11), which would dictate a departure from customary methods of preparation (see Mic 3:3).
31. The rendition of the NRSV reads the two Hebrew terms in succession as a case of hendiadys: see, also, Houtman, *Exodus*, 2:207. The alternative understanding of two distinct parties of temporary status in Israel is more common: Propp, *Exodus 1–18*, 417–18; Durham, *Exodus*, 169; McNeile, *The Book of Exodus*, 77.
32. The statement, effectively, muddies the categories. Conceivably, it allows Egyptians to enter the 'house' if they submit to circumcision. Conversely, the privileged parties indoors might surrender their privilege. The divine voice, here, affirms the realm within doors as Israel's space designated and clarified by God and prophet. Here Israel's unity, by submission to circumcision, is forged. Here Israel, as one 'house' with invited guests, shares God's protective embrace.
33. Childs, *The Book of Exodus*, 202–04.
34. Ibid., 203.
35. Ibid., 203. The instructions here are considered, largely, the work of the Deuteronomist (D): Van Seters, *The Life of Moses*, 119–22; Durham, *Exodus*, 176; Noth, *Exodus*, 101–02; McNeile, *The Book of Exodus*, 78.

REFERENCES

Baden, Joel S. 2012. *The Composition of the Pentateuch: Renewing the Documentary Hypothesis*. The Anchor Bible Reference Library; New Haven and London: Yale University Press.

Bakhtin, Mikhail. 1984. *Problems of Dostoevsky's Poetics*, trans. Caryl Emerson. Theory and History of Literature 8; Minneapolis: University of Minnesota Press.

Bar-On, Shimon. 1995. 'Zur Literarkritischen Analyse von Ex 12,21–27.' *Zeitschrift für die Alttestamentliche Wissenschaft* 107: 18–31.

Blenkinsopp, Joseph. 1992. *The Pentateuch: An Introduction to the First Five Books of the Bible*. The Anchor Bible Reference Library; New York and London: Doubleday.

Brettler, Marc Zvi. 2008. '"Fire, Cloud and Deep Darkness" (Deuteronomy 5:22): Deuteronomy's Recasting of Revelation.' In *The Significance of Sinai: Traditions about Sinai and Divine Revelation in Judaism and Christianity*, ed. George J. Brooke, Hindy Najman and Loren T. Stuckenbruck. Leiden: Brill.

Brooke, George J. 2006. 'Prophecy and Prophets in the Dead Sea Scrolls: Looking Backwards and Forwards.' In *Prophets, Prophecy, and Prophetic Texts in Second Temple Judaism*, ed. Michael H. Floyd and Robert D. Haak. Library of Hebrew Bible/Old Testament Studies 427; New York: T & T Clark.

Brooke, George J. 2008. 'Moving Mountains: From Sinai to Jerusalem.' In *The Significance of Sinai: Traditions about Sinai and Divine Revelation in Judaism and Christianity*, ed. George J. Brooke, Hindy Najman and Loren T. Stuckenbruck. Leiden: Brill.

Cassuto, U. 1967. *A Commentary on the Book of Exodus*, trans. Israel Abrahams. Jerusalem: Magnes.

Childs, Brevard S. 1974. *The Book of Exodus: A Critical Theological Commentary*. Old Testament Library; Louisville: Westminster.

Coats, George W. 1999. *Exodus 1–18*. Forms of the Old Testament Literature 2a; Grand Rapids: Eerdmans.

Driver, S.R. 1953. *The Book of Exodus*. Cambridge: Cambridge University Press.

Durham, John I. 1987. *Exodus*. Word Biblical Commentary 3; Waco: Word.

Eerdmans, B.D. 1910. *Das Buch Exodus*. Giessen: Alfred Töpelmann.

Friedman, Richard. 2001. *Commentary on the Torah*. San Francisco: Harper.

Fretheim, Terence. 1991. *Exodus*. Louisville: John Knox.

Green, Barbara. 2000. *Mikhail Bakhtin and Biblical Scholarship: An Introduction*. Semeia Studies 38; Atlanta: Society of Biblical Literature.

Heinisch, Paul. 1934. *Das Buch Exodus*. Bonn: Peter Hanstein.

Holquist, Michael. 1997. *Dialogism: Bakhtin and his World*. London: Routledge.

Honeyman, A.M. 1936. 'Hebrew סַף "Basin, Goblet".' *Journal of Theological Studies* 37: 56–59.

Houtman, Cornelis. 1993–2002. *Exodus*, trans. Sierd Woudstra. 4 vols.; Kampen: Kok.
Janzen, Waldemar. 2000. *Exodus*. Waterloo: Herald, 2000.
Knohl, Israel. 1995. *The Sanctuary of Silence: The Priestly Torah and the Holiness School*. Minneapolis: Fortress.
Levinson, Bernard M. 1998. *Deuteronomy and the Hermeneutics of Legal Innovation*. Oxford: Oxford University Press.
May, H.G. 1936. 'The Relation of the Passover to the Festival of Unleavened Cakes.' *Journal of Biblical Literature* 55: 65–82.
Morgenstern, J. 1917. 'The Origins of Massoth and the Massoth Festival.' *American Journal of Theology* 21: 275–93.
McNeile, A.H. 1908. *The Book of Exodus*. London: Methuen.
Mroczek, Eva. 2008. 'Moses, David and Scribal Revelation: Preservation and Renewal in Second Temple Jewish Textual Traditions.' In *The Significance of Sinai: Traditions about Sinai and Divine Revelation in Judaism and Christianity*, ed. George J. Brooke, Hindy Najman and Loren T. Stuckenbruck. Leiden: Brill.
Najman, Hindy. 1999. 'Interpretation as Primordial Writing: Jubilees and Its Authority Conferring Strategies.' *Journal for the Study of Judaism* 30: 379–410.
Najman, Hindy. 2003. *Seconding Sinai: The Development of Mosaic Discourse in Second Temple Judaism*. Leiden: Brill.
Noth, Martin. 1962. *Exodus*, trans. J.S. Bowden. Old Testament Library; Philadelphia: Westminster.
Pedersen, J. 1940. *Israel: Its Life and Culture*. 2 vols.; London: Oxford University Press.
Propp, William H.C. 1999. *Exodus 1–18: A New Translation with Introduction and Commentary*. Anchor Bible 2; New Haven: Yale University Press.
Segal, J.B. 1963. *The Hebrew Passover from the Earliest Times to A.D. 70*. London: Oxford University Press.
Ska, Jean-Louis. 2006. *Introduction to Reading the Pentateuch*, trans. Sr. Pascale Dominique. Winona Lake: Eisenbrauns.
Stackert, Jeffrey. 2014. *A Prophet Like Moses: Prophecy, Law, and Israelite Religion*. Oxford and New York: Oxford University Press.
Tso, Marcus. 2008. 'The Giving of the Torah at Sinai and the Ethics of the Qumran Community.' In *The Significance of Sinai: Traditions about Sinai and Divine Revelation in Judaism and Christianity*, ed. George J. Brooke, Hindy Najman and Loren T. Stuckenbruck. Leiden: Brill.
Van Seters, John. 1994. *The Life of Moses: The Yahwist as Historian in Exodus-Numbers*. Louisville: Westminster.
de Vaux, R. 1961. *Ancient Israel: Its Life and Institutions*, trans. John McHugh. London: Darton, Longman & Todd.

de Vaux, R. 1961. *Les Sacrifices de l'Ancien Testament.* Paris: Gabalda.
Vice, Sue. 1997. *Introducing Bakhtin.* New York: Manchester University Press.
Wambacq, B.N. 1976. 'Les Origines de la *Pesah Israélite.*' *Biblica* 57: 206–24, 301–26.
Watts, James W. 1998. 'The Legal Characterization of Moses in the Rhetoric of the Pentateuch.' *Journal of Biblical Literature* 117: 415–26.
Winnett, Frederick V. 1949. *The Mosaic Tradition.* Toronto: University of Toronto Press.

CHAPTER 3

On Sacred Heads and Sullied Wombs: Bouncing Between Leviticus and Numbers

An affinity for integrity inhabits the process of reading. We scan blocks of text in sequence, quite habitually, searching for overarching semantic categories, forging lines of thematic continuity, a sense of a whole to the text. This linear progression of ideas seems fundamental to a meaningful experience in reading. Where gaps exist—unstated motives for action, unexpected changes in behavior—prognostications abound. Projections of possible metanarratives multiply in the face of a perceived listlessness to a tale.[1] This scrutiny of the text is bidirectional: backward for the discernment of patterns and trajectories and forward for confirmation of putative patterns. Many projections in the quest for 'meaning' are discarded. Some are retained, almost always revised. A tentative posture superintends all adoptions. Additional data and evaluation will test all perspectives and construals of sense. The text is fraught with potential clues teasing the probings of a restless imagination. Here a lead opens; there another runs dry. Readers dangle between speculation and expectation—sometimes despair—in wrestling with the minutiae of plot. Where despair triumphs boredom ensues. The choice to read is, essentially, the will to persist in prognosis and to explore fresh vistas of significance. The implicit assumption in all this is that the 'meaning(s)' of a work, the cogency of its message(s) and its appeal, *is* its coherence! A systematized whole, established and locked away, is a goal. At times, this seems to me an accomplishment *in spite* of the text.

Such habits of reading—perhaps especially on this last point—are evident in the numerous interpretations of the odd collection of rules to Numbers 5:1–6:21. The divine voice in these chapters interrupts the appointment of the Levites as servants to the priests, having the semblance of an incongruous legal excursus nestled between the enumeration of the cultic assistants and their installation. The speeches are a pastiche of rite and regulation of variant interests: purity in the camp (5:1–4), restoration for acts of ill faith (5:5–10), clarification where adultery is suspected (5:11–31), and the regulatory strictures for Nazirites (6:1–21). The rules seem to many a scholar haphazard, bearing little connection one to another, and even less as a group to the broader context. Martin Noth speaks for a scholarly consensus in dubbing the prescriptions a miscellany of laws, an aggregation of rulings left over and inserted as late addenda to the Sinai/Horeb revelation.[2] Indeed, this 'malady' to Numbers 5–6, a result of the text's generic heterogeneity, afflicts the book as a whole. Noth's perception is that

> the book lacks unity, and it is difficult to see any pattern in its construction. Seen as a whole, it is a piece of narrative, but this narrative is interrupted again and again by the communication of more or less comprehensive regulations and lists which are loosely linked to the narrative thread by the short, stereotyped introductory formula, 'Yahweh said to Moses' ('in the wilderness of Sinai' or 'in the plains of Moab').[3]

Tortuously, the narrative persists in

> long stretches where the thread of the narrative fades so much into the background that it is almost lost to view. What then appear in the foreground are not larger, self-contained units but, for the most part, collections of very varied material with little inner cohesion.[4]

The disarray in Numbers 5–6 keeps company with the rest of the book. But the structural malaise Noth decries does little to stem the tide of scholarly speculation on the book's order. Indeed, Numbers is the locus of febrile scholarly contention on matters structural and systematic. Readers press on to *make* meaning out of the book. Thomas Römer speaks of Numbers as 'the only book of the Pentateuch where commentators need several pages to justify their idea of the structure of the book and to refute others.'[5] The pitched debate reflects the struggle to ascertain a coherent design to the work as an ongoing pursuit—a labor of Sisyphean proportions, it seems, with a constant litany of voices unmasking weaknesses in the putative constructs of their predecessors. Numerous commentaries, even Noth's, bear witness to the graded movement toward the plains of Moab and the transition from one generation to the next—a consensus of sorts—as markers of comprehensive units in the book.[6] Closer to the particular portion of the book of interest (Num 5–6), the election of the Levites—the enveloping context for the instructions of Numbers 5–6—is considered a source of inspiration for legislation on cultic purity, holiness, and other matters of priestly interest. A singular concern for moral and ritual purity in the precincts of the tabernacle animates the prescriptions of Numbers 5–6.[7] The laws betray the interests of a fastidious spirit in specifying the distinction between the holy and the profane on a range of issues. And so, Numbers 5–6 suits the broad agenda of Numbers 1–10! Scholarly confessions of disorder to the text herald arguments for the opposite in the compass of a close reading: the motley collection of rules to Numbers 5–6 makes sense after all. The incoherence of the text frustrates, yet speculations of a basis for the combination of laws persist.

The Task at Hand and Its Place in the Book

I offer *another* projection of coherence to the laws of Numbers 5–6, one enhanced by a reading in conjunction with an earlier series of instructions from the deity in Leviticus 21–22 on sacerdotal form (and deportment), sacred foods, and offerings. Within Numbers 5–6, a series of terms and their attendant concepts create lines of thematic intersection across laws and rites of different stripes. The words are nexi for semantic associations across the units of Numbers 5–6, highways for the cross-fertilization of ideas. Semantic categories expand, twist, and warp, as concepts find fresh expression. One case becomes an analogue for another, enticing readers to impute further associations between texts. The view from the top, looking down on Numbers 5–6, is kaleidoscopic. Connections move in multiple directions with links generating fresh interpretive possibilities. The flow of ideas triggers novel conceptions of the circumstances of cases and alternative possibilities to their attendant solutions. The same conceptual interpollination characterizes the reader's inclusion of Leviticus 21–22 in extending the semantic compass of Numbers 5–6. The inquiry uncovers a mode of distillation and dispersion in the negotiation of themes and topoi across texts. Single legislative units host concepts and lexica spread across multiple members in the other and vice versa. In this manner, the passages mutually reinforce inferences of coherence between the parts of the other. Each passage speaks to the other, uncovering and clarifying foundational principles in its counterpart.

My interests here intersect with those of the last chapter in two ways. First, the mutual interrogation and interpenetration of perspectives germane to the mode of inquiry of the last chapter are essential to my approach here. The quest for 'meaning' in acts of interpretation takes multiple vantage points, exchanging views from one text for another; all seen against a dynamic, eclectic background of (inter)texts. The inescapable consequence is the vulnerability of any projection of a meaningful motivational coherence—the varied productions of Iser's 'wandering viewpoint'—across texts as fresh vantage points substitute others in a concatenation of interpretive rubrics. Furthermore, the suggestion of thematic familiarity across series of legal and cultic prescription, the fruit of juxtaposition, falls short of explicit denotation in the texts. The analogies inferred cross categories—ritual and moral, sacerdotal and lay. They arouse suspicion and fall prey to ambiguity at the numerous turns of the readerly imagination. Coherence is phantasmagoric and subject to dissolution under scrutiny. Reticence intersperse moments of certainty.

Second, the context of the genesis of a distinct class of cultic servants—the Levites—to Numbers 5–6 evinces a rationale identical to that for the divine claim to Israel's firstlings (compare Num 3:40–44 and Exod 13:11–15), the culmination of the series of semantic metamorphoses in the Moses-God exchange of Exodus 11–13. Both consecrations—human and beast—are constructed as analogies to the smiting of Egypt's firstborn. To the degree that Numbers 5–6 bears significance for elaboration upon the logic behind the election of the Levites, the selection of laws extends the religious and legal argumentation by analogy extent in Exodus 11–13. In other words, the metamorphosis of ritual constructs through the Moses-God exchange of Exodus 11–13 spawns a new chapter in Numbers 5–6, drawing fresh material into the orbit of its mytho-religious framework.

This chapter, succinctly stated, expands the interpretive sensibilities and the exclusionary logic resplendent in the Moses-God dialectic of Exodus 11–13. In doing so, it lays out—extends—the binary optic and the metonymic habits of mind that will be challenged by the emancipative hermeneutics of subsequent chapters.

A Rationale for Reading Against the Horizon of Leviticus 21–22

There is something to Noth's explanation for the genetic and thematic disarray of Numbers that speaks to a rationale for reading between Numbers 5–6 and Leviticus 21–22. In his view, the encounter with divinity at Sinai/Horeb—the place where Numbers picks up the story—presents an opportunity for the insertion of extraneous material deemed authoritative.[8] The majesty of Israel's congress par excellence elevates the gravity of legal promulgation and religious exhortation in its immediate vicinity, rendering this point in Israel's epic narrative appropriate and opportune for the insertion of a slew of loose material—drawn from various sources—ill befitting the flow of the unfolding narrative elsewhere. Numbers, by Noth's reckoning, is something of an addendum, an editorial appendix exploiting a propitious opening in (an earlier version of) the story.

The Nothian vision of the book's literary provenance touches off a broadening stream of scholarship, mostly European, that places the book among the final strata in the formation of the Pentateuch/Hexateuch. Numbers, by this view, is a 'rolling corpus' of exegesis and commentary and part of a broader initiative to bridge the theological ethos of Deuteronomic (D) and Priestly[9] trajectories in redaction with a view to solidifying Israel's sacerdotal preeminence in a postexilic order.[10] In an era where David's line is obscured, Aaron's sons reign supreme. In accord with this vision, the marshaling of the tribes and the organization of the camp, in Numbers, foregrounds the tabernacle and the cadre of Levites. Servants of the cult find themselves leaders in a martial formation on the trek through the wilderness, with priestly figures at the forefront of encounters with hostile parties. A priestly hierarchy, sans monarch, has pride of place.[11]

This present tack in Numbers research, while exploring fresh vistas, is in the vein of currents in biblical law studies by its attention to the book's orientation toward the other legal corpora of the Pentateuch. The specification of a text's literary forebears and its novel theological tendencies remain the mainstay of a temperament that precludes the isolated reading of *any* law. Indeed, the diachronic labors in interpretation are in response to the degree of topical and lexical overlap between the legal texts of the Pentateuch, the evidence of literary dependence. The blocks of prescription in Numbers, as Römer and others observe, are components in the intertextual matrix which is pentateuchal law, a patchwork of inner-biblical allusion, explication, extension, and contention.[12] And so, the consecration of the Levites in Numbers 8:5–7 reprises themes of election and ordination in Leviticus 8–9; the prescriptions for the Passover supplement those of Exodus 11–12, 25, and 37; the rulings on oaths and vows extend the reach of Leviticus 27 by considering the legitimacy of a vow and the circumstances under which some might be rescinded. In texts of immediate interest in this chapter, the wayward wife of Numbers 5:11–31 is reminiscent of rulings on adultery in Exodus (20:14), Leviticus (18:20; 20:10), and Deuteronomy (22:22). The redirection of portions from the well-being offering in Numbers 5:6–10 builds on directives in Leviticus 6:2–19. Measures for the segregation of impure persons in Numbers 5:1–5 resonate with Leviticus 12–15 and 21:1–10. Regulations for the Nazirite in Numbers 6:1–21 correspond to the details of those for the chief priest in Leviticus 21:10–15. Nary a ruling of Numbers 5–6 escapes the shadow of Leviticus.[13]

Furthermore, the narratorial framework of Numbers casts the cultic and legal ruminations of the book as post-Leviticus reflections. The events and speeches of Numbers take place in the wilderness of Sinai (Num 1:1), this in contradistinction to the discourses of Leviticus delivered *on* Sinai (Lev 7:38; 25:1; 26:46; 27:34).[14] The temporal succession of Numbers is noted also at points of transition in its narrative (Num 1:1; 9:1). The chronological and topological distinctions distinguish the two bodies of law and narrative, rendering analeptic all reprisals of the subject matter of Leviticus in Numbers. So framed, the legal and religious discourse of Numbers looks back to Leviticus. Similar notes of temporal and geographical import in Deuteronomy (1:1–8; 4:1–4; 5:1–5; 29:1) and at the conclusion of Numbers (36:13) set the discourses of Deuteronomy in a temporal position posterior to Leviticus and Numbers.[15] Deuteronomy emerges as Mosaic commentary and elaboration on divine jurisprudence at the terminus of an arduous journey from Sinai to Moab, from Exodus through Numbers.[16] The cultic and legal precepts of Leviticus, Numbers, and Deuteronomy constitute a trilateral conversation on a range of issues. Here, synchronic and diachronic expository vectors converge: both interpretive positionings stand as studied responses to the fine nuances of the biblical text. Numbers, as a stretch in the unfolding fabula, *wants* to be read against the horizon of Leviticus. I can do no less.

But why Leviticus 21–22 in particular out of a slew of texts of topical and thematic proximity to Numbers 5–6? Here, as stated in the introduction to this book, I confess a measure of arbitrariness. I happened upon Numbers 5–6 having recently perused Leviticus 21–22 and was struck by the profusion of linguistic, thematic, and conceptual connections—most of which have been noted just now—between the two readings. Quite simply, I choose to examine these texts in tandem because it strikes my fancy to do so. The connections, it seems, impressed themselves upon me; and this, after all, is a study that prizes readerly intuition and speculation. Of course, I shall argue that the collation of these texts in my mind is a reasoned and reasonable response to the texts. Both prescriptive bodies eschew the same constellation of things defiling—bodily emissions, dead bodies, and illicit coital contact. Also common is the concern for the sanctity and sanctification of items pledged. Moreover, the resonance of Leviticus 21–22 in Numbers 5–6, as we shall see, is in at least one case seriatim. The interpenetration of the texts triggers the sensation of a *déjà lu* reading one after the other, an inescapable sense of familiarity so often part and parcel of the experience of a work.[17] The topical sequence, its imageries and lexical constitution, evokes visions and patterns of thought previously aroused, stamped in memory. The uncovering of one correlate sparks a quest for others. The consequent frenetic shuttling between the texts separated by some distance juxtaposes the legislative chunks. The assiduous comparison yields ever more similarities. The imaginary here, by the reckoning of Mary Douglas, is one wholly at home in Leviticus.[18] The (ana)logic to the legislation of the book shuns explanation for a ruling in preference for the addition of 'another similar instruction, and another and another, thus producing its highly schematized effect.'[19] The legal reasoning is a concatenation of imputed equivalences, a 'presentational' discourse of 'abstract projections lifted from one context to another' in the presumption of a Pythagorean expectation of a universalistic harmony of a sort that links all branches of learning.[20] The scheme to Leviticus, by the insistence of Douglas, is a production impossible, inconceivable, apart from the 'synaesthetic' propensities and the 'organizational activity' of a reading subject.[21] It is the reader's natural penchant for metonymic substitution that drives the imaginary to find echoes across the range of phenomena.

But, alas, the abstractions of theoretical formulation fail to convey fully the mental operations they seek to describe. Concrete examples must pick up the slack. Let us press on to the texts I have in view. The point of departure for this dwelling between texts, prior to postulating connections with Leviticus 21–22, is a poring over Numbers 5:1–6:21 with a view to the terms and concepts that lend a sense of coherence, a *feeling* of internal consistency, to that collection of rulings.

NUMBERS 5:1–6:21: THE WORDS THAT WEAVE

Four distinct units make up Numbers 5:1–6:21. The first two call for the evacuation of persons defiled from the camp (5:1–4) and the transfer of the items of reparation to a kinsman in cases where the defrauded party is deceased (5:5–10). Procedures for determining a woman's guilt (or innocence) in cases of suspected adultery (5:11–31) and for maintaining the status of a Nazirite (6:1–21) complete the section of legislation. These laws, previously noted, stand at the center of a program for the enumeration of the Levites and the assignment of their duties (Num 3–4), the dedication of items for the tabernacle (Num 7), and the consecration of the Levites to service (Num 8). The broad sweep of plot in the larger literary context (Num 3–8), therefore, is the election of the Levites.

Interlocking lexica, ideas, and themes bind the laws of Numbers 5:1–6:21. The conglomeration of ritual and law is a matrix of fertile concepts flowing *into* each other in various directions. Words and phrases echo through the course of the passage, their semantic freight unleashed to birth fresh nuances. The conceptions these interactions spawn breathe life into each prescriptive iteration, fresh significances provocative but, ultimately, unstable. We enter this web of ideas by way of the lexemes of the root *ṭm'*, 'to defile' in verbal expression.

'Defile,' 'Defiled,' 'Defilement' (Ṭm')

The laws of Numbers 5:1–6:21 maintain the Priestly category of 'defiled' and 'defiling' substances as designated by the inflections of *ṭm'* in Leviticus 13–15. Defilement by exposure to a corpse is a point of interest on the edges of the prescriptive series (Num 5:1–4 and 6:1–21). The passage kicks off with instructions for the removal of parties deemed unclean from the camp (5:1–4)—including those infected by exposure to a corpse (Num 5:2b)—and concludes with the rites for the restoration of Nazirite status following contamination by exposure to the dead (6:9–12).[22] The extremities of Numbers 5:1–6:21, so to speak, reek of dead bodies. The defiling miasma of decay is the enveloping structure to our text, a grave concern on both ends.

But 'impurity' reaches further into Numbers 5:1–6:21. The law of the jealous husband (5:11–31) identifies the wife's infidelity an unclean act: 'If any man's wife goes astray and is *unfaithful* (*wm'lh*) to him . . . she has *defiled* herself (*nṭm'h*)' (vv. 12b–13; emphasis added). Illicit sexual congress pollutes. But the language of adultery goes further in designating the anatomical locus of the contamination. This precision begins with the idiom for sexual intercourse, *škbt zrʿ* (5:13), a phrase bearing reference to the emission of semen.[23] The phrase is hardly euphemistic, given its explicit properties. The encounter, the lying together, involves the spilling of seed. The prescriptive gaze falls squarely on the reproductive organs, male and female. But there is more that foregrounds genital contact in the (hypothetical) illicit coupling. In the case that the rite reveals a guilty subject, the prescribed procedure is destructive to the woman's abdomen: physical distortions materialize in the area of the midriff, the receptacle of the seminal emission (5:22, 27). In the case that the woman is innocent, notably, she retains the ability to bear seed/children (*zrʿ*; 5:28b). The destruction of the reproductive capabilities of the guilty woman, in the logic of the rite, is apropos in that the instrument of transgression is the target of destruction. The unhappy end for the errant womb is a case of tit for tat.[24] The cluster of pubic references, it seems, supports a view to the woman's pelvis as the site of pollution and the seminal infusion as the polluting agent in the illicit tryst.[25]

The uterus, therefore, joins the Nazirite head and the camp as protected zones in the unfolding legislation. Three of the four passages have a brand of *ṭm'* in the focus of their protective attention.

The directions for reparation in Numbers 5:5–10 is the sole detraction from the matter of defilement. The term *ṭm'*, in any inflection, does not show up. What is one to do when a trope so prominently displayed elsewhere is missing in a stretch of the prescriptive thread? Iser's reader, no doubt, would read the absence as a 'blank,' an invitation for the ideational faculties to supply a connection to the broader thematic flux.[26] The impetus derives from the reader's penchant for discerning, inventing, broad semantic categories—inclusive schema—that might govern *all* the parts of a text. What might this totalistic orientation find in the law of Numbers 5:5–10 as an index to impurity to secure the membership of the rule in the prescriptive drift of the broader context? As it often does, the text proves felicitous. The nebulous category of transgression designated *mʿl*, 'malfeasance,' jumps to the fore: this is the misdeed against the deity that requires compensation (Num 5:6a). Might this be the 'defiling' act to secure the law's membership in the larger grouping? But this hermeneutical gesture is problematic. 'Malfeasance,' *mʿl*, in the Priestly vision pertains to *desecration* (Lev 5:15–16; 6:2–7), not defilement.[27] The error involves the (usually illegitimate) transfer of things or persons out of the sacred sphere. Profanity's intrusion into the holy realm by way of the misappropriation of sancta is the offense in view. The interpretive move I suggest in deeming 'malfeasance' a contaminating act mixes categories of things offensive to divinity in cultic parlance. But even on this point of difficulty the law's location appears to present something of a solution. Two of the surrounding pericopes pair 'defilement' *and* 'malfeasance.' The errant wife who *defiles* herself with another man commits *malfeasance* against her husband (Num 5:11–13); the Nazirite *defiled* by a corpse (Num 6:9) must bring a guilt offering (Num 6:12), the designated remedy for 'malfeasance' according to Leviticus 5:15–16 (and 6:2–7). A 'malfeasance-defilement' pairing is in the environs of Numbers 5:5–10. Might the mention of one member of the dyad suggest the other? Could *mʿl* become the law's way into the subject matter of impurity? How might this connection play out in Numbers 5:5–10? Perhaps the 'wrong' against a neighbor (Num 5:6) is the defiling of a sacred portion, thus requiring its removal from sanctity. We might imagine the foul deed to be the misappropriation of the property of a member of a priestly household.[28] I am suggesting that the law's immediate environment—its location in legislation simultaneously evocative of the concepts of defilement and desecration—*forces* 'defilement' *on* the law, leading a reader to concoct a connection. The words, their association in the near context, spark the imagination. The solution, not without its problems, seems to suggest itself. Such is the pressure of a lingering theme in the broader context to a law.

In sum, 'defile'/'defilement' is salient in Numbers 5:1–6:21. The category displays an elasticity that bridges a series of prescriptions, drawing together sources (corpses, disorders of the epidermis, unnatural genital discharges, 'misplaced' semen, acts of malfeasance) and objects (the Israelite camp, an adulterous wife, the Nazirite head) of contamination. The idea, as the sense of the term denotes, is contagious, even spreading to places where its lexical host (*ṭmʾ*) is not.

'Malfeasance' (Mʿl) *and 'Guilt Offering'* (ʾšm)

The guilt offering, *ʾšm*, is the prescribed remedy for *mʿl* ('malfeasance') according to Leviticus 5:14–6:7.[29] The specific offense in the purview of 'malfeasance'—a point already noted—is sancta trespass (Lev 5:15), up to and including the disregard or misuse of the divine name (Lev 6:2–3).[30] The breach of trust and the guilt offering, thus, are tandem concepts in the protocols of ritual in Leviticus 5–6. The prescriptions for restitution of Numbers 5:5–10 is the sole pericope that alludes to both components in the cultic nexus—the transgression of *m'l* leads to the commissioning of the *'šm*. The other laws of the set mention only one member of the lexical pair. The ruling of Numbers 5:5–10 invokes an alternative term with reference to the guilt offering: 'the ram of expiation' (*'yl hkkpprym*; v. 8b). Notwithstanding this variance in nomenclature, the similar requirement for the addition of twenty percent to the amount restored (Num 5:7; Lev 5:16, 24) is evidence that the guilt offering is in view.[31]

Two other units—the Nazirite law (Num 6:1–21) and the case of the jealous husband (Num 5:11–31)—name but one of the elements of the 'malfeasance-guilt offering' continuum. The sacrifice concludes the procedure for the restoration of Nazirite status following corpse contamination (6:12). That the defilement of the Nazirite head, notwithstanding the absence of 'malfeasance,' is tantamount to sacrilege is evident given the qualification of the Nazirite crown as 'holy' (*qdwš*) in 6:5. The inadvertent contact with or proximity to a dead body forces the removal of the Nazirite from sacred bounds; God's (premature) loss must be compensated. The law of the jealous husband, by contrast, does invoke 'malfeasance' designating by it the wife's suspected sexual indiscretion (5:12). But here, when guilt is established by divine agency, there is no allowance for a guilt offering to assuage a more severe consequence; the 'fallen thigh' and 'distended belly' follow (vv. 21–22, 27). The preclusion of the sacrifice is in order, perhaps, given the distinction that the victim of infidelity is the husband, *not God* (see Num 5:12; compare Lev 5:15, 17; 6:2; all cases where the deity is the explicit target of the act of ill faith). This difference to the case sets it apart from the pack as one of 'ill faith' of a different order—the term is deployed for general acts of miscreancy. Sacrilege, a crime quite *directly* against God, is not the issue here in the case of the jealous husband. Nonetheless the invocation of the term is felicitous for making a connection to the other laws that reference desecration, the regnant implication of the lexeme. The immediate effect of the association with sanctum trespass in the case of the jealous husband, perhaps, is to strike a note of kinship with God's outrage. Indignation is the lot of both parties deprived, husband and God.

The specifications for campsite purity (Num 5:1–4) are bereft of the lexica of interest in this segment of our study. Neither 'malfeasance' nor the guilt offering comes up. But even here an oblique allusion to the sacrifice may be construed. The mention of skin disorder (*ṣrwʾ*) in verse 2 is evocative of the requirement for a guilt offering as part of the process of restoration to the community (see Lev 14:10–13). Jacob Milgrom's opinion on this matter is that the requirement is a precaution on the off chance that sacrilege had taken place in the state of defilement.[32] The contagion of impure substances and parties sullies the tabernacle, its sacred personnel, and the appurtenances of the cult. The same precautionary gesture is applicable to the case of Numbers 5:1–4. Might the unclean individual have come too close, unwittingly, to any one of the sanctified entities in the encampment? Impurity is a constant hazard in the orbit of Israel's sacred precincts and sacrilege is a danger ever present. Again, the schematic imaginary, buoyed by the salience of a recurring notion in proximate literary units, fills a blank. The rules for campsite purity—by the way of Leviticus 14—are drawn into the semantic compass of the 'desecration-reparation' topos of the prescriptive milieu.

An alternative, or complementary, path to the same effect is to invoke the Nazirite crown as an analogue to the precincts of the camp: both loci are designated defilement-free zones in their respective texts. If the guilt offering following defilement is prescribed for the sullied Nazirite, can the pollution of Israel's 'holy' camp require less? If both guarded spaces—the camp and the sanctified crown—require the expulsion of uncleanness, how far apart can Israel's habitus and the Nazirite locks be on the holy-profane continuum? The comparative glance, conceivably, nudges Israel's camp a notch closer to the pedigree of a sanctum, rendering it vulnerable to the ravages of sacrilege. This precise association is not foreign to the concluding exhortations of Hebrews 13 (vv. 9–14) that conflate the temple precincts with the camp and the city (Jerusalem), implying the extension of the sanctity of the former to the latter. Indeed, the cultic determinations of the Halakhic Letter from Qumran (4QMMT^a) come close to doing the same. In striking the correspondence of the tabernacle-camp dichotomy to the temple-city pair, the banning of dogs from the camp lest they consume the remains of sacred offerings is supported by the proclamation that the camp is a *holy* place.[33] The camp, with the holy abode intact, is a holy space.

But this interpretive move in Numbers 5, if in the correct direction, might be one step too far. Pegging the camp a sanctum flies in the face of the directions to the Aaronide high priest to refrain from exceeding the bounds of the tabernacle while on duty (Lev 10:7). The Mosaic prescriptions, there at least, set a sharp distinction between the holy precincts of the sanctuary and the spaces external to its limits. The parturient, accordingly, is cautioned from touching 'anything sacred' and—quite specifically—from approaching the sanctuary in her defiled state (Lev 12:4). The camp is by implication *not* sacred terrain. In this vein, it seems wrongheaded to consider the camp as such in our associative optic on Numbers 5. Of course, one might get around the difficulty by prescribing differing degrees of holiness that sustain the boundaries without precluding a sliver of sanctity to Israel's camp. But the tableau of pentateuchal instruction presents challenges to a wholesale inclusion of the camp in the divine sphere. Our reservations here are a timely reminder that the concoction of a gestalt to a set of rules may be a reader's prerogative, but its defense is always a tricky affair. In the final analysis, texts and intertexts show themselves malleable under the configurative, harmonistic calculus of readers. The assemblage of affiliations to pave the path to coherence, however, is not trouble-free, and there is no shortage of gaps to fill.

'Vow' (Ndr) *and 'Oath'* (Šbʿt)

The semantic penumbra of the Priestly construct of sacrilege and reparation (guilt offering) covers another common element across the complex of ritual and law: the 'oath' (*šbʿt*). The overlap looks back to Leviticus 6:1–7 where the abrogation of an oath is deemed a variety of sacrilege.[34] The 'vow,' (*ndr*), is a parallel term, though strictly promissory, in that vows, like oaths, are solemnized by the invocation of the divine name.[35] Numbers 30, therefore, considers the seriousness of both these actions together. The solemn word, so implied by either lexeme, shows up in two of the laws of Numbers 5–6: the prescribed protocols for the Nazirite turn on the profession of a vow (Num 6:2b, 21), and an oath to assert innocence stands at the climax of the ritual to determine the fate of the suspected adulterer (Num 5:21, 22, 27). 'Calling on the deity's name,' then, straddles the two laws as one more related member to the growing cluster of concepts—sacrilege, reparation, and uncleanness—that binds the larger set.

Swearing by the divine name, however, is only implicit in the supplementary instructions for reparation in cases of fraud (Num 5:5–10). Its virtual presence is organic to the law's literary dependence on Leviticus 6:1–7, which cites the regard for an oath as a case of 'malfeasance' (v. 3).[36] To the extent that Leviticus 6:1–7 forms the literary horizon, the fraudulent act of Numbers 5:5–10 is inclusive of the failure to honor an oath.

The invocation of the deity's name, quite conceivably, looms in the background to Numbers 5:5–10. The connection, if slender, holds.

Once again, the requirement to ban the unclean from the camp (Num 5:1–4) slips a thematic band binding the complex of laws. But its inclusion is not impossible. The associative logic comes into play, again. Already, the camp's defilement has been viewed as akin to the contamination of the Nazirite's locks. A similar tactic informs the pursuit of a connection to the same law. Its logic is as follows. The consecration of the Nazirite crown is the effect of a vow (Num 6:2, 21). To the degree that the contamination disrupts the fulfillment of this vow *and* the substitutionary logic to the analogical vision enacts an equivalence between head and camp—both entities guarded and pristine—the defilement of the camp, too, is the 'transgression' of an oath, a devotion of sorts to God.[37] To sully Israel's living space is to take God's name in vain.[38]

Clearly, we are out on a limb with this last projection of a thematic echo in a law. My imagined connection, if warranted, is plausible *only* in the wake of the array of correlations on a stronger footing.

Of Words and Views

Numbers 5:1–6:21 is an interweaving of words and ideas into a complex of merging and emerging concepts. The thematic disparity of the passage at first blush yields to an articulation of conceptual conformity born of a readerly imagination fostering links with, and without, words across prescriptive units. In scrutinizing the schematics of this entanglement of rulings religious and cultic, five things stand out. Firstly and most obviously, the concepts borne by terms spread across the parts of the passage morph in adapting to the conditions of their application. 'Defilement' pertains to different substances, even as 'malfeasance' shifts from qualifying acts of sacrilege to adultery. Secondly, where a close relationship pertains to two or more terms and concepts—'malfeasance' and 'guilt offering'—the presence of one term in a passage draws the other within its purview. In other words, some terms and their attendant concepts may be construed as *virtually* present by virtue of the occurrence of a related lexeme. The third observable hermeneutical feature is related to the second. The presence of terms and concepts in one text may trigger the quest for (and postulation of) their relevance for (or even presence in) an adjacent or proximate text. Themes and ideas are susceptible to transfer when pressed up against a literary unit. Fourthly, a syllogistic logic may operate in fostering relationships between the units of legislation (if A is like B and B is like C, then C is like A). This manner of dissemination is distinct from the last in its incorporation of an additional step (the intercession of 'B' being essential to the syllogism) in the semantic transfer. The final note to our observations is that any readerly act of ideation in the genesis of a sense of resemblance between the laws has its obstacles to overcome. The comprehensive vision is, at the same time, an occlusive optic on the text and its intertexts. The view to an overarching order *is* a will to blindness.

The aforementioned movements of mind require the participation of readers in carrying values and ideas in one set of prescriptions into others. In this manner, the proximity of distinct procedures within a contiguous series of laws affords a degree of mutual infection between members. In the interstices between the perceived units of a passage, each member grows pregnant with possibility. The text comes alive under the scrutiny of a keen imagination seeking novel solutions and applications. Analogy is piled on analogy, and the web of corresponding, intersecting concepts grows. As in much literature developed over an extensive period the matrix of themes, though recast with each installment, is *strangely familiar*. Faint memories of similar interests in a distant text emerge in the perusal of Numbers 5:1–6:21. Casting a glance backward, Leviticus 21–22—among other texts—comes into view. Our wandering viewpoint responds to the sense of an iteration *already seen* and returns to an earlier point in the narrative to ferret out the significances to the echo.

Betwixt Numbers (5–6) and Leviticus (21–22)

Leviticus 21–22 comes hard on the heels of exhortations for Israel to pursue a holy lifestyle in keeping with the character of its god (Lev 18–20). Leviticus 18 regulates sexual relations and proscribes idolatry; a mixture of cultic and moral instructions comprises Leviticus 19. The desire to retain the privilege of residing in the land given by God motivates the social and religious mores set forth (Lev 20:22–26). Consonant with the thrust of this foregoing material is the concern in Leviticus 21–22 for protecting the sanctity of Israel's sanctuary—its personnel, sacrificial portions, and cultic accouterments. The narrator's reports of speech (Lev 21:1, 16; 22:1, 17, 26) mark the inception of each part to the legal promulgation of Leviticus 21–22. The marital restrictions and other guidelines for priests (21:1–15) are followed by restrictions on just who might preside over sacrifices and consume sacred foods (21:16–24; 22:1–16). Specifications for animals selected for sacrifice (22:17–25) and temporal guidelines for their slaughter and consumption (22:26–31) conclude this segment of legislation. The anchoring of the laws in divine holiness in Leviticus 22:31–33 reprises sentiments from a similar concluding admonishment in Leviticus 20:22–26. Both iterations of divine authority mark conclusions to the major segments of prescriptive discourse.[39] Leviticus 21–22 is, at once, a distinct literary unit *and* an extension of the prescriptive logic to the preceding chapters (Lev 18–20).

By distinctive terminology and theological tenor, Leviticus 21–22 is thought to derive from H(oliness Legislation), the hand credited for the bulk of Leviticus 17–26.[40] Recent discussions on the relative chronology of H reverse earlier trends, finding in H a recasting of ideas in Leviticus 1–16 (mostly P). In this view, H is a supplementary development overlying its literary patrimonies that fosters a new integrity to the refinished literary product.[41] The present shape of the Pentateuch, of course, projects the same impression: the legal discourses of Leviticus 17–26 (H) *succeed* those of Leviticus 1–16 (P). Numbers 5–6—according to currents in European scholarship, part of a series of late addenda to the religious constructions of Leviticus 1–16 in the formation of the Mosaic corpus—is in the same vein: both Leviticus 21–22 and Numbers 5–6, in historical development *and* the flux of plot, are the offshoots of the earlier prescriptive material of Leviticus 1–16. Both read as refinements and re-directionings of former (P's) literary-theological tropes, foisted on divine and prophetic (Moses) lips. In this qualified sense, Numbers 5–6 and Leviticus 21–22 are peas in a pod, and our project is nothing less than a comparative contemplation of parallel (and successive) literary reflexes to Leviticus 1–16.

My wanderings between the texts will follow diametrically opposite paths. For a start I wish to explore how a single pericope of Numbers 5–6 combines elements from diverse and distinct parts of Leviticus 21–22. Then, conversely, I will trace the scattering of components from a single pericope of Leviticus 21–22—thematic, conceptual, and lexical—across multiple members in Numbers 5–6. Movements of conversion and diversion, therefore, shall ply the paths between the texts. Quite ostensibly, as the following descriptions shall demonstrate, the intratextual maneuvers reinforce for the reader connections between units in either passage. Lexical and semantic entities juxtaposed through the combination of distinct segments in one text crystallize in the other. The conjunction of ideas implicit in one place is explicit in another. The conceptual correspondences between the texts are, in the final analysis, multifarious; the energies across the distance are centripetal and centrifugal. I begin with the collation of tropes from across Leviticus 21–22 in a single law of Numbers 5–6: the regulations for Nazirites (Num 6:1–21).

Aggregation: A Gathering of Leviticus 21–22 in Numbers 6:1–21

The Nazirite procedures of Numbers 6:1–21 admit points of contact with three distinct units of prescription in Leviticus 21–22: the regulatory strictures for priests (Lev 21:10–15), the consumption of sacred portions (22:4–16), and votive offerings (22:17–25). Shared vocabulary and themes facilitate connections with Leviticus 21–22. Of specific interest—our first foray into the spaces between the texts—are the stark similarities between the Nazirite protocols of ritual and those of the chief priest.

Numbers 6:5–8 and Leviticus 21:10–15

Regulations in both texts place constraints on headdress and mourning. The proscription of wine, additionally, connects with instructions for priests on duty in Leviticus 10:9. The similarity of the specifications for Nazirites and chief priests is striking and worth noting in some detail. Consider the procedural progression of the texts side by side.[42]

⁵All the days of their nazirite vow no razor shall come *upon the head*... they shall let *the locks of the head* grow long. ⁶All the days that they separate themselves to the Lord they shall not go near a corpse. ⁷Even if their father or mother, brother or sister, should die, they may not defile themselves; because their consecration to God is *upon their head*. ⁸All their days as nazirites they are holy to the Lord. (Num 6:5–8; emphasis is additional)	¹⁰The priest who is exalted above his fellows, *on whose head* the anointing-oil has been poured... shall not dishevel *his hair* nor tear his vestments. ¹¹He shall not go where there is a dead body; he shall not defile himself even for his father or mother. ¹²He shall not go outside the sanctuary and thus profane the sanctuary of his God; for the consecration of the anointing-oil of his God is *upon him*: I am the Lord. (Lev 21:10–15; emphasis added)

The sanctified head has focus across the prescriptive sets. Noteworthy is the similar double reference of each passage to the anointed portion of the anatomy: the head (see text in italics above). The twin indices to the sacred crown encase the stark direction to keep from mourning and the resultant contamination (Num 6:6–7a; Lev 21:11). The similarities go deeper. There is *within* the initial fixing of the reader's eye on the holy head in both laws (Num 6:5; Lev 21:10) a double reference, also, to the crown that envelops a statement underscoring the ordinand's separation. The relevant parts of both laws under narrowed scrutiny are as follows. We focus in on Numbers 6:5 and Lev 21:10.

All the days of his nazirite vow no razor shall come *upon his head* (*'l r'šw*); until the time is completed for which they separate themselves to the Lord, they shall be holy; they shall let the *locks of their head* (*ś'r r'šw*) grow long (*gddl pr'*). (Num 6:5; my emphasis)	The priest who is exalted above his fellows, *on whose head* (*'l r'šw*) the anointing-oil has been poured and who has been consecrated to wear the vestments, shall not dishevel (*l' ypr'*) *his hair* (*r'šw*) nor tear his vestments. (Lev 21:10; my emphasis)

Consecration/separation is encircled, once again, by twin indices (see text in italics) to the sanctified crown—in both texts. Both rulings return attention to the head in conclusion. Furthermore, the progression from consecration—with the double-notation of the sacred crown—to the matter of corpse contamination is the same across the laws. The caution against proximity to deceased family members follows immediately in both command sequences (Num 6:6–8; Lev 21:11). The similarity in these lines warrants closer scrutiny. Jacob Milgrom's rendition of the Hebrew clarifies the intertextual nexus.[43]

He shall not go near a dead body; for his father and his mother and his brother and his sister he shall not profane himself. (Num 6:7a)	He shall not go near a dead body; for his father and his mother he shall not defile himself (Lev 21:11)

The Numbers version, merely, adds two parties to the list of close relations. The echo is well-nigh verbatim.

Holy heads, holy orders, and holy strictures: the trappings of elevated status resound across the rulings. The priestly resonance in the construal of the Nazirite is unmistakable. In the echo, Nazirites take their place alongside the chief priest. There is compatibility between the sacred figures. What do we make of this strange juxtaposition? In shuttling between the texts, we might pose the question of whether the prescribed restorative measures of the Nazirite ritual could come into play—as Hilary Lipka suggests—if death does not follow the anointed priest's inadvertent departure from the holy precincts (Lev 10:7).[44] Certainly, Lipka's initiative fills a gap in the absence of a prescribed procedure for priestly reconsecration post-desecration. Might the Nazirite ritual provide a return to sanctuary service for deposed priests? To go further, could a Nazirite assume the functions and privileges of the chief priest?[45] Would this be a possibility under extenuating circumstances? Might a makeshift shrine in far-flung territories—this a troubling prospect in itself from Deuteronomy's perspective (see Deut 12:2–13)—ordain a Nazirite to priestly function, if only for a limited duration?[46] The coupling of a priestly function with a martial disposition so familiar to the warlike Nazirite, Samson (Judg 13:1–5), is not beyond the compass of biblical narrative. Eli's priestly sons accompany the ark into battle (1 Sam 4:1–11). Seven priests on horns trek around the city's walls with warriors awaiting their collapse in Israel's assault on Jericho (Josh 6:2–5, 12–14). Phinehas, the Aaronide, shrinks not from the use of a lance against the apostate Israelite and his Midianite lover (Num 25:7–8). The straddling of the roles, sacerdotal and soldierly, seems unproblematic in these instances. The beginnings of an argument for a priest/warrior seem in place in Numbers 6, should the conditions for innovation and improvisation arise. Necessity is the mother of invention.

But other passages defend priestly privilege. The elaborate rituals of ordination in Leviticus 7–9, buttressed by additional sanction in Numbers 18, obviate any suggestion that the Nazirite might approach the status of a priest, let alone the one elevated above his peers. The promise of privileges *exclusive* to the priestly line (of Aaron) in reward for the religious zeal of Phinehas (Num 25:11–13)—a passage used to make the opposite argument—strikes a similar tone. The spectacular defense of the Aaronide priesthood against the presumption of Korah and his faction—the Levite faction, it seems, wished to offer incense like priests (Num 16:39–40)—can hardly inspire the blurring of the line between priest and laity.

As elsewhere, the fruit of our interpretive enterprise is half ripe.

Numbers 6:13–21 and Leviticus 22:17–25

There are other adumbrations of Leviticus 21–22 in the rules for Nazirites. A specified series of gifts are to come at the conclusion of the period of sanctification (Num 6:13–21). The list of items to be transferred into the holy domain represents a minimum requirement. The instruction here underscores the fact that the offerings are integral to the *ndr*, the 'vow.'[47] Verse 21 invokes the word four times. That these animal offerings are *vouchsafed by swearing* brings the law within the purview of Leviticus 22:17–25, a unit of religious legislation insisting that freewill offerings and other animals dedicated (by vow) to the deity be blemish free. The promise, ratified by solemnization, binds the laws across the distance.

In this slew of offerings, the sacrifice of well-being, the *šlmym*, is common to both laws. In the rules for Nazirites (in both presentations of the offering), the sacrifice concludes the series of animal offerings (see vv. 14–15, 16–18). Its placement at the terminus agrees with the sequence in Leviticus 22:17–25 (see vv. 18b–25). This commonality in itself is unremarkable since the sacrifice of well-being often comes last in prescribed series of sacrifices in Priestly literature (e.g., Lev 9:3–4, 15–22; 23:18–19). The salience accorded the *šlmym* in *both* texts, however, is worth noting in some detail. I consider, first, its prominence in Leviticus 22. Compare that chapter's instructions for a burnt offering and those for the *šlmym*.

Lev 22:18b–20 (Burnt Offering)	*Lev 22:21–25 (Sacrifice of Well-Being)*
[18]When anyone of the house of Israel or of the aliens residing in Israel presents an offering, whether in payment of a vow or as a freewill-offering that is offered to the Lord as a burnt-offering, [19]to be *acceptable in your behalf* it shall be a male, *perfect ones* (*tmym*), of the cattle or the sheep or the goats. [20]You shall not offer anything that has a *blemish* (*mwm*), for it will *not be acceptable in your behalf*. (My emphasis)	[21]When anyone offers a sacrifice of well-being to the Lord, in fulfillment of a vow or as a freewill-offering, from the herd or from the flock, *to be acceptable* it must be *perfect* (*tm*); there shall be no *blemish* (*mwm*) in it. [22]**Anything blind, or injured, or maimed, or having a discharge or an itch or scabs—these you shall not offer to the Lord or put any of them on the altar as offerings by fire to the Lord.** [23]An ox or a lamb that has a limb too long or too short you may present for a freewill-offering; but it will not be accepted for a vow. [24]Any animal that has its testicles bruised or crushed or torn or cut, you shall not offer to the Lord; such you shall not do within your land, [25]nor shall you accept any such animals from a foreigner to offer as food to your God; since they are mutilated, with a *blemish* (*mwm*) in them, they shall *not be accepted in your behalf*. (Emphasis not original)

Evidently, the dyadic progression—the specification of a 'perfect' beast followed by the rejection of a damaged one—is common to the two parts of the prescriptive sequence. The reference to the agreeability of the offerings (or the opposite) underscores the purpose of the specifications (see relevant terms in italics in vv. 19, 20, 21, and 25). The requirement of a well-being sacrifice is disproportionately bloated for the extensive list of the exemplars of 'blemish' (see text in bold in vv. 22–25).[48] The loquacious elaboration—a parade of one example after another—leaves little room for doubt as to the semantic import of 'perfect,' 'blemish,' and 'acceptable.' This extensive excursus will bear fruit in conjunction with a reading of the regulations for would-be Nazirites.

The presentation of the well-being offering in Numbers 6 achieves something different. The directions linger over details in the preparation of the ram, setting these out intermittently, mixed in with instructions for offerings of cakes, wafers, and libations and for the shearing of the sacred locks. The drama shifts the reader's eye, swiftly, from item to item. There is a sense that the action comes to a crescendo with the setting of the hair in the fire (v. 18). The resumption of attention to the details of the sacrifice of well-being (v. 19 picking up the directions for the ram in v. 17) sets the sole reference to the burning locks at the apogee of the unfolding procedure (v. 18). The lines I have in mind are verses 17–19.

> [17]and [the priest] shall offer the ram as a sacrifice of well-being to the Lord, with the basket of unleavened bread; the priest shall make the accompanying grain-offering and drink-offerings. [18]Then the nazirites shall shave the consecrated head at the entrance of the tent of meeting, and shall take the hair from the consecrated head *and put it on the fire under the sacrifice of well-being*. [19]The priest shall take the shoulder of the ram, when it is boiled, and one unleavened cake out of the basket, and one unleavened wafer, and shall put them in the palms of the nazirites, after they have shaved the consecrated head. (Num 6:17–19; my emphasis)

The joint conflagration of sacrificial beast and hair (v. 18) is central to the rite. The cultic instructions here set in view a collocation of sacred things at a climactic point in the rite, its obtrusive prominence, perhaps, an effect of its encirclement by the directions for the preparation and the post-sacrificial distribution of the *šlmym*.[49] The flames consume, together, the strands and the bloodied portions of ram: Numbers has a knack for odd pairings.

The strange combination at this turn in the procedure leads some to suggest that the holy hair is, in fact, an 'offering' (*qrbn*) in keeping with a well-being sacrifice.[50] But the prescribed procedure makes no such claim, not explicitly. The omission is glaring for the fact that the text *does* designate the other commuted substances—the ram, the potables, and the baked items—by *qrbn* (see vv. 14–15). The Nazirite is directed, simply, to 'put' (*ntn*) the shorn locks in the flames beneath the offering of the ram. The divine voice here shuns the causative expression of *qrb*, 'to cause to approach' or 'to bring near,' a term in cultic parlance elsewhere in the procedure—see verses 14 and 16—for the consignment of things to the divine realm. For these reasons, the putative kinship to the hair and the well-being offering is problematic, prompting several scholars to see nothing more than a passing reference to the disposal of sancta.[51] Yet, the ritual's tarrying on this combination at the altar remains, teasing the reader to *invent* a connection beyond the shared space. And so, with Gray, McNeile and others, I take the bait and explore the ramifications of the association. The pairing of the hair with the sacrifice suggests that the former is without *mwm* ('blemish')—this is an effect of reading against the emphatic elaborations on physical defect in Lev 22:17–24. The hair, as the well-being offering, must be free of fault. But it is difficult to imagine hair with scabs or bruised testes. 'Blemish,' by dint of Numbers 6:9–12, must be recast to include contamination by proximity to dead bodies. Defilement, accordingly, is a kind of *mwm*. But this is a preposterous filiation by the dictates of Leviticus 21:17–23 which *permit* 'damaged' priests to partake of holy donations—a privilege denied those unclean (Lev 22:6–8). Pentateuchal legislation does *not* conflate animal (or priestly) defects with defilement: blemished priests may approach (and consume) holy food; individuals defiled may not. My tack in making sense of the arrangement on the Nazirite altar (Num 6:18), alas, is a confusion of distinct categories of abjection in cultic parlance, a misappropriation of one exclusionary calculus for the support of another.[52] Leviticus 21–22, as intertext, presents in this instance as many problems as it does solutions. But perhaps we have been too scrupulous for our own good. A blemish is *like* an unclean thing. Accordingly, priests should be careful with both unseemly quantities. Let us leave it at that.

Numbers 6:9–12 and Leviticus 22:4–16

The procedure for the Nazirite's transition out of a state of defilement and reinstatement in Numbers 6:9–12 opens a third point of contact with Leviticus 21–22. The requirement for the *'šm*, the guilt offering (Num 6:12b), is reminiscent of the same requisite restitution for the inadvertent desecration of holy food in Leviticus 22:4–16 (see vv. 14–16).[53] The association of the sacred strands—with the guilt offering as a touchstone in the nexus—with sacred food underscores the perception, again, of the sheared locks as an offering. The ostensible surplus to this connection is the expansion of the list of contaminants well beyond the singular focus of the Nazirite rules on corpse contamination. That genital discharges, skin disorders, and teeming things communicate uncleanness—the very defiling agents of concern to Leviticus 22:4–16—is a matter of record, already, in the former discourses of Leviticus 11–15. The implication of the association with the sacred edibles of Leviticus 22:4–16 is that the extensive restorative procedures of the Nazirite legislation *should* apply to cover the broader spectrum of defilement. Effectively, the interaction with Leviticus 22 on this point forces an abstraction in legal reasoning beyond the particulars of the Nazirite law of Numbers 6. The suggestion, then, is that the prescriptions of Numbers 6 should be (seen as being) concerned with the *full* range of substances unseemly in the priestly scope.

A less likely development from the retrogressive glance to Leviticus is the postulation that the profane parties beyond the priestly household barred from sacred foods (Lev 22:10–13) would have a similar desecrating or defiling effect on the Nazirite crown. If individuals beyond the sacred sphere desecrate God's food (Lev 22:15), might these persons not also by contact effect the removal of Nazirites from their sanctified state? This, of course, would limit Nazirite deportment to the priestly compound. Contact with laity would be proscribed! The tightened strictures, should we follow this path, moves the Nazirite ever closer to the compass of the chief priest, a pairing we have pursued elsewhere. An objection might be that ingestion enacts a closer degree of contact, thus necessitating tighter scrutiny and punctilious arduousness in boundary keeping. The profane persons in a Nazirite's environs, so the counter statement goes, are hardly his or her food. The scrupulous attention to the sanctity of the priest's table is not warranted for the company the Nazirite keeps (nor, for that matter, the priest), defiled parties aside. Nevertheless, however tenuous (or difficult) the cross-textual maneuvers—this is my point!—the building blocks of an argument await only a motivated reader and reading community to close the gaps and to override the inconsistencies.

Putting It Together: 'Aggregation' in Numbers 6:1–21

In sum, the aggregation within a single legislative periscope (Num 6:1–21) of terms and concepts littered across distinct units of prescription in Leviticus 21–22 forces the juxtaposition of cultic and legal categories: the Nazirite and the chief priest; the Nazirite locks, the well-being sacrifice, and sacred food. The accomplishment of the Nazirite law is the *crystallization* of possible (even probable) lines of association inherent, already, to the longer, more complex, collection of rules in Leviticus 21–22. In this convoluted fashion, reading *between* Numbers 6:1–21 and Leviticus 21–22 is also a reading *within* Leviticus 21–22. The same movements of mind—abstractions and metonymic associations—ply the paths within and without the Leviticus passage. But our ludic intertextual wanderings are the same habits of mind resplendent in the focused perusal of Numbers 5–6: the spying of lexical and conceptual correspondences; the *imputed* presence of a trope by analogy; the syllogistic reasoning in inventing fresh significances. But also, in all this, the contrived correlations and their spin-offs must admit caveats, the novel trajectories obstacles and impracticalities. In the wake of the reader's intertextual productivity are the seeds for the dissolution of the schemata of the holistic, totalizing imaginary. The disconnects between priest and Nazirite, cultic contagion and animal defect, remain. The compelling correspondences and their potential offshoots prove phantasmagoric, the schemes ephemeral. Somewhere, at some juncture contrived or implied, the web of correspondences fails.

Disaggregation in Numbers 5–6: The Dispersal of Leviticus 21:1–15

The collapsing of the prescriptive analogies of Leviticus 21–22 into the single law of Numbers 6 has been our interest so far. The opposite effect of a scattering of literary tropes, however, might be perceived in the transition from Leviticus to Numbers. The attendant concepts to priestly sanctity regarding mourning and marriage in Leviticus 21:1–15 spread across distinct pieces of legislation in Numbers 5–6 bearing significance for fresh arenas of legal argument. The spectacle is centrifugal.

Leviticus 21:1–15 in Numbers 5:1–4 and 6:1–21

The issue of corpse contamination frames the prescriptive series of Numbers 5:1–6:21. The polluting presence of dead bodies is of concern in the directions for campsite purity (Num 5:1–4) and the law of the Nazirite (Num 6:1–21). This subject matter at the limits of the larger literary entity is in common with the regulations for priests in Leviticus 21:1–15. The robust literary assonance of the sacerdotal figure in the figuration of the Nazirite—a matter previously in discussion—secures the link to Leviticus. In a trilateral dialectic on corpse contamination, the directions for campsite purity (Num 5:1–4) enter the mix as the third member in conversation. The holy heads of chief priest and Nazirite have been explored earlier. My task here, then, is to explore the novel terms the campsite rules (Num 5:1–4) bring to the intertextual trilectic.

The divine word to Moses in the campsite legislation exceeds earlier instruction (in Lev 12–15) which prescribes removal from the camp only for those with epidermal disorders, ṣrʿt (Lev 13:46). Patients with genital disorders only need to be segregated *within* the camp (Lev 15:31). But God goes further here, calling also for the evacuation from Israel's habitus of those with abnormal discharge (*zb*) and those unclean from contact with (or proximity to) the dead. The focus on contagion is pointed, twice commanding the removal of persons defiled (vv. 3, 4) on the heels of an initial directive (v. 2). Corpse contamination in Numbers 5:1–4—the point of contact with Leviticus 21:1–15—is an area for legal innovation in Numbers 5.[54]

The purchase of a trilateral reading encompassing Numbers 5:1–4, 6:1–21 and Leviticus 21:10–15 is the collation and juxtaposition (in the reader's imagination) of three pollution-free zones: the priestly crown, the Nazirite's locks, and Israel's camp. The equivalences raise questions and suggest avenues for speculation. If death is a consequence for the desecration of sacred spaces through priestly indiscretion (Lev 21:12; but also see Lev 22:9; 10:7), might the same apply to the failure to send away from the camp polluting parties in a timely manner? Certainly, Numbers 19 (vv. 13, 20) appears to move in this direction in its stipulation of excommunication (*krt*) for allowing pollution from dead bodies to fester.[55] Conversely, the penalty of excommunication—by the nexus to Numbers 19—might be applied to oversights in the management of contagion from corpses in the rules for priests and Nazirites. This, while lenient for priests, raises the stakes for Nazirites. Is death, by human or divine agency, the lot of the negligent Nazirite by this connection? In any case, the consequence is grave.

But our speculations here hit a snag already flagged in previous discussion. The quest for a family resemblance across the sanctified heads (of chief priest and Nazirite) and Israel's camp in the wilderness must admit the inconvenience that much of pentateuchal legislation militates against the designation of the camp a sacred space. The camp, by virtue of its status as the *common* living space for all Israel, is profane. The chief priest, by consequence, must be vigilant in the compass of his deportment, taking care not to stray into profane territory *within* the camp (Lev 10:7; 21:12). Israel's habitus in the wilderness is not, in its entirety, a sacred space. Yet, the reader must grapple with the camp's liminal status in the grand scheme of things straddling the spectrum from holy to profane, pure to impure. As Israel's common space, divine instruction demands that it remain free from specified pollutants—from the contagion of corpses, skin disorders, genital flow (Num 5:1–4), and excrement (Deut 23:12–14). Alas, an interpretive gesture founded on the 'holy heads-clean camp' conceptual complex is shaky. The two pristine spaces are *not* an exact match. But analogies, of course, work with less.

Leviticus 21:1–15 in Numbers 5:11–31

The law of the jealous husband is another discrete segment of prescription fraught with semantic associations to the rules for priests in Leviticus 21:1–15. The priestly concerns over defilement (*ṭm'*) and *seed*/offspring (*zr'*) resurface as subjects of interest in the tangled procedures of Numbers 5:11–31. This seemingly chaotic conglomeration of repeated acts—usually ascribed to the conflation of two or more distinct rites in the formation of the current law—evokes defilement (an inflection of the root *ṭm'*) seven times (vv. 13, 14 [twice], 19, 20, 27, 28; compare Lev 21:11b).[56] Jacob Milgrom's scheme finds defilement at the center of the procedure (v. 20), where the accused woman claims innocence under oath. At this very juncture is the insinuation that the source of the uncleanness is the semen (*zr'*) of the woman's illicit lover.[57] This inference—a point noted in earlier analysis—is borne by the focus of the destructive and retributive elements of the draught on the woman's organs of reproduction. Notwithstanding the obscurity of the described consequences for the guilty woman's midriff and thighs (vv. 21–22 and 27), the positive consequence that the innocent party, in contrast, 'shall be immune and be able to conceive children (*zr'*)' clarifies the reproductive capacity of the errant wife as the very object under attack.[58] The womb, the vessel for the illicit seed, suffers the deleterious effects of the cocktail.[59]

The law as a whole is peppered with allusions to fertility and sexuality. The idiomatic expression for copulation lends explicit focus to the woman's pubic region. The occasion for the woman's departure from the straight and narrow (v. 13a) is a liaison involving 'an effusion of semen,' *škbt zr'*.[60] The expression is hardly euphemistic. The reference to sexual congress later in the priestly adjuration to the woman (v. 20) is a touch more lurid: the woman's lover is depicted as the man who 'has placed (*wyytn*) his effusion (*škbtw*)' in her (*bh*). (Harry Orlinsky's rendition of *škbtw* by 'his penis' is more daring.)⁶¹ The locus of fertilization and the mechanics of insemination figure prominently in the pastiche of images, thanks to the choice of terms. This aspect to the procedure has not been lost on scholars.

Susan Niditch, for example, finds other indices to the motif of fertility. The requisite grain offering consists of barley unmixed with oil and spices (v. 15); the potable concoction combines water and dirt (v. 17).⁶² The mix of elements raw and primary smacks of agricultural fecundity. The law's vision of the wife's 'turning' is cast in this context of images dripping with connotations of the genesis of new life. And so, for Niditch, the law's central concern 'is the depositing of inappropriate seed in the improper place.'⁶³ It is 'the use of his wife's womb by a man other than himself' that worries the husband, the contamination of the husband's gestational device for growing *his* likeness.⁶⁴ Alice Bach has similar sentiments. The clay vessel that bears the odious concoction the woman imbibes (v. 17) 'is metonymic for the womb containing semen, for a sexually pure wife guarantees her husband a womb vessel filled solely with his seed.' The ritual is required, quite simply, because this exclusive right has been impinged upon and the purity of the womb has been impugned!⁶⁵ In the case of innocence the contents of the cup—to stay with Bach's construal of the ritual's symbolism—do the bidding of God, who assumes the role of the father defending his daughter's honor in the law of Deuteronomy 22:19 by producing evidence of his daughter's innocence: a functional, seed-bearing womb.⁶⁶ The matter of the woman's defilement, as the law puts it, cannot be separated from that of the insemination of her womb. The strange seed is contagion!⁶⁷

Bach goes further in unmasking the sexual connotations to the law. Even the prepositional phrase 'under her husband' (v. 19), the standard expression denoting authority, is double entendre, bearing oblique reference to the woman's 'proper' position in amorous embrace.⁶⁸ Bach's poetic rendition of Numbers 5:19 captures the sexual undertones.

> If no man has *profaned your body*,
> If you have not *turned aside to uncleanness*
> While *you should have remained underneath your husband*,
> Be free from this *bitter water that brings forth the agony*.⁶⁹

The flourish of sexual imagery by denotation and connotation, so astutely noted both by Bach and Niditch, finds an echo in the Mishnah's commentary to the law (Sotah 1:5–6). Legalistic discourse, as Bonna Devora Haberman puts it, gives way to 'a macabre textual enactment of adultery.'[70] The text lingers over the priest's undressing of the woman, exposing her bosom and thighs in tearing away her raiment.[71] The effect of this brutal and lewd treatment in the Mishnah, by Haberman's analysis, is the obsolescence of the adulterous woman's individuality and her objectification as an 'other,' a target of derision.[72] The ritual, in its literary milieu, serves as a deterrent to adultery.[73]

The concupiscent undertones to the Numbers law moves closer to a rhetoric for endogamy when seen in tandem with the marital restrictions for priests in Leviticus 21:1–15. The regulations of Leviticus 21:1–15, minus the accent on copulation, display a similar concern for the vessel that would bear sacerdotal seed. The restrictions for the chief priest guard against women with a history of sexual intercourse: the widow, the divorcee, the sexual miscreant, and the one 'defiled' (*ḥllh*; v. 14).[74] The list for the regular priest is slightly less stringent with the omission of the widow from the roster of proscribed parties (v. 7).[75] The purpose to the constraints appears to be the assurance of parentage in the priestly household, with the tighter restrictions for the chief priest requiring an unsullied, virgin uterus *of priestly provenance* (vv. 13, 14).[76] The purity of bloodlines on both sides in agnatic succession to the priestly office is paramount. Accordingly, the expressed reason for the chief priest's abstention from the types of women listed is 'that he may not profane (*ḥll*) his offspring (*zrʿ*) among his kin' (v. 15). The degradation—from holy to profane—flows both ways; the priest's daughter 'that plays the whore' desecrates (*tḥl*) her father (v. 9).[77] Clean wombs and wholesome seed/offspring, then, are crucial in preserving the holiness of priests. Priestly privilege is coterminous with the security of the boundaries that guard holy progeny from the ravages of strange, foreign seed. The view on intrusive semen, a sight so abhorrent in the presentation of Numbers 5, is alive here in the marital restrictions for priests. The venereal soundings of the Numbers law gain fresh significance in Leviticus 21. Leviticus puts an ethnicized genealogical spin in conceptualizing seminal and amniotic purity—the sanctity of the priestly uterus is *inextricably* tied to the requisite endogamy for the chief priest. The prospective incubator of the next generation to serve in Israel's most holy place must be free from the taint of profane seed. And so, the sexual tones of Numbers 5 blend into the stringent anti-miscegenation arguments that secure sacrosanctity and tribal integrity for the priestly class in Leviticus 21. The jealous husband's posture, his scrupulous scrutiny of his wife's vaginal tract, is the prescribed animus—a vigilance *par excellence*—for guarding holy seed in Leviticus 21.

This smuggling of ideas across texts, of course, is aided by the semantic spectrum to *m'l* ('malfeasance' has been our translation of choice), that choice term for cases of desecration. While the word is not seen in Leviticus 21:1–15, its application to the desecration of members of the priestly house is not out of place. Such deeds, by the words of divine inflection (Lev 5:15), force a transfer of holy persons to the common sphere. 'Malfeasance,' though absent in Leviticus 21:1–15, is present in the law of the jealous husband: the wife's 'turning aside' is dubbed an act of *m'l* against the husband (Num 5:11). But there the broader sense of an act of ill faith applies: God is not the direct victim of the foul deed. Sacrilege is not the crime. 'Malfeasance' in its typical semantic hue does not transfer easily across the laws. The word has not the same precise nuance between Leviticus 21 and Numbers 5. The to-and-fro schematizing imaginary, however, could make light this discrepancy. The common tropes of the purloined uterus and the wayward female—not to mention the concomitant outrage to the prescriptive tone—are enough to allow, perhaps, the projection of a generic category of 'misappropriation' across the prescriptive discourses. In both cases, something has been stolen. The disconnect to the imputed equivalence—a confusion of creator and creature, God and husband, in the victim's slot—seems minor. Never mind that a man, not divinity, is the victim in Numbers 5. A liberal reading of *m'l* bridges the cases, forging a likeness without claims of identity. Analogies in nimble minds have the flexibility of yogic masters. The husband's loss cannot be too unlike God's, can it? In the wake of the intertextual nexus the cuckold's cry for vengeance reaches heaven, obliging God to act with the outrage appropriate to the abuse of a divine possession, with the ferocity that would send a wayward daughter of a priest to the pyre (Lev 21:9). The adulterous expropriation of a husband's reproductive apparatus—the wife's uterus—is a rapacious deed on a par with sancta trespass.

Our traipsing through the marital rules for priests with adultery-soiled shoes, thanks to Numbers 5, enacts a familiar combination of tropes: misplaced sexuality is (a form of) covenantal infidelity, a betrayal of Israel's holy one. 'Whore,' *zwnh*, is the sememe of choice for the sexually promiscuous female in Priestly literature (Lev 19:29; 21:7, 9, 13). But the term, as is known, breaks free of coital denotation and applies also to the misplaced reverence for foreign deities (Lev 17:7; 20:5; see also Exod 34:15–16; Deut 31:16).[78] Indeed, the collocation of forbidden sexual congress and idolatry in Leviticus 20, placed on the divine tongue, bears witness to the association of the two perfidious acts in the religious imagination of the scribes. The prophet Jeremiah follows this trajectory, developing the act of illicit and unsavory sexual liaison, the province of the harlot, as a metaphor for idolatry. The vociferous invectives of the prophet against Israel liken the latter's affinity for foreign gods to the unbridled overtures of an ass in heat (Jer 2:23–24) and the salacious proclivities of nomads (Jer 3:2). Israel's idolatry defiles the land (Jer 2:7; 3:2), the very consequence of sexual improprieties in Leviticus 18 and 20. Israel is a *zwnh*, and there is scarce a place where its 'harlotry' has not been witnessed (Jer 3:2). Not to be outdone, the oracular indictment of Jerusalem in Ezekiel 16 casts the idolatry of Israel as the sexual wantonness of an adulterous wife. The sexual attention of the promiscuous woman—*znh*, again, characterizes the woman's amorous affections—is, as in Jeremiah, widespread and indiscriminate (Ezek 16:15). Ezekiel's whore is no less insatiable. In Ezekiel too, there is a connection with Leviticus 18 and 20; this time through the devotion of children to various lovers, the recipients of Israel's idolatrous attention (Ezek 16:20–21; compare Lev 18). Quite inseparable from the notion of a pining for foreign deities is the illicit conclusion of alliances. Jacob's relations with Egypt (Ezek 16:26–27), Assyria (Ezek 16:27–28), Babylonia (Ezek 16:29), and Tyre (Isa 23:17) are the objects of prophetic ire. Political advantage and financial gain, presumably, obstruct Israel's devotion to its god. 'Whoring,' then, means quite a bit more than illicit sex and religious apostasy by the term's acquisition of political significances. But the semantic range to 'whore' goes farther even. Isaiah extends Israel's harlotry to include immoral acts: murder, deception, thievery, bribery, and the oppression of the weak (Isa 1:21–23). But Isaiah might not be too much of an iconoclast in his rhetoric. The prophet's expansive interpretation of 'harlotry,' quite likely, is implicit to Leviticus 20 already. The divine dictates that construe the devotion of children to Molech as a 'prostituting' of oneself (Lev 20:5) joins idolatry to cursing one's parents (Lev 20:9), the failure to observe distinctions between pure and impure animals (Lev 20:25), and the consultation of soothsayers (Lev 20:6; there also deemed precisely a case of 'prostitution') along with a slew of sexual improprieties (Lev 20:10–21). The regard for said strictures, apparently, all comes under the banner of observing God's statutes and ordinances (Lev 20:22), all essential to becoming holy to God (Lev 20:26). 'Whoring,' thinking biblically, is a versatile metaphor indeed. The 'bad sex-desecration' tropological complex of our Leviticus–Numbers interexchange, then, is of the cloth of biblical literary-religious cross-pollination. (Certainly, the proliferation of hyphenated expressions just now should be a clue to the truism of this last statement.) By metaphorical extension, the lurid details of sexual misadventure vivify and animate the priestly and prophetic polemic against religious apostasy, moral turpitude, and political misjudgment, all acts of covenantal unfaithfulness. Failure in guarding Aaron's heritage, Eleazar's line, slips with ease under the wide and generous penumbra of 'whoring,' the cuckolding of God.

But what novel avenues of cultic and legal reasoning might the association of illicit sex, priestly exogamy, and the misappropriation of holy things engender? A chief priest's suspicion of a daughter's sexual misadventure might call for the elaborate procedures afforded by the jealous husband. Perhaps a man's aversion to capital punishment—born, we imagine, of a lingering tenderness for his spouse and/or the influence of an emergent distaste for vengeance in another time—might seize upon the likeness of sancta desecration in adultery and find satisfaction, instead, in a guilt offering with financial compensation. But the 'malfeasance' of Numbers 5, with respect to this last point, is *not*, strictly speaking, a case of desecration. The victim of perfidy is a layperson. This point keeps tripping us up! Contrary also to our liberal interpretive instincts on the subject is Deuteronomy's trenchant insistence on death for adultery or sexual intercourse with a woman betrothed (Deut 22: 13-27) that militates against any leniency for a wife's misguided erotic attentions. The husband's prerogative in such a case has no bearing whatsoever on the stipulated consequence of guilt. The adulterous woman is put to death. As always, there are holes in the correlations readers invoke and the applications they seek.

My argument succinctly stated is this. The erotic overtures of the jealous husband rite enact a 'pristine uterus-sullying seed' binary that is reminiscent of the marital restrictions for priests in Leviticus 21. In the cross-textual exchanges facilitated by a reading subject, adultery, exogamy, and desecration coalesce and conspire in the genesis of novel legislative trajectories—a guilt offering in lieu of capital punishment for adultery and a detective procedure for a suspicious priest vis-à-vis a sexually active and unwed daughter. As elsewhere, the correlative intertextual imaginary encounters barriers to its inventions. Yet, it persists.

The Accomplishment of Disaggregation in Numbers 5:1–6:21

The transposition of semantic relations in Leviticus 21:1–15 to the literary complex of Numbers 5:1–6:21 fortifies the bonds within *both* passages. The network of concepts that suffuse the figuration of the Nazirite crown, Israel's camp, and a woman's womb are bundled in the person of the chief priest and his relations. Even as the sanctity of the priestly mien and that of their vessels for reproduction must be maintained, so should the Nazirite head, Israel's abode and a wife's sexual organs be free of pollution. The vertical dimension (the nexus between Leviticus 21 and Numbers 5–6) motivates the genesis of meaning on the horizontal axis (the concepts that foster coherence *within* each passage). The overall accomplishment is an *expansion* of the sacerdotal realm, an encroachment of the priestly animus on the lay domain. Adultery is cast in parlance germane to the usurpation of priestly privilege in agnatic succession. The very things that endanger holy ordination must be kept apart from the living quarters and the holy orders of the broader community. A judicial consistency inheres to the religious reasoning that bridges the distance between laws. In this respect, the effect of the dispersion of themes and terms, of centrifuge, is no different from the literary maneuver—aggregation—witnessed in preceding analysis. Both movements, in concert, effect a *symmetry* in theological formulation that fosters the mutual transfer of paradigms in legal reasoning. Each text distils *and* expands the (theo)logical correlations inherent to the other. The spectacle is a multifarious crystallization and projection of the tropes that animate a collective reasoning, a calculus vivid and vivifying with its repertoire of ideas ever fruitful in novel arenas.

Also similar in previous analysis is the perception of difficulties in inscribing analogies by reading between texts. The problems involved in prescribing a reparation offering of sorts for adultery, an offshoot of the qualification of adultery as 'malfeasance' or a type of sacrilege is a case in point. The biblical text as a whole throws up as many obstacles as it does leads for innovation in jurisprudence and religious reasoning at large. The strength of an analogy in readers' minds, by consequence, stands in direct proportion to their ability (and willingness) to suspend attention to elements of discord in the metonymic transfer between texts. Insight, it seems, is the purchase of (willful) blindness in biblical interpretation.

Levi's Election, Egypt's Abjection, and the Road Ahead

Through this chapter, my interest has been to chart some ways in which Numbers 5–6 recalls Leviticus 21–22 and to trace potentialities for a sense and sensation of congruence across these texts. Defilement, desecration, and reparation are the abstract terms for the semblance of a thematic order. Heads, wombs, vows, camps, and offerings—the concrete items in the negotiations of the abstract notions just named—have been the esteemed entities in the cross-textual exchange. In the mix also are the toxic quantities—genital discharges, unnatural and strange, skin disorders, bodies dead and defective, profane persons. These, all, are the cloth of a permeating, spreading legal logic abetted by a willing reader.

Mapping the full spectrum of interpretive trajectories and the minutiae arising from these interactions, of course, is beyond the scope of this brief chapter. Rather, the normalizing imaginary posing lines of association between prescriptive segments and its concomitant blindness to the non sequiturs of the schemes imputed (and computed) have been foremost in my investigations. Texts are putty in the hands of readers. And readers, in the capacity of Bloom's Emersonian lector, are asking constantly of texts and reading: 'what is it good for, what can I do with it, what can it do for me, what can I *make it mean*?'[79] Pragmatic interests, I insist with Bloom, garnish texts in literary consumption. 'Strong readers' *misread*; their apprehension of every word is a 'prejudgment,' a swerving of an inherited trope toward a familiar series of experiences with texts.[80] Insight, wherever it occurs, is the child of volition, a choice to suspend momentarily the pursuit of alternatives. These propensities brought to a reading of our texts enact a seamless transfer of ideas and tropes from the cultic concerns of Leviticus 21–22 to the pastiche of rulings comprising Numbers 5–6. The impetus for substitution comes *naturally* to an imagination baptized in the to-and-fro between Numbers and Leviticus, hooked already on the stark likeness of the Nazirite to the chief priest.

The same proclivities, of course, lead the imaginative interaction with the broader, immediate context for Numbers 5–6: the enumeration of the Levites and their installation as cultic servants (Numbers 3–4, 8). Within the larger literary section of Numbers 1–8, the divine directives of Numbers 5–6 and the rhetoric of Levite election are mutually infectious.

This interaction is richer for the predication of the priestly claim to the Levite males on the divine demand for firstling offerings, itself modeled on the events of the night of Egypt's terror (Num 3:11–13, 40–41, 44–45; 8:15–19; compare Exod 13:11–16). In the emergent literary matrix is a potent tapestry of exclusive entities bridging the select legal discourses of Exodus, Leviticus, and Numbers. The installation of the Levites is seen against the rescue of Israel's sons, the divine claim on Israel's firstlings and, finally, the preservationist and protective instincts that inhere to the mixed rules of Numbers 5–6. The Levites and the guarded items of Numbers 5–6, from another angle, join the sacrificial lamb and Jacob's firstborn sons in the protected spaces of Israelite homes in Egypt, its limits under the guard of the lamb's blood. On the safe side of the threshold with the Levites—to include Leviticus 21–22—are the things, persons, and spaces prized and pure: Israel's camp (Num 5:1–4), the heads of Nazirites (Num 6:1–21), priests (Lev 21:1–15), the uterus (Num 5:11–31), sacred foods (Lev 22:1–8), and holy offerings (Lev 22:17–25). Outside in the 'destroyer's' arena are Egypt's sons, physical deformity, forbidden semen, sexual deviance, the pollutants that sully Israel's holy heads and habitus and the agents of profanity: the panoply of deeds and things that offend sacredness and elevated status.[81] The Levites bask in the glow of priestly and Nazirite consecration (Lev 21:1–15; Num 6:1–21). The urgent necessity for a clear distinction between the pure and the impure, the holy and the common, the seemly and the unruly underwrites their legitimacy as esteemed servants of the cult. Implicit to their standing and membership in the binary productions of the reader's wandering viewpoint, the Levites must keep the tabernacle and its furniture free of pollutants with the same vigilance accorded Israel's camp, its sacred food, and a woman's womb against the intrusion of incompatible substances (Num 5:1–4; Lev 22:1–16). Like the priestly and Nazirite crown (Lev 21:10, Num 6:), sacrificial beasts (Lev 22:17–25), and priestly lineage (Lev 21:7–9, 13–15), the Levites must remain free of deformity, contagion, and profane influences. This is what it means to keep company with priests, Nazirites, sacred offerings, Israel's camp, and the wife's organs of reproduction. The leveling and imbricating imaginary, then, fixes the Levites in a frame of treasured things and abject objects that shapes (and grows) the edifice of a biblical religiosity. By its ensnarement, the Levite ministry *makes* (and *receives*) sense.

The correspondences noted are not without warrant and reflex in biblical texts. My claim here is not of direct literary influence between the texts in discussion, but rather that select points within the Hebrew

Bible *facilitate* the analogical imagination in conceiving resemblances across texts. The ceremonial lustration of the Levites which renders them pure (Num 8:5–7) recalls, perhaps, the exhortation to purge the camp of defiled persons in Numbers 5:1–4. The concern that those mourning the dead might contaminate the Passover offering in Numbers 9:9–14 is reminiscent of the cautionary instructions to priests and their families to stave off defilement in Leviticus 21 (vv. 1–6, 10–12). That the Levites are a 'wave offering' (*tnwph*) by the people (Num 8: 11, 13, 15) is evocative of a category applied to sacred foods, holy offerings (Lev 8:29; 14:12; 23:11–15, 17), and even Moses's manipulation of Aaron's limbs at his ordination (Lev 8:27). Aaron is a wave offering on behalf of the people. That a similar gesture commits the Levites to their task insinuates a status approaching priestly standing. Several texts, in fact, seem to conflate the functions and the privileges of Levites and priests (Deut 18:1–3 [compare Lev 22:10–13]; Jud 17:7–13; Malachi 3:1–3; 2 Chron 29:5, 15; Ezra 6:20). The connections stated and implied here are among those I have pursued through this chapter. I don't believe that I'm the first to have had these instinctive responses to these texts.

Of course, the rich repertoire of possible associations between the setting apart of the Levites and the coterie of rules and rites we have surveyed is fraught with difficulties. This is not surprising. The Nazirite is not granted access to the appurtenances of the tabernacle; and God, in the wilderness, defends Aaron's honor in the face of a Levite presumption of priestly privilege (Numbers 16). Alas, the schemes of association only work up to a point. The correlative optic slips under intense scrutiny. While the gaps blunt the force of the schematic constructs, the latter continue to tease and to entice readers on a quest for a holistic view on seemingly disparate texts.

Later, in the unfolding of Israel's canonical story, the tropes of purity and privilege will converge further in fostering fresh exclusionary logics. The religious polemics of race, gender, sexual propriety, and physical proportion will conspire in metrical productions of genealogical fitness and moral disposition to out 'otherness.' Ezra's program of enforced separation (Ezra 9:1–2, 10–12; 10:1–17)—an example oft cited along such lines—will bend the Mosaic declaration of Israel as 'holy seed' (Deut 7:6; 14:21; 28:9) to embrace the divine prescription for priestly endogamy (Lev 21:1–15). Persia's demagogue for Yehud's reconstitution will purge Jacob's brood of an ethnic admixture (deemed) dangerously conducive to religious apostasy and sexual debauchery. Ezra's compatriot, Nehemiah, oblivious to Isaiah's inclusive gestures (Isa 56:3–8), will mutter Deuteronomy's injunctions (Neh 13:1–2) in cursing and abusing the foreigners that would taint Israel's blood (Neh 13:25). But well before the exile, the Aaronide Phinehas, true to his priestly calling, will pierce Moab's wanton female who dares bring her tarnished gods and her corrupting uterus into Israel's camp. And before Phinehas, Moses will blend sexual misadventure, racial 'defect,' and moral intransigence into a rhetoric for the marginalization of select groups—our immediate concern in the next chapter.

The ingredients for such powerful intersectional brandings of 'otherness'—and the habits of reading to concoct the exclusions—are in place. The language of abjection awaits the harnessing of the inventive, fence-staking imaginary. But, always, the inevitable blind spots that eviscerate the contrived schemes follow the waves of gestalt building, the relentless imaginings of *meaning*. The disturbing hybridities and ambivalences, over and against which the figurations of a 'natural purity' are forged, remain to ruffle the wrinkle removing, (overly) abstracting fiats of identity formation. Israelite subjectivity and its repertoire of resemblances may hold, but the cracks remain in view. The fault lines to the analogies of the rhetoric will show themselves to the countervailing sensibilities that would seek them out. The contrived network of correspondences and their sponsoring binary oppositions, then, may prove the Achilles heel to Israel's Othering project. The web will come undone.

Notes

1. On gap-filling in the interstices of textual segments as a phenomenon of reading see, again, Wolfgang Iser, *The Act of Reading: A Theory of Aesthetic Response* (Baltimore: The Johns Hopkins University Press, 1978), 182–95. The 'hermeneutic code' of Roland Barthes, *S/Z: An Essay* (trans. Richard Miller; New York: Hill and Wang, 1974), 19, 75–76), in recognizing this aspect of a reader's participation, envisions the formulation of enigmas and suspense as an operation in some tension with the grouping of actions already encountered under generic terms (*a walk, a meeting, greeting*), the function of his 'proairetic code.'
2. Martin Noth, *Numbers: A Commentary* (trans. J. D. Martin; Old Testament Library; London: SCM, 1968), 6, 44–45. For similar sentiments, see, among others, George Buchanan Gray, *Numbers* (International Critical Commentary; New York: Charles Scribner's Sons, 1906), xxiv; Rolf Rendtorff, *The Old Testament: An Introduction* (trans. John Bowden; Philadelphia: Fortress, 1986), 147.

3. Noth, *Numbers*, 1–2. Certainly, Noth's comments are the strongest statement in this vein. But scholarly deliberations elsewhere on the structure of Numbers are often preceded by acknowledgment of the difficulty to the task, due in no small measure to the complex historical development of the text. Beyond Noth, see Calum Carmichael, *The Book of Numbers: A Critique of Genesis* (New Haven and London: Yale University Press, 2012), 26–27; Nathan MacDonald, 'The Book of Numbers,' in *A Theological Introduction to the Pentateuch: Interpreting the Torah as Christian Scripture* (ed. Richard S. Briggs and Joel N. Lohr; Grand Rapids MI: Baker Academic, 2012), 115–18; Adriane Leveen, *Memory and Tradition in the Book of Numbers* (Cambridge and New York: Cambridge University Press, 2008), 22–23, 25; Thomas Römer, 'Israel's Sojourn in the Wilderness and the Construction of the Book of Numbers,' in *Reflection and Refraction: Studies in Biblical Historiography in Honour of A. Graeme Auld* (ed. Robert Rezetko, Timothy H. Lim and W. Brian Aucker; Supplements to Vetus Testamentum 113; Leiden and Boston: Brill, 2007), 427; Jean-Louis Ska, *Introduction to Reading the Pentateuch* (Winona Lake; Eisenbrauns, 2006), 35–36; Jacob Milgrom, *Numbers* (New York: Jewish Publication Society, 1990), xiii; Rendtorff, *The Old Testament*, 147–50; Philip J. Budd, *Numbers* (Word Biblical Commentary 5; Waco: Word, 1984), xviii–xxi; Gray, *Numbers*, xxii–xxvi.
4. Noth, *Numbers*, 2.
5. Römer, 'Israel's Sojourn,' 427.
6. S. R. Driver, *Introduction to the Literature of the Old Testament* (9th edn.; Edinburgh: T&T Clark, 1913), 60; Noth, *Numbers*, 1–4; Gray, *Numbers*, xxiii–xxiv; Brevard S. Childs, *Introduction to the Old Testament as Scripture* (Philadelphia: Fortress, 1979), 195–97; Budd, *Numbers*, xx–xxi; Dennis T. Olson, *The Death of the Old and the Birth of the New: The Framework of the Book of Numbers and the Pentateuch* (Brown Judaic Studies 71; Chico: Scholars Press, 1985), 121; Milgrom, *Numbers*, xiii–xv; Baruch A. Levine, *Numbers 1–20* (Anchor Bible 4a; New York: Doubleday, 1993), 64–66.
7. Childs, *Introduction to the Old Testament*, 196–97; Budd, *Numbers*, xxi; Olson, *The Death of the Old*, 118, 122; Milgrom, *Numbers*, xiv, 34, 359; Levine, *Numbers 1–20*, 65.
8. Noth, *Numbers*, 5–6.
9. In this chapter the capitalized term 'Priestly' bears reference to texts, themes, and concepts ascribed to literary sources designated by both the sigla 'P' (Priestly source) and 'H' (the Holiness Legislation) of the established nomenclature in modern biblical criticism. The term, here, is not specific to either literary strand. Where desired, greater specificity in source-critical analysis shall make distinction between those sources by reference to the established terminology. The capitalized form 'Priestly' as a designate of

literary sources is also to be distinguished from the categorical and generic denotation of matters sacerdotal inherent to the adjective 'priestly.'

10. The language and the sentiments here are those of Thomas Römer, 'Israel's Sojourn,' 436–41. For similar perspectives on Numbers consisting largely of the latest material supplementing earlier texts in the final shaping of the Pentateuch, see Reinhard Achenbach, *Die Vollendung der Tora: Studien zur Redaktionsgeschichte des Numeribuches im Kontext von Hexateuch und Pentateuch* (Beihefte zur Zietshrift für altorientalische und biblische Rechtsgeschichte 3; Wiesbaden: Harrassowitz, 2003), 442–635; idem., 'Numeri und Deuteronomium,' in *Das Deuteronomium zwischen Pentateuch und deuteronomistischem Geschichtswerk* (ed. Eckart Otto and Reinhard Achenbach; Forshungen zur Religion und Literartur des Alten und Neuen Testaments 206; Göttingen: Vandenhoeck & Ruprecht, 2004), 123–34; Christophe Nihan, 'The Holiness Code between D and P: Some Comments on the Significance of Leviticus 17–26 in the Composition of the Torah,' in *Das Deuteronomium zwischen Pentateuch und deuteronomistischem Geschichtswerk* (ed. Eckart Otto and Reinhard Achenbach; Forshungen zur Religion und Literartur des Alten und Neuen Testaments 206; Göttingen: Vandenhoeck & Ruprecht, 2004), 121–22; idem., *From Priestly Torah to Pentateuch: A Study in the Composition of the Book of Leviticus* (Forschungen zum Alten Testament 25; Tübingen: Mohr Siebeck, 2007), 570–72; Eckart Otto, *Das Gesetz des Mose* (Darmstadt: Wissenschaftliche Buchgesellschaft, 2007), 201–04; idem., 'Scribal Scholarship in the Formation of Torah and Prophets: A Postexilic Scribal Debate between Priestly Scholarship and Literary Prophecy—The Example of the Book of Jeremiah and Its Relation to the Pentateuch,' in *The Pentateuch as Torah: New Models for Understanding Its Promulgation and Acceptance* (ed. Gary N. Knoppers and Bernard M. Levinson; Winona Lake: Eisenbrauns, 2007), 174 n. 12; Konrad Schmid, *The Old Testament: A Literary History* (trans. Linda M. Maloney; Minneapolis: Fortress, 2012), 177–81. See also the essays of Christian Frevel, Thomas Pola and Aaron Schart (ed.), *Torah and the Book of Numbers* (Forschungen zum Alten Testament 2. Reihe 62; Tübingen: Mohr Siebeck, 2013). Frevel's introduction to the volume (pp. 1–37) offers a concise and judicious summary of the main positions on the pivotal role of Numbers in the final editorial shaping of the Pentateuch. In contrast, Israel Knohl, 'Who Edited the Pentateuch?' in *The Pentateuch: International Perspectives on Current Research* (ed. Thomas B. Dozeman, Konrad Schmid and Baruch J. Schwartz; Forschungen zum Alten Testament 78; Tübingen: Mohr Siebeck, 2011), 359–67, ascribes to H (HS, Holiness School, is Knohl's preferred choice of a siglum) the final editorial touches, including Numbers 5:1–4 and 27:12–14, in drawing together the major blocks to form the Pentateuch. On the compromise between Deuteronomic and Priestly redactional sentiments in the formation of the

Pentateuch/Hexateuch, see Erhard Blum, *Studien zur Komposition des Pentateuch* (Beihefte zur Zeitschrift für die alttestamentliche Wissenschaft 189; Berlin: de Gruyter, 1990); Thomas Römer and Mark Zvi Brettler, 'Deuteronomy 34 and the Case for a Persian Hexateuch,' *Journal of Biblical Literature* 119 (2000): 401–19; Eckart Otto, 'The Pentateuch in Synchronical and Diachronical Perspectives: Protorabbinical Scribal Erudition Mediating between Deuteronomy and the Priestly Code,' in *Das Deuteronomium zwischen Pentateuch und deuteronomistischem Geschichtswerk* (ed. Eckart Otto and Reinhard Achenbach; Forshungen zur Religion und Literartur des Alten und Neuen Testaments 206; Göttingen: Vandenhoeck & Ruprecht, 2004), 14–35; Reinhard Achenbach, 'The Pentateuch, the Prophets and the Torah in the Fifth and Fourth Centuries B.C.E.' in *Judah and the Judeans in the Fourth Century B.C.E.* (ed. Oded Lipschits, et al.; Winona Lake: Eisenbrauns, 2007), 253–61; Konrad Schmid, 'The Late Persian Formation of the Torah: Observations on Deuteronomy 34,' in *Judah and the Judeans in the Fourth Century B.C.E.* (ed. Oded Lipschits, et al.; Winona Lake: Eisenbrauns, 2007), 237–51.

11. The notion of a priestly sponsored theocracy behind the theological flavoring of Numbers is most pronounced in the arguments of Achenbach, *Die Vollendung der Tora, 557–59*; idem., 'Numeri und Deuteronomium,' 132–34; idem., 'The Pentateuch,' 253–85.

12. For concise notations of the literary developments involving all or some of the texts mentioned below, see Römer, 'Israel's Sojourn,' 428–30; Nihan, *From Priestly Torah,* 570–72; Schmid, *The Old Testament,* 177–78; Otto, *Das Gesetz,* 202–03.

13. It cannot be overstated that my approach—in keeping with diachronic interests in inquiry—eschews facile harmonistic maneuvers in favor of attention to the inconsistencies and the divergent rhetorical agenda between texts on similar or proximate subject matter. I do not envision a unified and consonant entity at the terminus of an extensive series of editorial combinations. The loose ends, indeed, are of grave importance to my approach. However, the postulation of provenance and the sequence of literary development between texts—and thus, the direction of influence—is beyond the scope of this chapter. Rather, it is the disquieting effect of the 'cacophony' and the reader's exertions of will (to meaning) in taming the text that pique my interest.

14. Schmid, *The Old Testament,* 178; Römer, 'Israel's Sojourn,' 428.

15. The prophet's introductory remarks of Deuteronomy 4:1–4, pointedly, follow the lengthy summary of Israel's sojourning in Deuteronomy 1:19–3:29.

16. Otto, 'The Pentateuch,' 20–23, makes the argument eloquently. His brief statement on page 21 is to the point: 'In the Pentateuch's plot Dtn 4,44–26,68 was the mosaic interpretation of the Sinai-torah in Ex 20–24.

Lev 26,46; 27,34 closed the Sinaitic law as the basic revelation in the Pentateuch, which also in a synchronic perspective downgraded Deuteronomy into a secondary legal corpus. Num 36,13; Dtn 1,1 separated Deuteronomy from the legal stipulations of the Tetrateuch and Dtn 1,1–5; 4,1–44 functioned as the hermeneutical key for the deuteronomic law as mosaic interpretation of the Sinai-torah.'

17. Roland Barthes, *The Rustle of Language* (trans. Richard Howard; New York: Hill and Wang, 1986), 60. The term *déjà lu*, 'the already read,' is the Barthesian designation for *all* things previously heard, seen, and read that come to bear on the reader's experience with and through the text. The encounter, thus, is always with a host of images, texts and iterations often untraceable and anonymous.

18. Mary Douglas, *Leviticus as Literature* (Oxford and New York: Oxford University Press, 1999), 15–20.

19. Ibid., 18.

20. Ibid., 19.

21. Here, Douglas rests her argument on the theoretical productions of Suzanne Langer and Immanuel Kant. For a similar sensibility to sixteenth-century scientific discourse, see Michel Foucault, *The Order of Things: An Archaeology of the Human Sciences* (New York: Random House, 1970), 17–45. *Convenientia*—the Foucaldian term for the calculus of the age—finds in the universe a 'whole system of mirrors and attractions,' a tapestry of mutual emulation and resemblance across cosmic phenomena (pp. 28–29). Learning, in this milieu, is the ability to collate and read the signs of similitude and to uncover the laws that govern the likenesses. Something of this thinking, if Douglas is right, is at work in Leviticus.

22. Milgrom's scheme (*Numbers*, xxiii–xxiv, 359) places this procedure for reinstatement at the center of a chiasmus in Numbers 6:1–21: A, introduction (vv. 1–2); B, prohibitions (vv. 3–8); X, defilement (vv. 9–12); B', completion (vv. 13–20); A', summary (v.21). The required removal of those impure through contact with dead bodies and genital emissions is extraneous to legislation in Lev 13:1–15:33 which specifies removal only for those with epidermic infections (*ṣrwʿ*; see Lev 13:46). Israel Knohl sees in this innovative feature an initiative of the Holiness Legislation to expand the sacred realm to encompass the precincts of the camp (Israel Knohl, *The Sanctuary of Silence: The Priestly Torah and the Holiness School* [Minneapolis: Fortress, 1995, 184–85]). If this, indeed, is the case, then the metonymy betwixt 'camp' and the Nazirite's head of this legal complex is a part of Knohl's putative rhetoric of legal innovation, an effusion of the tabernacle's sanctity.

23. Milgrom, *Numbers*, 37, with reference to Lev 15:16a, argues that *škbt zrʿ* means 'semen.' Levine, *Numbers 1–20*, 192, prefers the translation 'a layer of semen' in conforming to his understanding of the phrase in Lev 18:20. In

either case, the application of the term is concise and, being such, contributes to the location of the contagion to the pubic region in the case of Numbers 5:11–31.

24. Milgrom, *Numbers*, 350, follows Numbers Rabbah (9:24) and Tosefta (Sotah 3:1–19) on this point.
25. I am struck by the paronomastic correspondence between *zeraʽ* ('seed') and *ṣārû(a)ʽ* ('scales disease'), a phonetic resemblance that underscores the kinship of 5:1–4 and 5:11–31, and of the items as defiling substances in the cultic economy.
26. Iser, *The Act of Reading*, 182–195.
27. See Lev 5:14–6:7; Josh 7:1; 2 Kings 16:14–17; 2 Chron 26:16–18; 28:19–25. My rendition 'malfeasance' reflects the later, broader use of the term in the sense of a general act of ill faith against the deity, a violation of covenantal stipulation: see Lev 26:15; Ezek 14:13; 17:18, 20; 18:24. On *mʽl* as sacrilege and the related uses of the term, see Jacob Milgrom, *Leviticus 1–16* (Anchor Bible 3; New York: Doubleday, 1991), 345–61; idem., *Cult and Conscience: The Asham and the Priestly Doctrine of Repentance* (Leiden: Brill, 1976), 16–21; Baruch A. Levine, *In the Presence of the Lord: A Study of Cult and Some Cultic Terms in Ancient Israel* (Leiden: Brill, 1974), 91–101.
28. Properly understood, 'malfeasance' (desecration) in Num 5:6 most likely has to do with the misappropriation of the (holy) divine name under the pretext of a false oath in the act of defrauding another (see Lev 6:2–7): so Milgrom, *Numbers*, 34–35; Noth *Numbers*, 46. Alternatively, the term here may designate a breach of trust in a broader sense without the precise meaning of 'sacrilege' as it most certainly does in Num 5:12: see Levine, *Numbers 1–20*, 188. None of this, however, subtracts from the ability of the conceptual pairing—'malfeasance' and 'defilement'—to spur readerly *speculation* of a connection in Num 5:5–10 to the theme of impurity in the larger legislative sequence.
29. My enumeration follows the English. The Hebrew has these verses as Lev 5:14–26.
30. On the use of 'malfeasance' to denote sancta trespass, see above (n. 28).
31. So, among others, Levine, *Numbers 1–20*, 187–91; Milgrom, *Numbers*, 34–35; Gray, *Numbers*, 41. That Num 5:5–10 supplements Lev 6:1–7 is evident in the former's attention to the unique circumstance of a deceased defrauded party *and* its abbreviated references to the varieties of fraud and the requisite offering of Lev 6:1–7. On the relationship between the laws, see Budd, *Numbers*, 56; Milgrom, *Leviticus 1–16*, 368; Noth, *Numbers*, 47.
32. Milgrom, *Leviticus 1–16*, 363–64, concocts this explanation with reference to Lev 5:17–19, which prescribes a guilt offering on suspicion that sancta trespass has occurred.
33. 4Q394 1 II, 16–17; 4Q394 3, 8–10.

34. Milgrom, *Leviticus 1–16*, 365–73.
35. On the conjunction and the semantic overlap of 'oath' and 'vow,' see Milgrom, *Numbers*, 488–90.
36. The supplementary capacity of Num 5:5–10 is evident in the law's attention to the unique circumstance of a deceased defrauded party *and* its abbreviated references to the varieties of fraud and the requisite guilt offering of Lev 6:1–7.
37. It might be noted that the hermeneutical effort to this interpretation is not unlike that which extends a concise signifier for sacrilege—*m'l*, 'malfeasance'—to cover *any* variety of covenantal infraction.
38. Douglas, *Leviticus as Literature*, 199–208, makes a similar move by associating the blasphemy of Leviticus 24 with the desecration of the sanctuary in Leviticus 10 in her parsing of the book's structure.
39. So noted by Nihan, *From Priestly Torah*, 482.
40. On the distinctive traits of H, see Knohl, *The Sanctuary of Silence*, 168–98; J. Joosten, *People and Land in the Holiness Code: An Exegetical Study of the Ideational Framework of the Law in Leviticus 17–26* (Supplements to Vetus Testamentum 67; Leiden: Brill, 1996), 5–9; Nihan, *From Priestly Torah*, 559–62. On the dependence of H on P's literary and theological heritage, see Knohl, *The Sanctuary of Silence*, 111–23; Jacob Milgrom, *Leviticus 17–22* (Anchor Bible 3a; New York: Doubleday, 2000), 1349–52; Nihan, *From Priestly Torah*, 401–545.
41. Knohl, *The Sanctuary of Silence*, 1–23.
42. The following comparison is indebted to the detailed observations of Jacob Milgrom (*Numbers*, 355; *Leviticus 17–22*, 1814–15). The correspondences across texts have been noted in early Jewish exegesis (see Sifre [Numbers] to Num 6:6–8; Numbers Rabbah 10:11) and, in varying degrees, by modern scholarship: Gray, *Numbers*, 63; Paul Heinisch, *Das Buch Numeri* (Bonn: Peter Hanstein, 1936), 30; Noth, *Numbers*, 55; Budd, *Numbers*, 70–71; Levine, *Numbers 1–20*, 221; Anne Katrine de Hemmer Gudme, 'How Should We Read Hebrew Bible Ritual Texts?: A Ritualistic Reading of The Law of the Nazirite (Num 6, 1–21),' *Scandinavian Journal of the Old Testament* 23(2009): 80.
43. Milgrom, *Leviticus 17–22*, 1814–15.
44. Hilary Lipka, 'Profaning the Body: *HLL* and the Conception of Loss of Personal Holiness in H,' in *Bodies, Embodiment, and Theology of the Hebrew Bible* (ed. S. Tamar Kamionkowski and Wonil Kim; Library of Hebrew Bible/Old Testament Studies 465; New York and London: T & T Clark, 2010), 97–98.
45. The expansive thinking across categories here, perhaps, is not unlike Kristel Clayville's account of Charles Darwin's widening of the familial bonds of affection (Kristel A. Clayville, 'Landed Interpretation: An Environmental

Ethicist Reads Leviticus,' in *Leviticus and Numbers* [ed. Athalya Brenner and Archie Chi Chung Lee; Minneapolis: Fortress, 2013], 14–15). Clayville's gathering of the personified 'land' under the communal umbrella mimics Darwin's extension of a 'basic bond of affection and sympathy' germane to immediate groups of kin to more distant relations. The impetus for the enlargement of 'kinship' is an affective energy predicated on an acute awareness of one's 'own intrinsic value,' which 'then *generalizes* and *analogizes* from that awareness to include others' (p. 15, my emphasis). The new equivalence, then, is not so much an invention *ex nihilo* as it is an imitation of an earlier connection, a likeness *already* manifest.

46. The initiative of one Micah in the hill country of Ephraim (Judges 17) comes to mind.
47. Discussions in rabbinic exegesis take this as a premise: so Sifre (Numbers) to Num 6:21 and Numbers Rabbah 10:24. For a similar position on this point in modern scholarship, see Gray, *Numbers*, 71; Levine, *Numbers 1–20*, 226; Milgrom, *Numbers*, 50.
48. The list picks up on elements of one in Lev 21:18–20, which disqualifies priests from participation in the sacrificial cult. The absence of a similar list in Lev 5: 4–7, according to Milgrom, is due to the fact that the passage addresses priests, a party not involved in the selection of the animal for slaughter (*Leviticus 17–22*, 1873).
49. Neither the additional detail in the Aramaic Versions of a pot (*dwd'*) as the receptacle for the flesh of the sacrificial beast nor the likelihood that the flames are those of a separate hearth, not the sacred altar, detracts from the juxtaposition of the sacrifice and the hair at this juncture in the text. On the illegitimate use of embers from a different hearth, see Gray, *Numbers*, 68; Milgrom, *Numbers*, 49.
50. Gray, *Numbers*, 68–69; A. H. McNeile, *The Book of Numbers* (Cambridge: Cambridge University Press, 1911), 35; William Robertson Smith, *The Religion of the Semites* (New York: Shocken, 1972), 332; Eliezer Diamond, 'The Israelite Self-Offering in the Priestly Code: A New Perspective on the Nazirite,' *Jewish Quarterly Review* 88 (1997): 6–18.
51. David P. Wright, *The Disposal of Impurity: Elimination Rites in the Bible and in Hittite and Mesopotamian Literature* (Society of Biblical Literature Dissertation Series 101; Atlanta: Scholars Press, 1987), 143; Rolf P. Knierim and George W. Coats, *Numbers* (Forms of Old Testament Literature 4; Grand Rapids: Eerdmans, 2005), 89; de Hemmer Gudme, 'How Should We Read,' 76–77.
52. Knohl, *The Sanctuary of Silence*, 175–86, 189–96, outlines a similar transgressive imaginary to H's expansive vision that conflates, among other things, holiness and moral behavior. See also Milgrom, *Leviticus 17–22*, 1397–1404, 1409–14; Nihan, *From Priestly Torah*, 545–47, 559–62.

53. The reference to the guilt offering by *'šmh—'šm* being the common term of choice (Lev 5:15–16, 18–19; 6:5–6; Num 6:12)—raises the question of whether the abstract sense of 'blame' or 'penalty' apart from an offering (Lev 4:3; 22:16; 2 Chron 28:10, 13) is in view. Thus, Milgrom, *Cult and Conscience*, 63–66, construes the word to obtain to the financial value of the 'purloined' priestly emolument that must be repaid. On the balance, *'šmh* clearly designates the sacrifice in Ezra 10:19 in reparation for *m'l* ('malfeasance' pertaining to desecration; Ezra 9:2; 10:10) in accordance with the specifications of Leviticus 5:14–19. Furthermore, the additional requirement of a fifth to the capital value is in keeping with the stipulations of Lev 5:14–19. At the very least, the broad strictures of the guilt offering are in view even if the animal offering is not required in Num 6:16.
54. Similarly, restorative rites for those exposed to dead bodies alone among the three sources of pollution mentioned in Num 5:1–4 are missing in Leviticus 13–15, an omission remedied in Numbers 19.
55. Jacob Milgrom considers this a case where tardiness in the performance of the mandated rites of cleansing elevates the level of pollution generated, obliging the commission of a purification offering, *ḥṭṭ't*, for the removal of impurity from the tabernacle (Milgrom, *Numbers*, 161).
56. On the complex literary history of the law, see, B. Baentsch, *Exodus, Leviticus, Numeri* (Handkommentar zum Alten Testament 2; Göttingen: Vandenhoeck & Ruprecht, 1903), 363–64; Michael Fishbane, 'Accusations of Adultery: A Study of Law and Scribal Practice in Numbers 5:11–31,' *Hebrew Union College Annual* 45 (1974): 25–46; Herbert Chanan Brichto, 'The Case of the *Sota* and a Reconsideration of Biblical "Law,"' *Hebrew Union College Annual* 46 (1975): 55–70; Tikva Frymer-Kensky, 'The Strange Case of the Suspected Sotah (Numbers V 11–31),' *Vetus Testamentum* 34 (1984): 11–13; Jaeyoung Jeon, 'Two Laws in the Sotah Passage (Num. v 11–31),' *Vetus Testamentum* 57 (2007): 182–85. For a concise overview of the interpretation of Num 5:11–31 in modern scholarship, see Richard S. Briggs, 'Reading the *Sotah* Text (Num 5:11–31): Holiness and a Hermeneutic Fit for Suspicion,' *Biblical Interpretation* 17 (2009): 288–319. Among other postulations, the law has been considered a conflation of procedures leading, separately, to the determination of guilt (vv. 16–24) and innocence (vv. 27–28); of a rite requiring direct divine judicial intervention (vv. 19, 21) and another where judgment is mediated by magical water (vv. 26–27); and of a case with grounds for suspicion (vv. 12–13, 29, 31) and a second of unsubstantiated jealousy. Three times, the law is introduced (vv. 12–13; 14; 29–30); twice, the woman partakes of the potion (v. 24; 26–27) and submits to adjuration with an oath (vv. 19, 21b–22; 21a). There is a trend toward a view of the law as an orchestrated drama leading the reader through multiple aspects of a single procedure—the

studies by Fishbane, Brichto, and Frymer-Kensky just named are in example. The ethical ramifications of the rite have been the subject of discussion in a stream of studies in recent years: Alice Bach, 'Good to the Last Drop: Viewing the Sotah (Numbers 5.11-31) as the Glass Half Empty and Wondering How to View It Half Full,' in *The New Literary Criticism and the Hebrew Bible* (ed. J. Cheryl Exum and David J. A. Clines; Sheffield: JSOT Press, 1993), 26–54; Bonna Devora Haberman, 'The Suspected Adulteress: A Study of Textual Embodiment,' *Prooftexts* (2000) 20: 12–42; Deborah L. Ellens, 'Numbers 5.11-31: Valuing Male Suspicion,' in *God's Word for Our World I: Theological and Cultural Studies in Honor of Simon John de Vries* (ed. J. Harold Ellens, Deborah L. Ellens, Rolf P. Knierim and Isaac Kalimi; Journal for the Study of the Old Testament Supplement Series 388; London: T & T Clark, 2004), 55–82; Roland Boer, 'The Law of the Jealous Man,' in *Voyages in Uncharted Waters: Essays on the Theory and Practice of Biblical Interpretation in Honor of David Jobling* (ed. Wesley J. Bergen and Armin Siedlecki; Hebrew Bible Monographs 13; Sheffield: Sheffield Phoenix Press, 2006), 87–95; Susan Niditch, '*My Brother Esau is a Hairy Man*': Hair and Identity in Ancient Israel (Oxford: Oxford University Press, 2008), 121–32; Briggs, 'Reading the *Sotah* Text,' 288–319.

57. Milgrom, *Numbers*, xxiv–xxv, 351, moves in this very direction. Other arguments in a similar vein come into discussion subsequently.
58. Frymer-Kensky, 'The Strange Case,' 20–21, proposes that the woman's 'fallen thigh' (vv. 21b, 27b) refers to the condition of a prolapsed uterus placing pressure on the cervix. While the details of the malady as a consequence of guilt (an aborted fetus, sterilization, etc.) remain obscure, the region of the anatomy (and its relation to the nature of the crime) in view is clear.
59. The analysis by Ellens identifies four spheres of interest in the husband's malady of a 'jealous spirit': the vagina, the womb, the community, and the male perpetrator (Ellens, 'Numbers 5.11-31,' 76–77).
60. 'Effusion' understands the nominal construct form *škbt* to derive from the causative expression of the verb with the sense of 'to pour out': BDB 1012; *HALOT* 4:1379. Accordingly, Levine (*Numbers 1–20*, 192) opts for the translation 'layer of semen' as part of a euphemism for sexual intercourse; Milgrom (*Numbers*, 37) simply takes the phrase as referring to seminal fluid.
61. Harry M. Orlinsky, 'The Hebrew Root *ŠKB*,' *Journal of Biblical Literature* 63 (1944): 40.
62. Niditch, '*My Brother Esau*,' 123.
63. Ibid., 123.
64. On the conception of the uterus as a mere receptacle in a monogenetic construal of reproduction in parts of rural Turkey, see Carol Delaney, 'Seeds

of Honor, Fields of Shame,' in *Honor and Shame and the Unity of the Mediterranean* (ed. David D. Gilmore; Washington DC: American Anthropological Association, 1987), 35-48. The vulnerability of the womb by this view is inseparable from the conception of the seed as bearer of 'the essential identity of a man' that leaves 'an indelible imprint which no amount of washing can erase' (p. 42). For a similar interpretation of the 'contaminating' properties of semen in biblical rules for sexual congress, see Eve Levavi Feinstein, *Sexual Pollution in the Hebrew Bible* (Oxford and New York: Oxford University Press, 2014), 64-65, 95; Sarah Schectman, 'The Social Status of Priestly and Levite Women,' in *Levites and Priests in Biblical History and Tradition* (ed. Mark Leuchter and Jeremy M. Hutton; Ancient Israel and Its Literature 9; Atlanta: Society of Biblical Literature, 2011), 87-88. On the trope of 'contaminating seed' and the matter of genealogical purity in Lev 21:1-15 and related texts, see Christine E. Hayes, *Gentile Impurities and Jewish Identities: Intermarriage and Conversion from the Bible to the Talmud* (Oxford and New York: Oxford University Press, 2002), 27. On the phallocentric conception of sexual intercourse and the stigmatization of the penetrated party in homoerotic encounter, see Michael Carden, 'Homophobia and Rape in Sodom and Gibeah: A Response to Ken Stone,' *Journal for the Study of the Old Testament* 82 (1999): 85-88.

65. Bach, 'Good to the Last Drop,' 27-28.
66. Ibid., 36.
67. And so Feinstein, *Sexual Pollution*, 45, sets the graphic denotation of sexual intercourse and its qualification as 'defilement' here in Numbers 5 in the emotive domain of 'disgust.'
68. Bach, 'Good to the Last Drop,' 37.
69. Ibid., 40. Text in italics is Bach's.
70. Haberman, 'The Suspected Adulteress,' 24. See also Bach, 'Good to the Last Drop,' 33-34. Noteworthy is the Mishnah's postulation that the place of forced disrobement is the same as that of purification rites for the parturient and those with scales disease, evidence perhaps of a degree of association across the categories of 'uncleanness' in the Amoraic imagination.
71. The suggestion by R. Judah that the uncovering of the woman's bosom be aborted if her breasts be deemed attractive confirms the erotic undertones to the Mishnaic commentary on the rite.
72. Calum Carmichael finds double entendre in the loosening (*pr'*) of the woman's hair (Carmichael, *The Book of Numbers*, 38; see v. 18). The act is one of shaming *and* a gesture to the Nazirite's sacred overgrown locks (Num 6:5; also *pr'*). The point of the doublespeak, for Carmichael, is a semicryptic allusion (in the law of Numbers 5) to Tamar's tabooed sexual

stratagem in pressing Judah to perform his 'sacred' obligation to her as a levir (Gen 38:12–30).
73. This also is the conclusion of Feinstein, *Sexual Pollution*, 47.
74. The meaning of this term is uncertain: BDB 319–21; *DCH* 3: 237; *HALOT* 1: 319–20; *TWOT* 1: 288–90. A rundown of various arguments is available in Milgrom, *Leviticus 17–22*, 1806–07. The possibilities include victims of rape, harlots, sacred prostitutes, a woman profaned, or any woman with experience of sexual intercourse. It has been suggested, with asyndeton between *ḥllh* and *znh* in verse 14b, that the term is hendiadys for the 'promiscuous woman' (*znh*). Feinstein, *Sexual Pollution*, 94, follows Milgrom (p. 1807) in noting the position of the term between the promiscuous woman (*znh*) and the divorcee (*grwšh*) in verses 7 and 13–14. Its place, by her reckoning, suggests a status above that of the promiscuous woman, a woman guilty of sex out of wedlock *without the sense of habituality*.
75. Ezekiel (44:22) closes this gap, allowing priests to marry only the widow of a priest.
76. John E. Hartley, *Leviticus* (Word Biblical Commentary 4; Dallas: Word, 1992), 348; Milgrom, *Leviticus 17–22*, 1805.
77. The expected consequence here (in accord with the result of deviant sexual behavior in Lev 18:20, 24 and Num 5:19–20) is defilement, not desecration. This, so Milgrom, *Leviticus 17–22*, 1818, is a case of the Holiness Legislation's (H) tendency to imprecision in its choice of terms. But *ḥll*'s ('to desecrate') appearance in this instance is in keeping with the wider legislation's orientation to the sanctity of the sanctuary precincts and the distinction between priest and laity in the broader context: so Nihan, *From Priestly Torah*, 483–86. Desecration *follows* defilement. Eve Levavi Feinstein (*Sexual Pollution*, 94) follows Milgrom (*Leviticus 17–22*, 1810)—quite contrary to the majority opinion represented by, among others, Hilary Lipka ('Profaning the Body,' 100)—in construing 'desecrate' a metaphor for 'disgrace' in this verse. The father's disqualification from cultic service, in Milgrom's view, is the father's self-perception. The disturbance to the decorum of the sacred realm, if this view is correct, is no less palpable.
78. The metaphorical application of the verb *znh* and its nominal counterparts (*zwnh* and *znwt*) is well recognized: see, for example, Naomi Koltun-Fromm, *Hermeneutics of Holiness: Ancient Jewish and Christian Notions of Sexuality* (Oxford and New York: Oxford University Press, 2010), 47–52; Lipka, 'Profaning the Body,' 98–100; Hayes, *Gentile Impurities*, 41–43; Milgrom, *Leviticus 17–22*, 1462; Phyllis Bird, 'To Play the Harlot: An Inquiry into and Old Testament Metaphor,' in *Gender and Difference in Ancient Israel* (ed. Peggy Day; Minneapolis: Fortress, 1989), 75–94.

79. Harold Bloom, *Agon: Towards a Theory of Revisionism* (Oxford and New York: Oxford University Press, 1982), 19. My emphasis.
80. Ibid., 21.
81. To the point is Steed Vernyl Davidson's observation that Rahab the 'prostitute' is kept *outside Israel's camp* ('Gazing [at] Native Women: Rahab and Jael in Imperializing and Postcolonial Discourses,' in *Postcolonialism and the Hebrew Bible: The Next Step* [ed. Roland Boer; Semeia Studies 70; Atlanta: Society of Biblical Literature, 2013], 83–84; see Josh 6:23). The Israelite house/camp analogy and the sullying effects of foreign/illicit sexuality and religiosity resonate in Joshua 6.

References

Achenbach, Reinhard. 2003. *Die Vollendung der Tora: Studien zur Redaktionsgeschichte des Numeribuches im Kontext von Hexateuch und Pentateuch*. Beihefte zur Zietshrift für altorientalische und biblische Rechtsgeschichte 3; Wiesbaden: Harrassowitz.

Achenbach, Reinhard. 2004. 'Numeri und Deuteronomium.' In *Das Deuteronomium zwischen Pentateuch und deuteronomistischem Geschichtswerk*, ed. Eckart Otto and Reinhard Achenbach. Forshungen zur Religion und Literatur des Alten und Neuen Testaments 206; Göttingen: Vandenhoeck & Ruprecht.

Achenbach, Reinhard. 2007. 'The Pentateuch, the Prophets and the Torah in the Fifth and Fourth Centuries B.C.E.' In *Judah and the Judeans in the Fourth Century B.C.E.*, ed. Oded Lipschits, Gary N. Knoppers and Rainer Albertz. Winona Lake: Eisenbrauns.

Bach, Alice. 1993. 'Good to the Last Drop: Viewing the Sotah (Numbers 5.11–31) as the Glass Half Empty and Wondering How to View It Half Full.' In *The New Literary Criticism and the Hebrew Bible*, ed. J. Cheryl Exum and David J. A. Clines. Sheffield: JSOT Press.

Baentsch, B. 1903. *Exodus, Leviticus, Numeri*. Handkommentar zum Alten Testament 2; Göttingen: Vandenhoeck & Ruprecht.

Barthes, Roland. 1974. *S/Z: An Essay*, trans. Richard Miller. New York: Hill and Wang.

Barthes, Roland. 1986. *The Rustle of Language*, trans. Richard Howard. New York: Hill and Wang.

Bird, Phyllis. 1989. 'To Play the Harlot: An Inquiry into and Old Testament Metaphor.' In *Gender and Difference in Ancient Israel*, ed. Peggy Day. Minneapolis: Fortress.

Bloom, Harold. 1982. *Agon: Towards a Theory of Revisionism*. Oxford and New York: Oxford University Press.

Blum, Erhard. 1990. *Studien zur Komposition des Pentateuch*. Beihefte zur Zeitschrift für die alttestamentliche Wissenschaft 189; Berlin: de Gruyter.
Boer, Roland. 2006. 'The Law of the Jealous Man.' In *Voyages in Uncharted Waters: Essays on the Theory and Practice of Biblical Interpretation in Honor of David Jobling*, ed. Wesley J. Bergen and Armin Siedlecki. Hebrew Bible Monographs 13; Sheffield: Sheffield Phoenix Press.
Brichto, Herbert Chanan. 1975. 'The Case of the *Sota* and a Reconsideration of Biblical "Law."' *Hebrew Union College Annual* 46: 55–70.
Briggs, Richard S. 2009. 'Reading the *Sotah* Text (Num 5: 11–31): Holiness and a Hermeneutic Fit for Suspicion.' *Biblical Interpretation* 17: 288–319.
Budd, Philip J. 1984. *Numbers*. Word Biblical Commentary 5; Waco: Word.
Carden, Michael. 1999. 'Homophobia and Rape in Sodom and Gibeah: A Response to Ken Stone.' *Journal for the Study of the Old Testament* 82: 83–96.
Carmichael, Calum. 2012. *The Book of Numbers: A Critique of Genesis*. New Haven and London: Yale University Press.
Childs, Brevard S. 1979. *Introduction to the Old Testament as Scripture*. Philadelphia: Fortress.
Clayville, Kristel A. 2013. 'Landed Interpretation: An Environmental Ethicist Reads Leviticus.' In *Leviticus and Numbers*, ed. Athalya Brenner and Archie Chi Chung Lee. Minneapolis: Fortress.
Davidson, Steed Vernyl. 2013. 'Gazing (at) Native Women: Rahab and Jael in Imperializing and Postcolonial Discourses.' In *Postcolonialism and the Hebrew Bible: The Next Step*, ed. Roland Boer. Semeia Studies 70; Atlanta: Society of Biblical Literature.
Delaney, Carol. 1987. 'Seeds of Honor, Fields of Shame.' In *Honor and Shame and the Unity of the Mediterranean*, ed. David D. Gilmore; Washington DC: American Anthropological Association.
Diamond, Eliezer. 1997. 'The Israelite Self-Offering in the Priestly Code: A New Perspective on the Nazirite.' *Jewish Quarterly Review* 88: 6–18.
Douglas, Mary. 1999. *Leviticus as Literature*. Oxford and New York: Oxford University Press.
Driver, S.R. 1913. *Introduction to the Literature of the Old Testament*. 9th edn.; Edinburgh: T&T Clark.
Ellens, Deborah L. 2004. 'Numbers 5.11–31: Valuing Male Suspicion' In *God's Word for Our World I: Theological and Cultural Studies in Honor of Simon John de Vries*, ed. J. Harold Ellens, Deborah L. Ellens, Rolf P. Knierim and Isaac Kalimi. Journal for the Study of the Old Testament Supplement Series 388; London: T & T Clark.
Feinstein, Eve Levavi. 2014. *Sexual Pollution in the Hebrew Bible*. Oxford and New York: Oxford University Press.
Fishbane, Michael. 1974. 'Accusations of Adultery: A Study of Law and Scribal Practice in Numbers 5:11-31.' *Hebrew Union College Annual* 45: 25–46.

Foucault, Michel. 1970. *The Order of Things: An Archaeology of the Human Sciences.* New York: Random House.
Frevel, Christian, Thomas Pola and Aaron Schart, ed. 2013. *Torah and the Book of Numbers.* Forschungen zum Alten Testament 2. Reihe 62; Tübingen: Mohr Siebeck.
Frymer-Kensky, Tikva. 1984. 'The Strange Case of the Suspected Sotah (Numbers V 11–31).' *Vetus Testamentum* 34: 11–26.
Gray, George Buchanan. 1906. *Numbers.* International Critical Commentary; New York: Charles Scribner's Sons.
Haberman, Bonna Devora. 2000. 'The Suspected Adulteress: A Study of Textual Embodiment.' *Prooftexts* 20: 12–42.
Hartley, John E. 1992. *Leviticus.* Word Biblical Commentary 4; Dallas: Word.
Hayes, Christine E. 2002. *Gentile Impurities and Jewish Identities: Intermarriage and Conversion from the Bible to the Talmud.* Oxford and New York: Oxford University Press.
Heinisch, Paul. 1936. *Das Buch Numeri.* Bonn: Peter Hanstein.
de Hemmer Gudme, Anne Katrine. 2009. 'How Should We Read Hebrew Bible Ritual Texts?: A Ritualistic Reading of the Law of the Nazirite (Num 6, 1–21).' *Scandinavian Journal of the Old Testament* 23: 64–84.
Iser, Wolfgang. 1978. *The Act of Reading: A Theory of Aesthetic Response.* Baltimore: The Johns Hopkins University Press.
Jeon, Jaeyoung. 2007. 'Two Laws in the Sotah Passage (Num. v 11-31).' *Vetus Testamentum* 57: 181–207.
Joosten, J. 1996. *People and Land in the Holiness Code: An Exegetical Study of the Ideational Framework of the Law in Leviticus 17-26.* Supplements to Vetus Testamentum 67; Leiden: Brill.
Knierim, Rolf P. and George W. Coats. 2005. *Numbers.* Forms of Old Testament Literature 4; Grand Rapids: Eerdmans.
Knohl, Israel. 1995. *The Sanctuary of Silence: The Priestly Torah and the Holiness School.* Minneapolis: Fortress.
Knohl, Israel. 2011. 'Who Edited the Pentateuch?' In *The Pentateuch: International Perspectives on Current Research*, ed. Thomas B. Dozeman, Konrad Schmid and Baruch J. Schwartz. Forschungen zum Alten Testament 78; Tübingen: Mohr Siebeck.
Koltun-Fromm, Naomi. 2010. *Hermeneutics of Holiness: Ancient Jewish and Christian Notions of Sexuality.* Oxford and New York: Oxford University Press.
Leveen, Adriane. 2008. *Memory and Tradition in the Book of Numbers.* Cambridge and New York: Cambridge University Press.
Levine, Baruch A. 1974. *In the Presence of the Lord: A Study of Cult and Some Cultic Terms in Ancient Israel.* Leiden: Brill.
Levine, Baruch A. 1993. *Numbers 1–20.* Anchor Bible 4a; New York: Doubleday.

Lipka, Hilary. 2010. 'Profaning the Body: *HLL* and the Conception of Loss of Personal Holiness in H.' In *Bodies, Embodiment, and Theology of the Hebrew Bible*, ed. S. Tamar Kamionkowski and Wonil Kim. Library of Hebrew Bible/Old Testament Studies 465; New York and London: T & T Clark.

MacDonald, Nathan. 2012. 'The Book of Numbers.' In *A Theological Introduction to the Pentateuch: Interpreting the Torah as Christian Scripture*, ed. Richard S. Briggs and Joel N. Lohr. Grand Rapids MI: Baker Academic.

McNeile, A.H. 1911. *The Book of Numbers*. Cambridge: Cambridge University Press.

Milgrom, Jacob. 1976. *Cult and Conscience: The Asham and the Priestly Doctrine of Repentance*. Leiden: Brill.

Milgrom, Jacob. 1990. *Numbers*. New York: Jewish Publication Society.

Milgrom, Jacob. 1991. *Leviticus 1–16*. Anchor Bible 3; New York: Doubleday.

Milgrom, Jacob. 2000. *Leviticus 17–22*. Anchor Bible 3a; New York: Doubleday.

Niditch, Susan. 2008. *'My Brother Esau Is a Hairy Man': Hair and Identity in Ancient Israel*. Oxford: Oxford University Press.

Nihan, Christophe. 2004. 'The Holiness Code between D and P: Some Comments on the Significance of Leviticus 17–26 in the Composition of the Torah.' In *Das Deuteronomium zwischen Pentateuch und deuteronomistischem Geschichtswerk*, ed. Eckart Otto and Reinhard Achenbach. Forschungen zur Religion und Literartur des Alten und Neuen Testaments 206; Göttingen: Vandenhoeck & Ruprecht.

Nihan, Christophe. 2007. *From Priestly Torah to Pentateuch: A Study in the Composition of the Book of Leviticus*. Forschungen zum Alten Testament 25; Tübingen: Mohr Siebeck.

Noth, Martin. 1968. *Numbers: A Commentary*, trans. J. D. Martin. Old Testament Library; London: SCM.

Olson, Dennis T. 1985. *The Death of the Old and the Birth of the New: The Framework of the Book of Numbers and the Pentateuch*. Brown Judaic Studies 71; Chico: Scholars Press.

Orlinsky, Harry M. 1944. 'The Hebrew Root ŠKB.' *Journal of Biblical Literature* 63: 19–44.

Otto, Eckart. 2004. 'The Pentateuch in Synchronical and Diachronical Perspectives: Protorabbinical Scribal Erudition Mediating between Deuteronomy and the Priestly Code.' In *Das Deuteronomium zwischen Pentateuch und deuteronomistischem Geschichtswerk*, ed. Eckart Otto and Reinhard Achenbach. Forschungen zur Religion und Literartur des Alten und Neuen Testaments 206; Göttingen: Vandenhoeck & Ruprecht.

Otto, Eckart. 2007. *Das Gesetz des Mose*. Darmstadt: Wissenschaftliche Buchgesellschaft.

Otto, Eckart. 2007. 'Scribal Scholarship in the Formation of Torah and Prophets: A Postexilic Scribal Debate between Priestly Scholarship and Literary Prophecy—The Example of the Book of Jeremiah and Its Relation to the Pentateuch.' In *The*

Pentateuch as Torah: New Models for Understanding Its Promulgation and Acceptance, ed. Gary N. Knoppers and Bernard M. Levinson. Winona Lake: Eisenbrauns.

Rendtorff, Rolf. 1986. *The Old Testament: An Introduction*, trans. John Bowden. Philadelphia: Fortress.

Römer, Thomas. 2007. 'Israel's Sojourn in the Wilderness and the Construction of the Book of Numbers.' In *Reflection and Refraction: Studies in Biblical Historiography in Honour of A. Graeme Auld*, ed. Robert Rezetko, Timothy H. Lim and W. Brian Aucker. Supplements to Vetus Testamentum 113; Leiden and Boston: Brill.

Römer, Thomas and Mark Zvi Brettler. 2000. 'Deuteronomy 34 and the Case for a Persian Hexateuch.' *Journal of Biblical Literature* 119: 401–19.

Schectman, Sarah. 2011. 'The Social Status of Priestly and Levite Women.' In *Levites and Priests in* Biblical History *and Tradition*, ed. Mark Leuchter and Jeremy M. Hutton. Ancient Israel and Its Literature 9; Atlanta: Society of Biblical Literature.

Schmid, Konrad. 2007. 'The Late Persian Formation of the Torah: Observations on Deuteronomy 34.' In *Judah and the Judeans in the Fourth Century B.C.E.*, ed. Oded Lipschits, Gary N. Knoppers and Rainer Albertz. Winona Lake: Eisenbrauns.

Schmid, Konrad. 2012. *The Old Testament: A Literary History*, trans. Linda M. Maloney. Minneapolis: Fortress.

Ska, Jean-Louis. 2006. *Introduction to Reading the Pentateuch*. Winona Lake; Eisenbrauns.

Smith, William Robertson. 1972. *The Religion of the Semites*. New York: Shocken.

Wright, David P. 1987. *The Disposal of Impurity: Elimination Rites in the Bible and in Hittite and Mesopotamian Literature*. Society of Biblical Literature Dissertation Series 101; Atlanta: Scholars Press.

CHAPTER 4

On Bad Sex and Bad Seed: Doubting Deuteronomy

The trek through the expanding and evolving network of rites and laws pertaining to the constitution of Israelite identity, sexuality, living spaces, vows, and sacred portions remains a mainstay in this chapter. The patchwork of Mosaic pronouncements on sexual propriety, divorce, the constitution of the assembly and campsite purity, among other things, are familiar topics in (or, at least, of thematic propinquity to those of) the journey thus far. Similar movements of mind across prescriptive sets in forging a semblance of coherence are conceivable. The analogical imagination continues to animate thinking across rulings in juxtaposition, denying semantic sacrosanctity to perceived literary units. No text is an island; indeed, texts, their (possible) *meanings*, are infectious and reading facilitates infection. And so, the argument for interpretation as deliberate(d) productions in the spaces between texts—that other constant in the volume—informs the approach of this chapter. Texts and intertexts, so the argument goes, present possibilities that reading subjects activate in accordance with individual interests. *Meanings*, the senses that may accrue to a passage, fester in that fertile space where texts and readers meet. Reading, in a word, is a *subjective* affair. So much for similarities with preceding chapters, how is this one different?

    This chapter advances the discussion about reading subjects in bringing to attention a particular class of consumer/producer. The theoretical and practical ruminations of Majority World feminist criticism form the horizon for our present foray into Deuteronomy. The narrowed focus specifies a reading subject that, so far, has been a loose construct, an abstract but implied sensibility at the confluence of select texts and the repertoire of semantic possibilities they bear—recall Iser's 'wandering viewpoint' of the introduction. The explicit introduction of a decolonizing hermeneutic (addressing ethnicity *and* gender) enriches the intertextual project, drawing into the orbit of the expanding corpus of texts in conversation extra-biblical material. The novelty of the chapter, to put it another way, is the expansion of the intertextual matrix into the space *in front of* the (biblical) text. This flirtation with postcolonial and feminist methodology occasions the onset of a deconstructive approach to the task. The altered orientation of the present chapter, of course, is opportune, given our approach toward hybridized registers of exclusion—racial, sexual, religious, and moral—in the preceding chapter. The turn to our current project is *from* a fortification of the rhetoric of prescription by analogy *to* an interrogation of the arguments for a coherence across prescriptive sets. The task is a disclosure of the logical inconcinnities and of the dubious assumptions behind the correlative imagination. The reader's suspicion, once triggered, acquires a sense (and sensibility) for the instabilities of the dichotomies propounded in reading across prescriptive sets. The boundaries seem, increasingly, porous and evanescent.

Our constituted reading subject wrought in conversation with postcolonial and feminist criticism—for the purposes of this chapter—runs up against another subject: Israelite and masculine. Subjectivity, in this last instance, is the apex of privilege implied in a reading of the laws. It is the party that is the primary beneficiary of legislation, the hegemon whose interests and authority the laws serve and protect, and, as such, a construct of the prescriptive discourses.[1] This chapter, thus, may be perceived, plausibly, as a contest of subjects, though not one between equals. My approach will give the counterhegemonic remonstrance of Majority World feminism the final word (to the degree that the reticent reading posture of this volume is able to declare a winner). It remains to be said, with all this talk of subjectivity, that in conceiving the subjects I follow Stuart Hall's construal of 'identity' as a fluid production, 'a process of articulation, a suturing, an over-determination,' always 'subject to the "play", of *différance*.'[2] Eschewed are essentialist notions of subject or identity as transparent entities, stable cores, fixed points on a map of phenotypical traits. The subject, rather, is an organism in motion, the fragmented effect (s) of discursive processes at the intersection of voices in contention. Here, the 'voices' of interest to our decolonizing optic confer at the interstices of

Mosaic articulations of Israelite identity (23:1–8) and the surrounding rhetoric on sexual and marital propriety (22:13–21; 24:1–4).[3] Mosaic promulgation here denotes the assembly, women's wombs, the 'people' (Israel) and its locus, and the land as recessed, exclusive entities. The specified loci are points in a larger litany of prized and pristine things or places across the broader context to Deuteronomy 22:13–24:4. The prophet's prescriptive discourse draws Israel's camp (23:9–14), its vows (23:17–23), the case of a runaway slave (23:15–16), and pilferage in a vineyard (23:24–25) into the mix. The constellation of items sacrosanct and/or the topoi of interest rehearse those of previous stipulations (but especially those of Lev 21–22 and Num 5–6). My line of inquiry is centrifugal. It proceeds from a perception of the ethnic exclusions in Israel's constitution of its assembly (Deut 23:3–8) as the center. From here, my critical attention fans outward to consider the adjacent, enclosing legal pronouncements on sexual and marital propriety (Deut 22:13–30; 24:1–4). So, the racialized restriction to assembly membership (Deut 23:3–8) is my point of entry into a critical reading of Deuteronomy 22:13–24:4.

The expansion into Majority World feminist criticism is balanced by a narrowing of focus in pursuing the biblical text. The passages on campsite hygiene (23:9–14), runaway slaves (23:15–16), and pilferage (23:24–25) receive scant attention; I pursue these only to the degree that they bear relevance to the protracted interest of this chapter on sexual/marital propriety and assembly membership. The choice to focus on the latter, in turn, is a result of my commitment to engaging the twin emancipative agendas of feminist critique and postcolonial theory. The interests of these sometimes mutually contentious interpretive stances are organic to the process. Accordingly, my engagement with specific aspects of the theoretical apparatus, the lens to the texts, shall be piecemeal and opportune. But first, what exactly are the inflections of my adopted view to the texts? How, precisely, does it skew my vision?

Priming the Vision

Mutual recriminations of myopia form the backdrop to the increasingly fertile exchange between the varying critical stances under the umbrella terms 'postcolonialism' and 'feminism.' The febrile exchange in certain quarters lends an impression of incompatibility between these spheres of scholarly inquiry. The brief survey of the interface between the critical camps by R. S. Sugirtharajah hits the mark in its succinct statements on the state of the discussion.[4] The charge of feminist criticism, speaking with a shared commitment of opposition to oppression, is that the critical scope of its companion remains mired in patriarchy, oblivious to power differentials between the genders in its construal of hegemony. The danger, thus, is a lopsided emancipative agenda that leaves a broad swathe of the exploited populace—women—in the chains of systemic oppression. The countercharge, led by feminist critics sympathetic to the developing world, is that feminism remains largely a province of the Western, developed world. The corollary to this misstep is the abstracted conception of *Woman* that overlooks the double victimization of many women of developing countries under the yoke of patriarchy *and* colonialism's detritus. This trend toward homogenization is most visible—to judge by the volume of, sometimes vitriolic, commentary on the matter—in the unreflective European or Euro-American feminist view on Third World Woman, one that unwittingly reifies imperialism's stereotypes.

Chandra Talpade Mohanty's programmatic essay on the issue follows such a tack. The essay sustains a diatribe against universality as a thematic in feminist discourse on women of the developing world across several categories.[5] Victimhood and dependency, all within an economy of development in accordance with Western social and economic norms, colors the view of the West to the rest. The nub of the problem, as she puts it, is that the postulation of *Woman* as a category of evaluation is an all-encompassing, totalizing entity.[6] The distinction by gender, thus, becomes an essential trait of the evaluative process, a monolithic commodity free of social–historical configuration. The problem, as Mohanty sees it, is that these scholars

> discursively colonize the material and historical heterogeneities of the lives of women in the third world, thereby producing/re-presenting a composite, singular 'Third World Woman'—an image which appears arbitrarily constructed, but nevertheless carries with it the authorizing signature of Western humanist discourse. [She] argue[s] that assumptions of privilege and ethnocentric universality on the one hand, and inadequate self-consciousness about the effect of Western scholarship on the 'third world' in the context of a world system dominated by the West on the other, characterize a sizable extent of Western feminist work on women in the third world.[7]

The unfortunate effect of this methodological trajectory is the conception of

> 'sexual difference' in the form of a cross-culturally singular, monolithic notion of patriarchy or male dominance [that] leads to the construction of a similarly reductive and homogeneous notion of what I call the 'Third World Difference'—that stable, ahistorical something that apparently oppresses most if not all the women in these countries. And it is in the production of this 'Third World Difference' that Western feminisms appropriate and 'colonize' the fundamental complexities and conflicts which characterize the lives of women of different classes, religions, cultures, races and castes in these countries. It is in this process of homogenization and systematization of the oppression of women in the third world that power is exercised on much of recent Western feminist discourse, and this power needs to be defined and named.[8]

The methodological universalism of the disputed vision and its penchant for abstracted, stable paradigms comes to the fore in Mohanty's indictment of the economic reductionism well represented in various works on women and development.[9] 'Development' here is narrowly construed as economic progress in line with the democratic and capitalist patterns of the West. From the outset, other paths are eschewed. Of greater prominence in Mohanty's incisive critique, though, is the pervasive blindness to the social–economic locations of the women of interest—class, ethnic identity, whether urban or rural—in the pursuit of a binary opposition based solely on gender (a distinction between the 'haves' and the 'have-nots'). 'Gender,' thus, is an essential, *a priori* categorical lens trained upon the data collated. In stark contrast is Mohanty's praise for Maria Miles whose study of the lace makers of Narsapur, India, unravels the 'ideology of the housewife' as a patriarchal construct for economic oppression.[10] The putative frame upon the women of the profession stands at the interstices of local and familial prejudicial discourses with evidence of regional variation. The strength (and accuracy) of Miles's analysis, as Mohanty rightly states, is its discernment of the inflection of constructed cultural norms through 'a certain historically and culturally specific mode of patriarchal organization.'[11] The same astute judgment pertains to her (Miles) ability to parse the varied responses of the flesh-and-blood women to the oppressive patriarchal imposition in accordance with distinctions in class.

That Mohanty's essay is 'programmatic' is evidenced in the prevalence of homogeneity as the cardinal sin of Western feminist scholarship in the penmanship of others. The ahistorical eye, too, is the *prima culpa* in Kwok Pui-lan's articulation—Mary Daly's *Gyn/Ecology: The Metaethics of Radical Feminism* is in her sights—of an imperialistic impulse to Western feminist scholarship shared with masculinism.[12] The specific practice in focus is foot-binding in China. Daly's purpose is the compilation of a series of cross-cultural sado-rituals—clitoridectomy, *sati,* polygamy, and veiling completing the list of heinous practices—designed to curtail female freedom and initiative, nothing short of a dismemberment of the Goddess.[13] A noble cause, however, produces a little shop of Oriental(ist) horrors with scholarly strokes too broad to capture the diversity of opinion in the historical subject(s). Abstract and monolithic, Daly's China fails to capture variance in the practice across regions, classes and ethnic groups. Foot-binding, as Kwok points out, was commonplace in the north, but less followed in the southern, coastal regions. The practice was the province of the upper classes, but not found among the Manchus, the Kejia, and the Mongolians.[14] The portrait is of a silent indigenous subject, void of dissonance on the practice and certainly lacking the initiative to pose a challenge of any sort: a singular, hapless mass awaiting (Western feminist) enlightenment and rescue.

Meyda Yeğenoğlu's criticism of the Western feminist view to the veiling of women follows a similar path.[15] But here, the homogenizing Western eye conflates modern North Atlantic constructions of motivation for the practice with those of the Mediterranean, with the former, of course, as the dominant vision. The fundamental misstep is a blindness to the particularity of Western women in the rush for a universality that (con)fuses progress and the act of unveiling. The singular vision affords 'a clinching example that interlocks "woman" and "tradition/Islam" so that it could be morally condemned in the name of emancipation.'[16] The move deftly erects a norm that effaces heterogeneity to the functions of veiling across regions, repeating the epistemic violence of colonialism. Yeğenoğlu's read on the practice in Algeria—here, she relies on Frantz Fanon—bucks the 'norm.' Evoking the Derridean 'hymen'—the signification of that liminal space that both conjoins and separates, that is *and* and *or*—the veil, in its Algerian guise, is fabric (external to the body) and skin (internal to the body) in a rite of passage that forms the adult, female, body. Unveiling leaves (the rest of) the body bereft of its protective epidermis, exposing its members to dissolution, an outcome that can hardly be construed as emancipation.[17] The simplified, totalizing frame of Western discourse on the matter does not hold. Veiling (and unveiling) does not submit to a monological Western reading.

Indeed, the move to check the homogenizing and occluding impulse of liberal feminism—a repeat of the phallocentric impulse—is common in postcolonial criticism. Valerie Amos and Pratibha Parmar dispute the applicability of white middle-class constructions of a 'feminist consciousness' in Britain to a black feminist situation, one that dissipates beyond the narrow social–economic concerns of whites in which privileges are secured often at the expense of blacks.[18] Ann Rosalind Jones questions, among other things, French feminism's dualistic and essentialist constructions of female sexuality—derivations of Freud and Lacan—apart from the particular social and symbolic matrices germane to a given moment in the evolution of a culture.[19] Laura Donaldson protests *We of the Never-Never*'s (a film based on a volume of the same name and *The Little Black Princess*) purchase of a redemption of sorts from sexism by way of a reinscription of imperialism's earnest postulation of indigenous impotence and dependency, an 'insight' born of a blindness to the complex and varied treatment of the native in the written works.[20] The productions under assault are nothing short of acquiescence to Leela Gandhi's perception of a 'metropolitan *demand* for marginality,' a hailing that is 'also troublingly a *command* which consolidates and names the non-West as interminably marginal.'[21] The (forcibly) constituted margins, in such cases, serve the interests of a center-seeking validation, the purchase of a moral high ground predicated on the imputed political immaturity and only just now nascent moral sensibilities of the Third World. By contrast, the lofty clarity of the educated Western feminist imagination—a beacon of light in the darkness—is implied. Feminist discourse, in such instances, rides the currents of an imperialism that sustains a cultural hierarchy on a self-assuring and self-congratulatory march toward a mirage of equ(al)ity.

But the criticism goes both ways. Postcolonial criticism suffers a similar onslaught for its tunnel vision to ethnicity and nationalism. Ania Loomba, for example, finds in Frantz Fanon's colonized subject a latent masculine vision. Where the sexual fantasies of black men for white women are historicized and contextualized, the erotic projections of colored women remain unexplored territory, a domain of undifferentiated 'private dreams' and 'inner wishes' void of social-historical connections.[22] The black woman comes in one perpetual shade. Meyda Yeğenoğlu takes aim at Homi Bhabha's blindness to sexuality in his insistent deployment of the sexual fetish as *signifier* of racial and cultural difference in colonial discourse, a dualistic hermeneutical gesture that sets the two (sexuality/gender and race/culture) in *separate* realms.[23] The oversight, as Ann Laura Stoler puts it to us, creates the sense that the asymmetries of sex 'convey what is "really" going on elsewhere, at another political locus.'[24] Power differentials in discussions of gender, thus, are but 'tropes to depict other centers of power.' Such an erroneous and artificial cleavage in postcolonial discourse leaves Valerie Cooper's read on the condition of African American women—an insight of her reflection on the plight of Jephthah's unnamed daughter—without that other front (gender) that renders it a case of double marginalization.[25] Postcolonial criticism's misprision of imperium—according to Musa Dube—overlooks the sexually oppressive agenda of postcolonial nationalisms.[26] The insidious side to nationalism's summon to 'liberty' is its direction to indigenous women to preserve and promote, wholesale and uncritically, native cultures that would return them to invisibility and subordination. Recriminations of occlusion, an essentialist slant to analysis and the proliferation of unyielding dichotomies, go both ways, clearly.

But Leela Gandhi is certainly correct in her assessment of the sparring between camps as 'a very old quarrel,' an extended in-house r/fumble in a meeting of minds with a shared vision for emancipation.[27] Gandhi is optimistic: the collaboration affords a vista on numerous possibilities and fresh trajectories; an expansion of the liberalizing agenda beyond the bounds of the respective movements; and a mutually beneficial adjustment of focus in 'a combined effort against the aggressive myth of *both* imperial and nationalist masculinity.' Elizabeth Schüssler Fiorenza, it seems, assumes a theoretical stance that captures well the ethos of a polydimensional/directional orientation to the task. The call—theologizing in biblical interpretation, particularly, is in focus—is for the implementation of a 'radical democratic ethos' to cull the winds of imperialism. The need for said ethos is dire in biblical interpretation for the simple fact that the Bible is an instrument 'in the service of empire, colonialist expansion, racist exploitation, and hetero-sexist discrimination.'[28] The list of obstacles to liberty, one might note, is expansive and indicative of Schüssler Fiorenza's perception of imperialism's place at the intersection of multiple hegemonic fronts. Feminism's nemesis, therefore, is *kyriarchy* (and *kyriarcentrism*), a beast of many faces. The neologism captures the range of oppressive vision(s), those of 'emperor, lord, master, father, husband, elite propertied male.'[29] Legion is the ways of imperialism, and domination comes in many guises. At multiple nodes, therefore, feminist criticism must pose its resistance, its view to the task kaleidoscopic. Accordingly, the movement, rightly so, finds variegated, localized expressions: womanist, *mujerista*, black, Asian, queer, LGBT, postcolonial.[30] Shunned, furthermore, is the divorce of cultural studies from Marxist (socioeconomic) discourse in envisioning the project.[31] Gender, in such emancipative stance(s), is a fluid concept within a social–political matrix of shifting, sometimes competing, structures of domination. The liberating imagination, if it is to hit the mark, must confront 'the embeddedness of wo/men's oppression in the entire domain of Western society, culture, and religion' and 'reveal that the subordination and exploitation of wo/men is crucial to the maintenance of kyriarchal or imperial cultures and religions.'[32] Oppression is intersectional and the response must be the same. The emergent hermeneutic must be an ever-inclusive anti-imperial optic respectful of a dynamic spectrum of identities and positions within an intercalated and imbricated structure of exploitation.[33] In esteem is Thomas Kuhn's theory of paradigm in scholarly discourse that reveals 'the conditioned nature of all scientific investigation,' dismissing the notion of neutrality to discursive evaluation.[34] Avoiding language of a 'value free standpoint' (and its attendant rigid dichotomies), Schüssler Fiorenza—with Kuhn—favors 'a typology of shifting interpretive practices' that stems the dogmatic certainty of parochialism.[35] It follows that Schüssler Fiorenza stands with Edward Said as an advocate of his 'contrapuntal reading'—an emancipative stance 'with a simultaneous awareness *both* of the metropolitan history that is narrated *and* of those other histories against which (and beyond which) the dominating discourse acts.'[36]

Schüssler Fiorenza's radically inclusive stance—one that encompasses even the metropole (the expansive hermeneutics of the decolonizing project makes for strange bedfellows)—is at the heart of her vociferous opposition to the 'dual systems approach' that is often the cleft in both postcolonial studies and feminist criticism.[37] The unfortunate analysis in these instances—a defect already indicated in aforementioned critical statements—unfolds with sole focus on patriarchy/gender *or* postcolonialism/imperialism. The malaise on the side of postcolonial studies stems from its homogenizing eye to Western scholarship that effects 'a reverse "othering"'—a logic forgetful of the Western (especially poststructuralist and feminist) epistemological premise to postcolonial theory.[38] The Manichean mania endemic to the view is reminiscent of mainstream/malestream scholarship, the very entity under assault in feminist studies *and* postcolonial critique.

Schüssler Fiorenza's ruminations on theory, a clarion call to reform in liberal feminism, repair a rupture in the logic of anti-imperialism. The intersectional, contrapuntal, and mutually interrogative demeanor she advocates captures the spirit of a broadening stream of feminist scholarship fleeing the shadow of a solipsistic North Atlantic configuration for the greener pastures of a multilateral approach. Talk of emancipation (and action) proceeds at the intersections of race, gender, class, sexual orientation, and economics. Banished are monochromatic configurations of subaltern subjects. Many share Schüssler Fiorenza's approach. Denise Noble, beyond examples already mentioned, charts a course to more refined and historically/culturally embedded engagements with the counterculture of an emergent Caribbean–British identity in her cross-examination of the sexual hedonism and homophobia of Bashment/Dancehall performance and performativity.[39] Lena Sawyer tracks transformations in conceptions of ethnic and social identity between black/African adoptees (and children of 'mixed race') in Sweden—a group conversant with the political articulations of (US) African Americans—and the adult immigrants (often with children) of a later generation.[40] Zheng Wang and Ying Zhang discuss implications to the shift in Chinese feminism from the Marxist formulations of the Chinese Communist Party to visions of autonomy and agency germane to the Western liberal political aspirations of a subsequent generation of activists.[41] David Eng brings psychoanalytic insights to disarming the racialized, sexualized, and gendered productions of Euro-America in construing Asian American males.[42] Eng's disposition on US racial discourse, with consummate erudition, puts heteronormativity in the dock, exposing its reach into cultural constructions on both sides of the racial divide.

Specimens of the new(er) affinity for historically embedded and regionally specific studies of gender-related cultural productions are ubiquitous. The vision of this matured (and still maturing) decolonizing eye is multilateral, ever ready to discern fresh configurations to the vectors of oppression and novel manifestations of old malevolencies. The imperialism in its sight is a *moving* target. To this vision reborn, the selected texts of Deuteronomy prove a suitable arena for charting the embattled, problematic, and problematizing energies germane to the emancipative project. The Mosaic rulings juxtapose gender and ethnicity as bases for exclusion in a manner that imbricates both registers. The imperialistic ethos of each is ineluctably bound to the other. Conversely, the undoing of one signals the demise of the other. The texts effectively force the interface, even confrontation, inherent to the collaborative efforts of feminist and postcolonial discourse.

The general parameters to our slant on the text are set. Let us proceed with a reading of Deuteronomy 22:1–24:4.

THE TEXT IN VIEW: DEUTERONOMY 22:13–24:4

The patchwork of regulations that is Deuteronomy 22:13–24:1–4 is preceded by a command series (22:1–12) prescribing tassels for coats and rulings against theft and undesirable mixtures (cross-dressing, mixed cropping, incompatible fabrics, etc.). Moses's pronouncements beyond Deuteronomy 24:4 take up the subject matter of exemption from military service, loans, defiling skin conditions, and kidnapping (Deut 24:5–13). The pronouncements on sexual and marital improprieties at the extremities of Deuteronomy 22:13–24:4—sexual infelicities in 22:13–30 and divorce and remarriage in 24:1–4—lend a sense of distinction to the passage of laws. Sex and marriage encapsulate the mixed rulings of Deuteronomy 23:1–25 on Israel's assembly, runaway slaves, vows, and misappropriations in the field. Coital relations are the brackets to our text of interest.

Bad Blood Out

The point of entry into the text, as stated, is that delectable morsel on the colonial platter: the ethnic constitution—the bloodlines—at the social-political apex. A perusal of texts across the Hebrew Bible finds the privileged lot of the assembly (Israel's *qhl* and/or *'dh*) charged with executive, judicial, and legislative responsibilities.[43] This elite group of arms-bearing and adult males (Num 14:1–4; 27:17–21; Josh 22:16; Judg 20:1; 21:5) confers for the election of monarchs (1 Kings 12:20; 2 Chron 23:2–3) and the conclusion of treaties (Josh 9:15). Where failures in external or internal relations occur, the assembly initiates military action (Num 22:4; Judg 20:1–2) and presides over the division of spoils (Num 31:26). The assembly's agency, also, is essential in allocating inheritance (Num 27:1–2) and restraining the dreaded blood avenger in cases of unintentional homicide (Num 35:22–25). While the term is at times coterminous with Israel as a whole (e.g., Num 19:20; Deut 31:30), its usage often suggests a narrower sense (Num 10:7; 20:10). The expressed interest in reproductive capabilities (in Deut 23:1–2) may be indicative of marriageability (with Israelites) as a requirement for admission to the assembly.[44] The restrictive measures propounded in Deuteronomy 23:3–8, at the least, underscore the selective status of the political entity.

That fecundity of a 'proper' variety is in view in the broader context—extending our scope of interest to the exclusion of eunuchs and the 'misbegotten' races of verses 1–2—lends greater relevance to the unifying, repeated sequence of 'shall not enter' clauses (vv. 1–3) comprising the legislation.[45] The coital undertones to the passage are assured. The legislative block stands guard over the tribal womb, a prescription for eugenics with no use for parties with equipment in disrepair and racial misfits for the gene pool. Two particular exemplars of the 'ill conceived' (*mmzr*)—Ammon and Moab—are the specific parties proscribed in the constitution of Israel's assembly. There is, however, speciousness to the definition of the assembly when the prescriptions are seen in a broader context. The stated motivation for the exclusion of both groups is their intractably pugnacious and inhospitable disposition toward Israel: the refusal of provision and their commission of that bad-mouther-for-hire, Balaam (Deut 23:4). The Moabites and the Ammonites are hostile to God's chosen race. While the charge of employing Balaam against Israel sticks—though Numbers 22–24 makes no mention of the Ammonites as a party to Moab's vindictive agenda—that of denying God's chosen sustenance runs aground on Deuteronomy 2. In Deuteronomy 2:28–29, Moses's rehearsal of Israel's wilderness wanderings lists Moab and Edom as models of hospitality! This double praise, of course, renders untenable the subsequent unequal treatment of the same two parties (Deut 23:3–4, 7) on the grounds that one—but presumably not the other—lacked charity in the wilderness. Elsewhere, in accounts of conflict with Sihon (Num 21:10–20, 24–25; Deut 2:19, 37), Israel makes no contact with Moab. The avoidance of the Moabites, it seems, stems from divine instruction to do such (Deut 2:19). By these accounts, there was no failure on the part of the Moabites in offering Israel refreshment *for there was no encounter*. And then, there is the strange matter of Israel's acceptance of the Edomites (Deut 23:7) in the light of Moab's (and Ammon's) expulsion. The inclusion of the Edomites is surprising for their vilification in Numbers 20:14–21 for reasons not unlike those for the rejection of the Ammonites and the Moabites. Israel's request for safe passage and provender—'if we or our livestock drink any of your water, we will pay for it' (Num 20:19)—is rebuffed (Num 20:20). The very act that places Moab and Ammon in the proverbial 'doghouse' (Deut 23:3–4) is Edom's transgression in Numbers 20. Yet, the Edomites are welcome in Israel's assembly. The distinguishing factor is their shared ancestry (Deut 23:7), a factor that does not help Moab as the offspring of Lot, the nephew of Israel's glorious ancestor (Gen 19:30–36). Perhaps this is because Lot's line is sullied by incest (more on this in a while). Also, Israel's embrace of Egypt, if only at arm's length, is alarming. The rationale is Israel's extended residence in Egypt as foreigners (Deut 23:7). Yet, the prominently stated motive for the rejection of Moab and Ammon is their hostility to Israel on its trip through the wilderness, a journey of escape from Egyptian oppression! Jacob's tarry in Egypt, after all, was marked by forced labor, genocide, and repeated calls for deliverance from a living hell (Exod 2:23–25; 3:9; 6:5–6). If any group would inspire images of unbridled and unrepentant brutality in Israel's retrospection, Egypt should have pride of place. In the broad sweep of pentateuchal narrative, the alleged inhospitality of Moab and Ammon—the disagreeable trait that keeps them from Israel's good graces in Deuteronomy 23—seems mild in comparison to Israel's protracted suffering under Egypt's auspices! Indeed, the patchwork of reasoning behind the erection of the fence around the assembly is inconsistent, to say the least.

The mixed review of Moab and Ammon across Numbers and Deuteronomy betokens an overall ambivalence toward Lot's lot. This dissonance, clearly, is but one aspect of a broader incoherence to the story of Israel's sojourn. This well-noted aspect to the narrative is ascribed usually to the conjunction of competing accounts (sources) and/or the accretion of various editorial glosses.[46] Jeffrey Tigay's delineation of the sources and their unique perspectives is not uncommon.[47] The narratives of Numbers are largely the work of the Yahwist (J) adapting strands of the Elohistic source (E), with some minor editorial interpolations mostly from the hand of the Priestly (P) scribe. This view has the Edomites refusing passage to Israel shortly after their arrival at Kadesh (Num 20:1), which forces a trek southward to the Red Sea via Mount Hor, bypassing Edom (Num 20:14–21:4). The Deuteronomist (D), who reworks J(E)'s account, roughly, accords with this view, with the glaring exception that Israel turned north from the Red Sea and secured passage through Edom (Deut 2:1–8).[48] Numbers 33, the work of P, describes a northward move *from* the Red Sea *to* Kadesh, proceeding from there to the eastern boundary of Moab (Num 33:36–44): no circumlocution of Edom and Moab is implied.[49]

But even within the smaller literary complex of Numbers 20–21, there is evidence of multiple hands. John Van Seters, in keeping with majority opinion, finds the hand of the Yahwist historian (J) in Numbers 20:14– 21:20 charting a course from Kadesh, bypassing Edom and Moab, to the eastern reaches of Moab.[50] In this sweeping portrayal of the journey are two glosses (21:10–11, 14–20) that—quite contrary to the gist of the account—suggest an incursion into Moab. In stark contrast to J's convoluted narrative is Edom's sanction of Israel's passage through its territory in Deuteronomy 2:1–8 (which the Yahwist deploys as a source by the account of Van Seters). Angela Roskop's survey of Numbers 21 largely agrees with Van Seters.[51] The itineraries of Numbers 21:4, 10–11a minimize contact with Canaanite groups, signaling a circumlocution of Edom and Moab. But contrary to this initiative are the later insertions of verses 12–13a and 18b–20—a portion of the secondary material Van Seters postulates—that place Israel in Moab. Editorial interpolation here, by Roskop's estimation, fosters connections with the Balaam Story Numbers (22–24) and Deuteronomy (2–3); both texts find Moab as locus. The aporia of a composite text inspires acts of harmonization that, ultimately, fortify the dissonance. By both accounts, the text is in disarray, its unwieldy fabulation on full display.

But Roskop's interest—and mine—passes beyond a detailing of the vagaries to Israelite–Moabite–Ammonite relations and the interrogation of genetic variety in textual composition. Her scrutiny lingers considerably over the literary affects of obfuscation. Invoking the contrastive Barthesian categories of *readerly* and *writerly* pleasures, Roskop's final assessment is that the little incongruities to a narrative are but the flipside to a perceivable coherence. Where the readerly pleasure delights in conjuring a tidy gestalt to a tale 'in spite of indications that it is a composite text,' the writerly whim finds *jouissance* (the Barthesian term of choice) at the points of *non sequitur* that betray the work of multiple scribes.[52] The semblance of conformity—the pleasure of the readerly disposition—across sources and editorial layers is *not* one that erases the dialectic between *traditum* and *traditio*, the ostensible traces of a text's history. The reading subject is cleft and attends to both proclivities, to the dual pleasure of reading:

> Fractures in the itinerary chain can therefore be understood *both* to create an impression of unity in the text *and* to point to disunity in the text due to diachronic development. Wolfgang Iser notes that part of the reading process involves accepting the illusion of the text, making differences

disappear. When we read passively, we experience the readerly pleasure of the illusion of a coherent itinerary chain. Of course, the illusion can also be broken... When we read analytically, breaking the illusion, the workings of the text begin to show themselves, and we experience the writerly pleasure of figuring out the puzzle of how the text was written.[53]

The double vision affords a view of the trees *and* the forest, the strokes of the brush *and* the holistic brilliance of a Monet from five paces back.[54] Indeed, the cues to the text's history—the editorial glosses bridging sources—are, strangely, also aids to reading the text *as a whole*.[55]

Roskop's writerly pleasure in the text uncovers the sinews that bind the pieces, the very bonds that also are the indices to the fractures. Her astute ability to hear the Janus tone to the editorial glosses—the building blocks of unity and diversity in the texts—is not unlike Mikhail Bakhtin's ear soused in 'an apperceptive background pregnant with responses and objections.' Bakhtin's perception is a listening ever cognizant of the 'alien words' in every utterance. Texts are assemblages of enunciations fraught with 'contradictory opinions, points of view and value judgments'; every utterance is a contested space 'present to the speaker not in the object, but rather in the consciousness of the listener.'[56] Such moments of realization bring bouts of euphoria—of orgasmic proportions—to the Barthesian reader. Cherished are such moments of 'loss,' an unsettling to 'the reader's historical, cultural, psychological assumptions, the consistency of his [sic] tastes, values, memories.'[57] The pleasure of the reading subject, here, is 'far from being pacified by combining... taste for works of the past with... advocacy of modern works in a fine dialectical movement of synthesis.' On the contrary, the reader is 'a split subject, who simultaneously enjoys through the text, the consistency of his [sic] selfhood *and its collapse, its fall.*'[58]

A somewhat similar sense of 'collapse' or 'fall' inhabits Roland Boer's quest for the subject of Ezra–Nehemiah (though I do not detect a sense of bliss in Boer's academic prose). Cycling through various registers—a political identity in response to divine election, the constitution of an 'other' to 'Israel,' social–economic distinctions of class—Boer comes up empty. The strident summon of divinity to peoplehood clashes with words of rejection. Delimitations of identity lead to outings of insiders. Who, precisely, is Israel? And what is subjectivity? One way out of the quagmire, for Boer, is to show that the subject is a useless category, destined for such an undoing every time it is examined closely. Or...the subject is not a self, an ego, or the symbolic entity produced through various processes of subjectification. No, the subject is the unstable process and unrealizable search itself. In other words, the subject is not centered but split...It is a little like the proverbial onion: I have attempted to peel the texts back, layer after layer, and all I have found is a void, a point of pure negativity...But we need to go one step further, for not only is the subject a negativity or void, *but it is also the process in which we come to the void*, that, is the failure of symbolization that is supposed to produce the subject. So the subject emerges as a negativity or void *that both forecloses the totality of the process of subjectification and simultaneously fuels the process.*[59]

Boer's 'void' is the end to our reading, the fruit of our *writerly* pleasure in shaking the foundations for putting Ammon and Moab out while embracing Egypt and Edom. The rhetoric, if forceful, languishes in the broader context, prompting several scholars to point out the discrepancies that mar the transparency of the law's logic.[60] If breeding *into* Israel is the privilege assembly membership affords—as some suggest—then the battery of prohibitions are a leaky prophylactic, effective only against the eunuch (who's not a threat!). The anchors to the fence are in shambles. Anyone might get through. Israel's bounds seem porous. The efforts at demarcation border on nonsense. Not inconceivably, the mangled portraiture of a somewhat more generous 'Israel' reflects Boer's quest for subjectivity as a futile undertaking 'that both forecloses the totality of the process of subjectification and simultaneously fuels the process.' The quest is Sisyphian in essence (or worse, one never gets to the apex of the hill). 'Israel' as subject, inclusive of its favored brood of allied parties, is a cipher, a moniker of dubious authenticity and varying hues in powerful hands for political gain. Ultimately, though, the term falls within the bounds of the well-worn phrase of that wise sage of Ecclesiastes: 'vanity of vanities' (Eccl 1:1–2). And so, 'Israel of the assembly' is but a wisp of smoke, the ephemeral effect of a text void of substance.

The shifting standards in 'othering' are reminiscent of colonial expediency in racial policy. That pragmatism is an undercurrent, Ania Loomba reminds us, should not cast aspersion on the fact that a trenchant racism underlies colonial practice.[61] Nonetheless, shifts in political–economic exigency are discernible in tracking the forces that accompany changes in the regulation of subaltern groups. What is needed is comprehension that 'the relationship between racial ideologies and exploitation is better understood as dialectical, with racial assumptions both arising out of and structuring economic exploitation.'[62] There was flexibility to colonial propaganda, a rich and labile rhetorical repertoire of invective and praise that attended imperialism's metamorphosis on the ground. English constructions of Aboriginal essence in Australia—one example Loomba cites—moves from docility to savagery as Anglo awareness of the indigenes as a veritable supply of labor grew. The very 'primitive excess of energy' that sets the aborigene beyond the compass of polite (European) society would be essential for the strength of England's expansionist agenda: 'wild' servants of the crown to tame a 'wild' land, fuel for developing a frontier to meet an English design.

Ann Laura Stoler's excellent study of sexuality and colonial protocol in Dutch Indonesia documents well the imbrication of evolving colonial sexual mores with the dynamics of Dutch East Indies Company commercial enterprise.[63] Tensions with Indonesian workers in the early twentieth century coincided with heightened European policing of indigenous male sexuality. In the wake of fears of insurgency, in colonial Southeast Asia and elsewhere, was a slew of invective casting native males as salacious beasts with eyes trained on European females. The Sumatran Dutch community 'expanded their vigilante groups, intelligence networks, and demands for police protection to ensure their women were safe and their workers "in hand."'[64] This pronounced vilification of indigenous males, however, was but a single gesture in an evolving landscape of regulated interracial (sexual) relations stretching back to the seventeenth century. Its development coincides with a shift in Dutch colonial policy to an enshrinement of European culture in which Dutch women were to play a pivotal role. Eschewed were earlier preferences for a range of domestic and sexual arrangements of varying economic and personal configurations—concubinage of different forms—for Dutch-male comfort. The perceived advantages to the absence of the distracting and impoverishing interests of Dutch females and to the 'healthier' offspring of miscegenation gave way to the glaring need for the fortified ethnic boundaries of endogamy. Protect the (Dutch) women; guard the race. The new calculus within an old formula—the maintenance of European supremacy, racial, political, and economic—recasts Dutch colonial vision in which select parties (Dutch women, the indigenous males, and the offspring of two cultures) play pivotal roles. The evolving image of the Other betrays a dynamic imperial vision born of economic and political expediency and urgency.

The construction of race (and gender) was grist for colonial policy and a pawn in the shifting tactics of commercial enterprise. Judith McKinlay's emphasis on 'process' and 'processes' in imperialism's construction of 'ethnicity' and 'ethnic identity' is to the point. The terms denote continual 'negotiating and re-negotiating what it is that allows them [colonizers] to identify themselves as an "us" and then maintain that self identity in the midst of changing circumstances.'[65] The stalwart component to the flux, of course, is the colonizer's privilege, a (dis)position anchored in foundational myths and tales from hoary antiquity fuelled—if Regina Schwartz is on the mark—by an acute cognizance of scarcity.[66] So much land and, yet, not enough! And if not enough, who should take precedence? Excommunication, in this economy of race and hierarchy, means diminished access (or none) to the land under 'one people' and—as the case with biblical Israel—one god. The selective, unequal distribution of resources and profit, so ordered, guarantees (Schwartz again) that the business of Other-ing will always be a violent affair.[67]

But constructions of 'race,' as the examples of Stoler and Loomba show, are not innocent of gendered biases. Our texts forge the same conjunction in delimiting 'Israel.' The portmanteau structure to Israelite identity—*both* racialized *and* gendered—comes clearer in the broader literary context. And so we cast our eyes at proximate legislation on sexuality and divorce that envelope the laws in focus thus far. Our perusal begins on a trail backward to the laws that initiate Moses's rulings on the assembly—the abjection of the eunuch and the child of illicit union (*mmzr*)—before proceeding to the regulations on sexual conduct in Deuteronomy 22:13–30 and beyond.

Bad Seed, Bad Blood

The double prohibition (Deut 23:1–2) at the inception of the prescriptive set respecting the assembly is something of a hinge between these regulations and the preceding unit on sexual misadventure (Deut 22:13–30). At the inception of Deuteronomy 23, we pass from pronouncements on 'bad sex' to 'bad blood.' The contribution of the twin rulings, the beginning to the novel topic, is the explicit foregrounding of fertility and (illegitimate) sexual congress at the seams of the units of discourse.

> [1] No one whose testicles are crushed or whose penis is cut off shall be admitted to the assembly (*qhl*) of the Lord. [2] Those born of an illicit

union (*mmzr*) shall not be admitted to the assembly (*qhl*) of the Lord. Even to the tenth generation, none of their descendants shall be admitted to the assembly (*qhl*) of the Lord. (Deut 23:1–2)

Quite visibly, a common concern for procreation unites the pair of rulings. Under this broad thematic canopy, a plausible rationale for the exclusion of males with damaged organs of reproduction is their inability to contribute to the fulfillment of the divine promise of innumerable offspring to Israel's patriarchs of yore.[68] While the precise semantic value to *mmzr* ('born of an illicit union')—the concern of the second prescription (v. 2)—eludes us, its application to the errant religiosity of the Philistines in Zechariah 9:6 lends a nuance of heterodoxy to the term. Bastards are religious outsiders! The proximity to the pejorative stabs at Lot's offspring (in Deut 23:3) brings, also, the suggestion of incest within the orbit of *mmzr* (Ammon and Moab being the issue of Lot's couplings with his daughters; see Gen 19:29–38). The association of illicit sex with religious waywardness, of course, is already a prominent aspect of the Moabite disposition by biblical account (see Num 24).[69] That Moab and Ammon, specifically named as groups not (quite) kindred to Israel—a point implied in the embrace of Edom *as kin* (Deut 23:7) by contrast—fortifies the tripartite rationale for exclusion showcased in, among other places, Leviticus 18 and 20: idolatry, race, and sexual deviance. The Moabites and the Ammonites are triply strange. This is the force of *mmzr*. 'Misbegotten' or 'bastard,' is the signifier for the idolatrous religious praxis and its attendant salacious deportment so very alien to Israel's ethnic DNA.

The three-pronged jeopardy to Israel's identity, as Randall Bailey recalls, is implicit to the near infringements on Israel's matriarchs, facilitated by the cowardly conduct of the patriarchs in passing their beautiful wives off as sisters (Gen 12, 20 and 26).[70] The threats of racial admixture, deviant sexuality, and religious apostasy are present at Israel's beginnings. The irony to the episodes, of course, is that the 'foreign' males prove themselves of superior moral fiber to that of Israel's ancestors in their expressions of outrage in discovering the ruse. Nonetheless, the stigma to foreignness remains a trope to the tales, albeit one subverted in course. The canonical stories, Judith McKinlay remarks, witness nothing short of a 'collapsing of language for illicit sex, illicit worship and intermarriage with foreigners, especially foreign women.'[71] The 'misbegotten' at the inception of Mosaic legislation on assembly membership, the point of transition from misplaced sexuality and inferior seed, is the lemma standing for the polysemantic matrix that renders select strangers suspect. Words—a word, in this case—are powerful for the potent cluster of concepts they invoke. 'Bastard' here is a term well placed.

The semantic cloud and clout to Deuteronomy 23:1–2 is appropriate to its function in the broader context as a bridge to the sex laws of Deuteronomy 22:13–30. The allusion to illegitimate sexual practice signals, quite precisely, a common thread through the prescriptive sets on sexual misbehavior (Deut 22:13–30) and the constitution of the assembly. 'Bad sex' is common to both sets of rules. But, of course, deviant sexual behavior, so clearly a matter of interest in the preceding laws and the initial rulings on assembly membership, is only implicit to the exclusion of Ammon and Moab. Incest as a reason for Moab and Ammon's abjection is the *suggestion* of the broader context.[72] The stated reason of 'hostility against Israel,' in fact, obscures the connection with incest, with deviant sexuality. The abjection of the *mmzr*, however, renders explicit in the rulings the taboo of sexual malfeasance—the clearest point of connection to the preceding sex laws—which hovers as mere connotation over Moab and Ammon, perceived only by intertextual reference.

Further to this function of a hinge between units, the specific exclusion of the misbegotten connects in a fashion more precise with the final member of the prescriptive sequence on sexual impropriety: 'a man shall not marry his father's wife, thereby violating his father's rights' (Deut 22:30). Conceivably, any offspring from the range of illicit sexual unions envisioned in Deuteronomy 22:22–30 might wear the mantle of *mmzr*. My point is that *mmzr*, fraught with the connotation of incest by association with Lot's brood, connects a tad more directly with the prohibited intergenerational coupling of Deuteronomy 22:30. To put it another way, the solitary prohibition to sexual relations with a close relative in the series of sex laws constitutes the most direct connection to the following set of laws by its association with the nefarious sexual escapades of Lot's daughters, the progenitors of the 'misbegotten' races—Moab and Ammon. Sexual deviation is the family value across the laws; incest is the bond.

To the point, the literary hinge that is Deuteronomy 23:1–2 cuts both ways. The mention of illegitimate children connects with the matter of sexual misconduct of preceding (Deut 22:13–30) and following (Deut 23:3–8) legal promulgation. The veritable nexus between distinct sets of laws facilitates a comingling of discourse on sexuality, race, and religiosity in defining the Israelite subject. As an introduction to the subject of assembly membership, the pivot between units injects sexual misconduct and the consequent genetic 'defect' of offspring into the following discussion of the negative Canaanite disposition, religious and civil.[73] The miscreance of the rejected pair (Ammon and Moab), so the inference holds, is congenital. Bad blood comes from bad seed and bad sex![74] The case for the exclusion of Ammon and Moab is multifaceted.

But Deuteronomy 23:1–8 is not an island. No text is! The potent mix of tropes inherent to Israel's national portrait(ure)—its invention of Others—mines the rich semantic field at play between Deuteronomy 22–24 *and* the texts seen thus far. To follow a few (possible) trajectories: we might associate the bad seed, the *mmzr*, beyond the assembly with the excrement (Deut 23:12–14)[75] and the unclean parties (Num 5:1–4; Deut 23:9–10) that must be removed from the precincts of the camp. As Egypt is beyond Israel's portals (Exod 12:2–3), so the 'misbegotten' are cut off from the house/assembly of Israel (Deut 23:1–8). Ammon and Moab of incestuous seed are 'contaminants' in the assembly *and* the compromised uterus (Num 5:11–31; Deut 22:13–29); their abjection is akin to the scouring of the misappropriated vagina under a husband's jealous surveillance (Num 5:20–22, 27). But Israel's assembly, that pristine tribal womb, is also the payment of a vow free of the taint of sexual indiscretion (Deut 23:17–18), the sort of tarnish left by the income of the whore whose defiling act sullies the priestly pate (Lev 21:7, 13). The Nazirite, whose hallowed crown resembles the priestly head, must consign his defiled locks to the flames, just as the priest must the desecrating presence of a promiscuous daughter (Lev 21:9). Should the payment of a vow from a sordid source (Deut 23:17–18) and the transgressing Moabite be assigned a similar fate? The dastardly Ammonite, like the emasculated male (Deut 23:1), is the defunct priest saddled by defect (Lev 21:16–24), a bearer of a blemish that renders a beast an unacceptable offering (Lev 22:21–25; Exod 12:27 [compare 12:5]).

Heads, camps, vows, gifts, houses, congregations, hair: the network of rites and prescriptions presents a mélange of equivalences, a dizzying swirl of correspondences to the reader pregnant with potential for expansion. Michael Riffaterre's *matrix*—a hypothetical web of periphrasis, a network of metonymic multiplication from a single term or concept—comes to mind.[76] The text(s) 'runs the gauntlet of mimesis from representation to representation...with the aim of exhausting the paradigm of all variations on the matrix.'[77] A single utterance triggers the search for analogues from already familiar texts by thematic connection. Riffaterre's casting of the phenomenon a 'neurosis' born of a repression of the matrix, whose 'displacement produces variants all through the body, just as suppressed symptoms break out somewhere else in the body' is not out of place.[78] The index to a mental state, even a malaise, approaches the sense of an ineluctable subjective state of affairs that is the experience of reading. This experience of texts, like a congenital degenerative condition, is inescapable. To read is to be drawn deeper, concept by concept, into a web. The 'neurosis,' perhaps, approaches the experience of Mikhail Bakhtin's sense of *polyphony* to an utterance: a socio-ideological *heteroglossia* 'of social groups, "professional" and "generic" languages, languages of generations and so forth.'[79] The panoply of voices is a stratification that insures its dynamics, a multilateral intersection to a single utterance that 'not only answers the requirements of its own language as the individual embodiment of a speech act,' but also 'the requirements of heteroglossia.'[80] The turns of phrase affect an *active participation* in the literary-ideological-cultural diversity of speech in its generic variety. There is a quirky imbalance of tones, a pebbly dissonance that is not quashed by the postulation of a singular subject to the utterance. To read is to be seeing/hearing double, always.

If Bakhtin and Riffaterre are on the mark, then the impassioned rejection of the 'misbegotten,' the excommunication of 'those incestuous bastards'—Bailey's quip that captures so well the indignation of the outburst—is evocative of the gamut of exclusions that inhabit our unsettled imagination; 'unsettled' for the *tendentiousness* to the interpretive trajectories required in forging the equivalences. The imagination that *makes the sense* is flawed for the holes it overlooks. The limited inclusion of Egyptians in the assembly, for us, seems to fly in the face of their exclusion from divine graces in the exodus affair. Has our scribe so quickly forgotten Pharaoh's pernicious deeds? We certainly haven't! The memory of it is positively jarring in the encounter with 'you shall not abhor any of the Egyptians' (Deut 23:7). The rationale for Egypt's inclusion only sharpens the disturbance of the memory: 'because you were an alien residing in their land' (Deut 23:7). Pharaoh's 'hospitality' is the solvent to any equivalence the *readerly* pleasure might infer through the intertextual network of dichotomies that sets Egypt on the 'right' side of things. A homology can only go so far. There is always, at least, one loose end.

The loose ends, therefore, the fissures to the Riffaterresque matrix are the points of erosion in the expansive (and expanding) literary horizon to the abjection of the Ammonites and the Moabites. This, the dissolution of the gestalt, is our interest. The imputed correlates—those assuring guarantors of consonance across legal corpora in the literary imagination—may function, also, as the conduits of chaos. If the exclusion of the Ammonites and the Moabites, to put it another way, are of a cloth with divine pronouncement elsewhere on a range of other topoi, then might the instability of the rhetoric for exclusion spread across the corpus? United they stand; together they fall. Will the semblance of connectedness across texts ferry the tenuous disposition to Israel's neighbors, that outcropping of the deconstructive *writerly* pleasure of the Barthesian imaginary, into the heart of Mosaic regulation on sex? Let us see.

Bad Sex, Bad Seed

It is not inconceivable that the jaundiced disposition born of a tussle with the disheveled logic of assembly constitution might drift forward and backward in our text of choice. Our conditioned view to the text pursues first a lexical regression to the sex laws of Deuteronomy 22:13–30 in tracking the outward ripples of the now aroused deconstructive gaze. The emboldened disassembling eye of suspicion, now, interrogates that other element in the double-helixed imperialistic construal of subalternity —gender. The deconstructive stance, I think, finds a text quite agreeable to its nose for dissonance: logical, aesthetic, and moral.

The seven laws of Deuteronomy 22:13–30 are a conglomeration of opinion on the protocols of sex and marriage. The prescriptions, quite easily, are grist for empire's insidious fusion of sexism and racism in the rhetoric of domination. The initial six cases address a husband's suspicions of premarital sexual activity on the part of the wife (two outcomes; Deut 22:13–19, 20–21), adultery with a woman married (Deut 22:22) or betrothed (two variants; Deut 22:23–24, 25–27), and coerced sex with an unmarried woman (Deut 22:28–29). The specification that the woman should remain with her husband in the apodoses of the first and last law (22:19, 29) lends an additional measure of integrity to the set beyond the common element of sexual coupling. The matter of payment or compensation to the woman's father is a third strand that binds the unit's inception to its conclusion. The literary distinction of the set holds.[81] The proscription of marriage to a father's ex-wife lies beyond this tight order to the set. The ruling, moreover, departs from the casuistic, if-then, style of the preceding laws. As the single representative of a larger corpus from Leviticus (18:6–18) on sex with near relations, its presence in

Deuteronomy 22 has prompted S.R. Driver to suggest its secondary incorporation.[82] Leviticus 18 and 20, nevertheless, witness the integration—if only by editorial manipulation—of this subset of interests within the broader parameters of sexual legislation. Deuteronomy, then, is not the sole witness to the conjunction of these categories.

The likening of sexual intercourse to assembly admission does not require a stretch of the imagination. In fact, the text facilitates the connection. The reference to coitus in the initial ruling—'he goes into her' (*wb' 'lyh*; Deut 22:13b; my translation) finds an echo in the language barring select parties from admission to the assembly. The eunuch, the seed of illicit union, and Lot's offspring, too, are the prohibited subjects of 'shall not enter' clauses (*l' yb'...bqhl yhwh*; 'he shall not enter...the assembly of YHWH'; my translation; Deut 23:1, 2). Lexical and syntactic correspondence is the lubricant for the semantic slippage, a metonymic ellipsis, from 'uterus' to 'assembly.' The repeated qualification of juridical determination in cases of sexual misadventure as a 'purging of evil' *from the community* (22:21, 22, 24) compounds the analogy. Bad seed is not welcome in location, assembly, or womb. The rulings regard a coalescing network of secluded/guarded spaces: the assembly, the womb, and the people.[83] The conjunction of these topoi effects an overdetermination to the trope of vaginal penetration. As elsewhere, sex is not just about sex—it almost never is the case! The proximity of guidelines to safeguard the camp area from the impurity of genital emissions (23:10–11) and 'the house of the Lord your God' from earnings from illicit sex (23:17–18) fortify the connection between errant sexuality and contagion in Israel's esteemed spaces. By sheer juxtaposition, the prescriptions for sturdy limits in the protection of these pristine loci bleed into each other. But the impression of connectedness facilitates also the transfer of a sense of Deuteronomy's shoddy boundary keeping in its ethnic distinctions. If Moses fails in his argument for an 'expurgated' assembly, might we expect his logic to hold elsewhere, in surrounding legislation?

As it turns out, the safeguards to sexual propriety in Deuteronomy 22 and 24 are easy prey, especially under the emancipative gaze of a decolonizing hermeneutic. The prescriptions are an affront to the operative *assumption* of an egalitarian view to gender relations. The premise to the rules is lopsided and shaky. Carolyn Pressler, Deborah Ellens, and Cheryl Kirk-Duggans, among others, have shown us how and why.[84] We follow Ellens's lead here. The prescriptions address males; the executioners of the wretched woman who cannot establish her virginity at marriage are the 'men of her town' (22:21).⁸⁵ The depictions of sex construe the women as objects: they are the ones taken or given (in marriage, vv. 13, 16, 30), entered into (v. 13a), lain with (vv. 13b, 22, 23, 25, 28), and violated (vv. 24, 25, 28, 29).⁸⁶ We might add that they are the disliked (vv. 13, 16), the slandered (v. 19), the defended (vv. 13-19), the executed (v. 21), and the ones sent away (vv. 19, 29). To the point, the woman is, consistently, the *object* of juridical deliberation. If agency and self-determination are measures of power and high standing, she has neither. Back to Ellens's list: the 'purging' of the people is a requirement *only* where female transgression is ascertained (vv. 21, 22, 24).⁸⁷ The absence of this requirement in cases where a man is the sole transgressor is telling (vv. 13-19, 25-27, 28-29). Only female error pollutes. That the errant woman is the one in the cross wires of the legislation is consistent with the persistent reference to women in relation to men.⁸⁸ She is 'her father's lass' (vv. 15, 16), 'his daughter' (v. 16), 'the wife to a man' ('the master's charge' comes closer to the Hebrew; v. 22), 'a woman betrothed to a man' (v. 23), and 'his father's wife' (v. 30). The women are attendant to males. The corollary to female obsolescence is the placement of female sexuality under the auspices of males, so that the rulings—in line with a related law in Exodus (22:16-17)—find male figures the *victims* of sexual acts against women.⁸⁹ And so the cases involving the defamation of a bride are portrayed as a tussle between the husband and the father. This is evident in that the parents are the defendants and the recipients of compensation should the charge prove false (Deut 22:19). If the case goes badly, however, the parental home—perhaps, the symbol of the father's authority—shall be the site of the bride's destruction (Deut 22:21). Not surprisingly, Pressler adds, the deflowering of a woman un-betrothed yields different consequences between genders: death by stoning for the woman (Deut 22:21), but, for a man, payment of the bride wealth (to the father) and the espousal of the woman—this is a case of rape!—without recourse to divorce (Deut 22:28-29).⁹⁰ If the vantage point and the interests of the rulings are measures of subjectivity, the heterosexual Israelite male is firmly installed in the driver's seat of legislation.

The sex laws find a counterpart on the other side of the rules for admission to the assembly. Deuteronomy 24:1-4 takes up the matter of remarriage following divorce. The rules here fare no better where gender relations are concerned. While the precise purpose of the legislation remains elusive, the lowered status of women remains germane to the legal parlance of the passage.⁹¹ The woman is cast in relation to a series of husbands and her standing—favored or not (Deut 24:1), married or divorced—is at the husband's discretion. *She* is the one sent away (Deut 24:1b, 3b), expelled from the house by a man's decree. *She* is the locus of the 'defilement' (Deut 24:4a), the resultant imputed state from the interceding marriage that bars her return to her first husband. That negligence in this matter brings sin *upon the land* (Deut 24:4b), a reprisal of the refrain in Leviticus 18 and 20, evidences one more strand in the nexus between sexual misadventure and 'Israel'—people and land, objects under masculine inspection. The vagina—that jewel of venereal veneration in the masculine gaze—is the object of delicate negotiation between interested males on *both* ends of our passage.

The broad survey of the text as whole (chapters 22–24), therefore, reveals skewed visions of gender and race conspiring in the conception of an interlocking, self-reinforcing, network of reserved confines across a complex of prescriptions. To put it another way, the well-ensconced masculine, Israelite subject is exposed and shamed by the ironizing lens to these texts. The liberalizing agenda contests the situated perspective of this self-assuring privileged group and lays bare the power differentials to the binary constructions of the texts.

An Intersectional, Decolonizing View to the Text

An imagination bathed in a decolonizing hermeneutic, of course, stands at the head of such a strategy in interpretation. Schüssler Fiorenza's intersectional eye to *kyriarchy* would spot at once the layered language to imperialism, the tangled relations of domination in the name of 'emperor, lord, slave-master, father, elite male.'[92] Perhaps the familiar paths of multilateral oppression inherent to the literary productions of European colonialism come to mind. The decolonizing optic is one, in part, shaped in response to the travelogues of colonialism oozing with eroticized and feminized images of the 'undiscovered' world. Laura Donaldson invokes Anne McClintock's putative genre of 'pornotropics' in recalling Columbus's vision of the 'unexplored' world as a female breast awaiting (colonial) male attention.[93] The trope, of course, is part of the repertoire of a gendered and racialized vision of hegemony that casts the non-European realm as a salacious whore desirous of a colonizer's embrace. The angle of vision is an arrow in the quiver of the 'Pocahontas Perplex,' Rayna Green's term for that conjuration of the noble, female indigene that stands guard over colonizers and their agenda.[94] She, as a central figure in this favored narrative of colonial mythologizing, is the 'good Squaw,' the astute observer of cultural currents ever cognizant of the tides of progress. This very sentiment is on flagrant display in Thomas Middleton's seventeenth-century pageant on Anglo expansionism that depicts the unbridled elation of an Indian queen's embrace of Christianity.[95] The riches, the spices, India's splendor—the queen's words—are fair exchange for the celestial heritage now hers, whose 'inner goodness' now radiates with sufficient brilliance to overcome the 'depravity, sin and filth' of her swarthy complexion. The good gospel is a lesson in self-loathing.

The trope comes to the fore in biblical literature in, among others, the figure of Rahab, whose 'house' becomes Jericho's Trojan horse. Strangely, as Judith McKinlay notes, dalliance at the woman's home seems the primary undertaking of the spies to judge by the narrative.[96] The sexual undertones to the night's tarry are assured in the deliciously ambiguous note that the spies 'slept' there (*wyyškbu šmmh*).[97] What is clear is the security of Rahab's allegiance in Israel's intercourse with the indigene. Imperialism's discourse dons the dregs of gender with a dash of lasciviousness. The path to cultural imperialism, as postcolonial and feminist criticism has uncovered, is peppered with misogyny. Colonial expansion *is* sexual conquest, and Israel's way to the land, naturally, is through Rahab's legs! The metonymic shift in Joshua, by Musa Dube's estimation, is a characteristic accomplishment of the colonial pen; the figure of Rahab is a prop in the 'script about the domestication of the promised land.'[98] The literary construct is nothing less than a vehicle for 'colonizing ideologies,' a personification of indigenous wantonness awaiting domestication 'by those with superior morals.' In empire's shadow Indigenous Woman's words of welcome—'I know that the Lord has given you the land' (Josh 2:9)—are avid acknowledgment of divine sanction for imperialistic incursion. Native resistance, ineluctably, melts before Israel's glorious mien.

The indigenous female—the land—is not without attractive traits in imperial eyes. She/it, after all, is a coveted object. This much is clear in Musa Dube's elaboration on Mr. Kurtz's perspective on the 'savage' and 'superb' African woman in Conrad's *Heart of Darkness*.[99] Unlike the British female, her jewelry, her vociferous displays, and her raised hands betoken 'her wildness and extravagance,' her 'immoderate passions.' Her impassioned soul matches the wild and wanton territory she inhabits, one which the colonizer covets. The woman's fervent affinity for Mr. Kurtz, Dube opines, signals, as always, the desire of the colonized (and the land) for European domestication.[100] The woman's primordiality—the very mark of her inferiority in vivid contrast to the placid and temperate demeanor of the English female—is her allure. European exploration, by extension, is the masculine animus gone wild.

Hegemony's putative line through its conceptions of ethnic identity (masculine 'Israel' as the scrutinizing subject), sexuality, and the coveted *terra copiosa* trades on the configuration of the lecherous female as the Achilles heel of a people. Certainly, Deuteronomy's kaleidoscopic superintendence over assembly, uterus, land, and people fits the mold. To guard the womb, so the good prophet preaches, is to secure the people, the land. The nexus from sexuality to territory—Steed Vernyl Davidson puts it well—entails the transfer of the 'gendered language of conquest' onto women's bodies, a conflation of the land and the female form 'reducing the territory to a single individual in the imperialist imagination.'[101] The cluster of images is a potent mix in a symbolic economy that facilitates sexual fantasy en route to domination. Empire's ensemble, naturally, includes the figure of the hypersexualized native woman who bears—craves—the seeds of racial and cultural 'regeneration.' She is 'not only sexually active but readily available.'[102] The colonizer's vessels in a harbor are but the harbinger of a new order to snuff out the old, the erasure of a culture that has outlived its usefulness. Kwok Pui-lan's gesture to foreign female sexuality 'as the boundary marker to define difference in the contact zone of different cultures' is to the point.[103] It is in Rahab's embrace and Ruth's nocturnal fumbling at the threshing floor that strange identities—Canaanite and Moabite—are effaced. The women are fodder for the conqueror's lust. This is the bitter irony to Indigenous Woman's love affair with the imperial master; that the very coupling calculated to elevate the indigenous female—the native culture—facilitates her demise. Ruth loses her child to the imperial matriarch (Ruth 4:16–17), even as Rahab is shown her place *beyond Israel's camp* (Josh 6:23)—Deuteronomy's designated space for excrement and other impurities.

The corollary to 'the indigenous female as strumpet' in imperialism's repertoire is the inadequate, feeble (also feminized) indigenous male. Davidson proffers the example of Sisera (of the Deborah–Jael story of Jud 4–5), who expires at the point of a tent peg—the throbbing phallus wielded by the libidinous Jael.[104] The sexual implications to the scene—the rape of Sisera—are tantamount to a feminization of the indigenous male standing for the impotence of indigenous culture. The emasculated native man, 'who remains inadequate to meet the insatiable appetite of his woman,' becomes the wretched condition from which the European male rescues the indigenous female.¹⁰⁵ Colonialism is imbued with benevolence; it assumes the air of charitable consolation for the frustrated indigenous female, a noble response to the flirtatious beckoning of virgin land with the potential to be *so much more*. Imperialism's discourses load the boat with numerous other images of feminization—the gender confusion of native men, their deviant sexual pleasures, and affinity for female manner—in its diatribe against native cultures.¹⁰⁶ Euro virility and masculinity are irresistible beside the degenerative conditions of Native Man. The amorous indigenous female—the invitation of the fertile lands that borders on pleading—is but the victim of circumstances. Her sexual hysteria is understandable, given her desperate deprivation.

Colonial penmanship, thus, parlays an expedient conjunction of patriarchy and ethnocentrism for hegemonic ends. To such vision, Deuteronomy's terse juxtaposition of feminine inferiority to genetic defect in the foreigner is complicit. Mosaic proclamation here, it seems, charts a course to imperialism's blended apologies of a later era. Female frailty, physical and moral, while exploited, is evidence of native weakness by genetic defect. The fence around the womb *is* a shield around the assembly, lest Israel suffer Canaan's fate in the hands of a higher race. Moab's degenerate seed must not enter Israel's womb to compromise its issue. Israel's genetic purity, its very moral fiber, and *manly* gumption—no eunuchs allowed—is at stake. Deuteronomic legislation, so perceived in the to-and-fro from text to colonial context, is a two-faced shield against imperialism's imagined threats to racial degeneration, the deplorable condition that mars the 'other'—female irresolution *and* indigenous incompetence. This sad state of affairs Israel must avert.

This brings us to another trope in the repertoire of imperial rhetoric, one already raised in passing. This literary figure, I think, cuts closer to Deuteronomy's legal calculus in the computation of gender and ethnicity. I have in mind the savage and hypersexual native man, the antithesis to the feminized indigenous male. It is not inaccurate to construe the figure a perversion of a trope that properly finds the European male as subject, the would-be paramour to (Native) Woman. A hint of this 'slipping of the leash' may be seen in Jenny Sharpe's revealing perusal of E.M. Forster's *A Passage to India* against the backdrop of the Sepoy mutiny of Anglo-India in 1857. The reading uncovers a mythography with the rape of the English woman, that icon of Victorian idealism, in focus.¹⁰⁷ Nothing stoked English ire like representations of 'leering Sepoys with their swords raised over the heads of kneeling women' and reports of sexual violations over extended periods; such reports often preceded by exclamations that the details exceed the boundaries of journalistic decorum.[108] There, imperial sophistry, as Sharpe puts it, deploys 'a range of signification that has the same effect as the missing details.' The strength of the violent imagery lies, surely, in its ability to signal a wholesale rejection of the ideals of civilization as captured in England's social mission.[109] The semantic import to the violence, in other words, exceeds that of an assault on a single individual or group. Insurgency, a contestation of European supremacy, is the connotation.

The reflex of this notion in the leaves of Forster's novel, Sharpe argues, is in the reactions of Adela's fellow expatriates on the news of her alleged assault in the hands of the native physician, Dr. Aziz. By their conception of English chivalry, Adela is afforded treatment 'as a mere cipher for a battle between men.'[110] Their read on the crime is predicated on the intimate association of female chastity with male honor (an echo of Deuteronomy's sex laws), the construal of the (European) female form as the embodiment of the Western civilizing project in colonialism. Forster's lines, in Sharpe's eyes, are an indictment of Anglo-Indian propaganda, a gruesome appropriation of female bodies for a masculinized imperial agenda.[111] The initiative constructs an institution on the torso of the English lady, casting her limbs as the streams of European moral supremacy and Christian charity. Such is the birth of colonialism's 'cult of the (great white) mother.' The gendered rhetoric had currency beyond England's colonial holdings.

The European female as symbol of national identity and colonial agency is salient in Anne McClintock's analysis of colonial discourse in Afrikaans nationalistic mythologizing.[112] The historical productions of a burgeoning nationalism invoke a gendering of nation and time that straddles nostalgia for the past and an urgent demand for progress. This bidirectional orientation blends the transformation of national identity with the preservation of an authentic kernel to the sense of peoplehood. Within the continuum the female is atavistic, the embodiment of national tradition. As a figure of imperial propaganda, she is 'inert, backward looking, and *natural*,' traits in stark contradistinction to the potent and progressive masculine animus.[113] Enshrined permanently in antiquated memory, she is the apotheosis of Occidental supremacy, the civilizing hope of the world, and an anchor in the prestige of hoary antiquity. The fetishizing narratives of the *Broederbond* (the brotherhood) give the Afrikaans female pride of place even as she is erased in patriarchal articulations of nationhood.[114] She, the national symbol, stands at the confluence of dialectal variety in the constitution of a national tongue. As the center of familial intimacy, she is installed in every *Vrou en Moeder* (wife and mother) wagon of the *Tweede Trek* celebrating the Boer mutiny of 1838. Vested in ancestral garb, the national *Moeder* takes her place in 'an orgy of national pageantry' across the land 'in a four-month spectacle of invented tradition and fetish ritual.'[115] The feminine figure seems a strange patriotic concoction arising from the ashes of, what McClintock terms, a 'masculinized memory, masculinized humiliation and masculinized hope.'[116]

Dutch colonial propaganda would place the Dutch woman in the same liminal space in a latter phase of Netherlands Indies policy. The figure, and the directives for Dutch women in the colonies derivative of the trope, played a central role in securing the boundaries between colonizer and colonized. Displacing the indigenous concubine, the Dutch wife/mother was installed as guarantor of Euro-supremacy—much like the Afrikaans 'woman of yore'—in an arena where wealth, religion, education, and even skin tone had fallen short as clear and critical registers of distinction.[117] As the bastion of Dutch cultural sensibility, she lit the path to civilization. Nubile imports from Europe in the twentieth century would fortify Dutch colonialism's promotion of the cultural construct. The accouterment to the figure was the cloistered compound furnished with the elements of European prestige and privilege. And so, Stoler notes, the bloated arrival of the marriageable females in Asia

> coincided with new bourgeois trappings and notions of privacy in colonial communities. And these, in turn, were accompanied by new distinctions based on race. European women supposedly required more metropolitan amenities than did men and more spacious surroundings for them. Women were claimed to have more delicate sensibilities and therefore needed suitable quarters—discrete and enclosed. Their psychological and physical constitutions were considered more fragile, demanding more servants for the chores they should be spared. In short, white women needed to be maintained at elevated standards of living, in insulated social spaces cushioned with the cultural artifacts of 'being European.'[118]

The colonial mother was the lifeline to the metropole, the vanguard of European sensibility under assault in a tropical clime in which the degeneration of such civilized disposition was deemed quite likely. If convalescence on Holland's immaculate shores—or, at least, repair to one of the temperate hill stations that dotted the colonial landscape—proved impossible, then mother's cultured garden, with its bevy of restorative rituals and victuals, would be the sole bulwark against dissipation in the tropical heat.[119] The fragile and gentle white female was integral to the salubrious and opulent *mise en scène* of the European colonial habitus.

There was, to be expected, a psychosocial aspect to this masculinist construct of 'female frailty' quite beyond Woman's diminished physical form. David Lean's filmic rendition of Forster's *A Passage to India* (1984) writes into the plot unattractive Adela's sexual hysteria that so taints her perception of the affair at the Marabar Caves. The sexually frustrated (and fresh of the boat from London) Adela, as Laura Donaldson puts it, 'withdraws her cathection of desire from "India" and transfers it' to the unenviable Dr. Aziz, the unintended victim of Adela's 'fantasy.'[120] White Female hysteria is in this case part of the montage of Anglo-European views on India. Jenny Sharpe, then, insists that Lean's 'frigid women suffer from sexual hysteria and unattractive women desire to be raped' optic on Forster's tale is only partially grasped within a feminist framework, and only fully realized as an 'historical category of rape within a system of *colonial* relations.'[121] Sharpe means, of course, that the construct of the 'wretched' Adela is part of a repertoire for the ideological sanction of a defensive posture in the face of vulnerability, which finds support also in the lecherous predisposition of indigenous males for white females. 'Rape' is, here, a 'master trope for the objectification of English women and natives *alike*.'[122] A trenchant concupiscence, moral defect (ion), is the shared dysfunction of both parties under masculine imperial surveillance.

The less pleasant aspect to the discipline of segregation in the enhanced supervision of Dutch females, then, is of little surprise. A cleavage had to be enforced between the susceptible, mutually infectious groups. The withdrawal of the European woman, by such reasoning, became an expedient complement to the maintenance of the chasm between the races. And so, neophytes to colonial society were chastised for indecorum in dress and speech. Constant warnings of social indiscretions were *de rigueur*. Fastidious attention to the possibility of misplaced familiarity with the locals, especially the menfolk, was appropriate to the colonial project. Harsh punishment, of course, was a requirement for transgressions by indigenous males; but blame fell, too, upon the white women for inflaming the already smoldering desires of the brown men. An accompaniment to the policing of female social mobility, of course, was the circumscription of their economic viability.[123] The eschewal of financial independence was the norm. Budding inroads to select trades—floral arrangement, tailoring—were discouraged. The protests of female missionaries and teachers—outliers to the order—fell upon deaf ears, even where such initiatives fell short of a questioning of the racial fundamentals to the arrangements. The cloistered compound was the *ideal* locus for a white woman. There her womb could be safe from undesirable seed.

Female vulnerability and male native venery, thus, were the touchstones on the tongues of the coterie of pedagogues on colonial deportment, the architects of the socioeconomic arrangements that underwrite European supremacy. Colonial stability was predicated on the security of the strictures to Dutch female social intercourse. Deuteronomy's collapsing of national security into (female) sexual propriety parallels the multinodal anxiety to European colonial governance. The conjunction of sexual–social protocol and the institutionalization of sociocultural ascendancy in Deuteronomy is natural to nineteenth-century colonial thinking. The 'national mother'—ennobled but naive, central yet marginalized, biblical, and modern—is the quintessence of the national spirit. Her fair limbs in the perfidious, rapacious hands of the Sepoy mutineers would arouse any hot-blooded son of Albion.

Stoler's and McClintock's findings on gender and colonial rhetoric confirm Sharpe's instincts on Forster's opus. Forster's invocation of Adela's plight as 'a sign for the victimage of imperialism' is not comprehensible apart from the nineteenth-century Anglo-Indian deployment of a Victorian ideal of womanhood as a trope in its diatribe against insurgency.[124] As the epitome of self-sacrifice and moral superiority—the mainstays of England's social gospel to the colonies—English Woman's intimated violation in barbarian hands stoked the flames of Anglo-colonial outrage. The lascivious Sepoys, in this milieu, assume the profile of specter —an ungrateful oaf of a degenerate race—in the colonizer's view.

The anticipated offense in such depictions of mutiny, it seems to me, trades on the comportment of these representations of feminine vulnerability *and* masculine aggression (and virility) with imperialistic narratives of conquest and subjugation. The offensive images, as those favored by colonialism's triumphant narratives, are a fusion of military prowess and erotic desire with territorial mastery as a desideratum. This is the common ground of the two, seemingly, antithetical sets of figures: the effeminate and impotent indigene against the hypersexualized, heterosexual native;

the submissive, appreciative subaltern against the brutish, irreverent colonial rebel; all gendered and sexualized productions. The configurations of the indigene, indeed, run the gamut of opposite and opposing characterizations. But within this mythic economy, where initiative and aggression are the foregrounded traits, the native male is the colonizing man's evil twin. It is the audacity of an Indian assumption of colonial privilege that is the brunt of imperialism's agonistic edge. The Anglo-Indian summon to action, in other terms, dresses the Sepoys in imperial garb. Empire's propaganda here springs from nothing less than the nub of colonial anxiety: the nagging fear of an indigenous adoption or realization of the imperial stance. This is the rebel's 'sin' in the cross hairs, the (mis)appropriation of the master's place. The face of Indian mutiny, so conjectured, is a darkened reflection of the colonizer's own demeanor. But, of course, the propaganda falls short of its mark once the nexus between subject and image is grasped, the symmetry betwixt colonizer and colonized. The facile exchange of roles is the argument's undoing. The (too) easy slippage from master to servant shows up the bigotry of the colonial contention. The criticism turns back on the master. Equally unhelpful, of course, is the inconsistency in framing the subaltern. The morass of conflicting figurations (already flagged) compromises the integrity of the portrait. Through multiple castings, the servants, eventually, resemble their masters. But the script, an inscription of the double helix of race and gender with all its jumbled reasoning, is an old one, as old as the Bible. The English masters, it would seem, take their cue from Deuteronomy. Not surprisingly, the dissolution of colonialism's arguments follows a similar course.

In Summary

The urgency of Deuteronomy's boundary-keeping—the erection of a fence around Israel, its assembly, its land, and its uteri, the incubators of future generations—is the production of a subject (in our reading) infused with an anxiety soused in the mythography of imperialism and its attendant tropes. The logic to the order is an assemblage of the signifiers of empire bent on ensuring that the way of hegemony stays a one-way street. But don't read too closely! The clumsy exclusion of Ammon and Moab—the choppy logic to the excommunication—proves the dangling thread in the Gordian Knot, the loose brick in the fence that would secure Israel's assembly. The disassembling assembly sets off a deconstructive wave through the larger prescriptive passage that shows the broader legislation little more than a concatenation of lopsided binaries. The sex and marriage laws are decidedly sexist. The disquieting inequities are the low-hanging fruit of a disenchanted, decolonizing view to the text. Moses's regulations, in the wake of the dissonant characterization and dismissal of Moab, seem arbitrary; the rules are a product(ion) of double standards. The prophet's arguments appear, on the balance, unbalanced.

The logic of European imperialism in modern times, I contend, mimics the Mosaic crisis in reasoning. If the Bible is the tree, the fruit of European colonialism does not fall far. Both hostile and submissive, intransigent and obsequious, the chameleonic subaltern ethos is the consistent inconsistency in the protean expressions of imperialistic discourse. The conflicting portraits of the 'other' span biblical mythmaking, the marginalizing discourses of Deuteronomy *and* European colonialism. As Moses's framing of the Moabites, imperialism's estimation of the colonized is mixed (and mangled) in its descriptions. The Euro-vision chokes and stutters on its iterations. The colonized realm is a woman both docile *and* savage beyond bounds. The indigenous male is threateningly virile *and* effeminately effete. The colonized mind, as aesthetic object, is as elusive as Moses's Moabite. The imperial countenance, when it turns on itself, is no less fractured. The European Mother is the emblem of cultural ascendancy, the face of imperial potency to the impotent subaltern. Yet, she is the soft underbelly of the empire, ever vulnerable to indigenous seduction. Master yet master-able, cloistered and enshrined she must remain. Imperialism's discrimination slips too in its surveillance of the colonizer/colonized divide. Its reports of Indian mutiny paint a picture of the Indian in hues *not unlike* England's understanding of its own colonial adventure. The Sepoys, though 'unfit' for the role, assume a pretense to privilege—so unseemly in British eyes—strangely familiar, strangely English. This portraiture is also biblical. England's (en)vision(ing) of the 'native' seconds Moses's veiling of the tribal uterus by a *reinscription* of Israel's audacity at Jericho—its penetration of Jericho's walls and Rahab's womb. Moses's fear, as England's, is that the native will do as Israel does. As through British lenses in this regard, the wall that divides outsiders from insiders is thin. The Sepoys and the Israelites, the English and the Moabites, they all collapse into one.

The texts, colonialism's and the Bible's, are a screen of mixed signals and shaky dichotomies. But still, their signifiers blaze a trail of equivalences from genetic defect to unruly deportment, sexual deviation to the anarchy of indigenous barbarism. The discourses of national pride enact their series of metonymic transfers—from women's bodies to land, from maternal affection to national essence—in its illusion of a wholesome ethnic whole. For all its ambiguity, the (il)logic of imperialism—in Deuteronomy and European colonial talk—is an ordering hierarchy, an imbrication of gender, race, and morality in the service of a regime that polices female sexuality and subaltern distinction. Sexual propriety, ethnic segregation, and strict compartmentalization are the hallmarks of good governance and national stability. As one goes, so the others.

But alas, the irregularities of Deuteronomy and European colonialism surface through the interrogative lenses of postcolonial feminist dialogue. The arguments seem forced, contradictory, and trite. The statements, spoken and unspoken, betray a nervous awareness that the ethnic distinctions are bald assertions in response to social, religious, and political exigencies on the ground. Hegemony, as it turns out, is a precarious undertaking, its narrative unstable. The gestalt, *always already an illusion*, comes apart.

Notes

1. For similar orientation to subjectivity, see Roland Boer, 'Thus I cleansed Them from Everything Foreign: The Search for Subjectivity in Ezra-Nehemiah,' in *Postcolonialism and the Hebrew Bible: The Next Step* (ed. Roland Boer; Atlanta: Society of Biblical Literature, 2013), 221–37; Philip Chia, 'On Naming the Subject,' in *The Postcolonial Biblical Reader* (ed. R.S. Sugirtharajah; Oxford and London: Blackwell, 2006), 171–85; Jeffrey Kah-Jin Kuan, 'Diasporic Reading of a Diasporic Text: Identity Politics and Race Relations and the Book of Esther,' in *The Bible and Postcolonialism, 3* (ed. Fernando F. Segovia; Sheffield: Sheffield Academic Press, 2000), 161–73.
2. Stuart Hall, 'Introduction: Who Needs "Identity"?' in *Questions of Cultural Identity* (ed. Stuart Hall and Paul Du Gay; London: Sage Publications, 1996), 3. Hall's understanding of identity or subject formation as a relative positioning within historically and geographically determined symbolic economies is current in cultural studies (over and against the now near moribund essentialized Cartesian subject). For concise surveys of this intellectual shift(ing), see José Esteban Muñoz, *Disidentifications: Queers of Color and the Performance of Politics* (Cultural Studies of the Americas 2; Minneapolis and London: University of Minnesota Press, 1999), 5–8; Lawrence Grossberg, 'Identity and Cultural Studies: Is That All There Is?' in *Questions of Cultural Identity* (ed. Stuart Hall and Paul Du Gay; London: Sage Publications, 1996), 89–92.

3. All references to biblical texts follow those of English translations.
4. R.S. Sugirtharajah, *Postcolonial Criticism and Biblical Interpretation* (Oxford: Oxford University Press, 2002), 28–29. The following paragraphs are but a cursory overview of salient points—ones relevant to our analysis— in discussions at the intersection of postcolonial studies and feminist criticism. For comprehensive overviews of the state of the dialogue, especially pertaining to biblical and theological studies, see Musa W. Dube, *Postcolonial Feminist Interpretation of the Bible* (St. Louis: Chalice, 2000); Kwok Pui-lan, *Postcolonial Imagination and Feminist Theology* (Louisville: Westminster John Knox, 2005). Concise depictions of the exchange are available in Elizabeth Schüssler Fiorenza, *The Power of the Word: Scripture and the Rhetoric of Empire* (Minneapolis: Fortress, 2007), 111–29; Leela Gandhi, *Postcolonial Theory: A Critical Introduction* (New York: Columbia University Press, 1998), 81–101.
5. Chandra Talpade Mohanty, 'Under Western Eyes: Feminist Scholarship and Colonial Discourses,' *Boundary* 2 (1984): 333–58.
6. Ibid., 344.
7. Ibid., 334–35.
8. Ibid., 335.
9. Ibid., 343–44.
10. Ibid., 344–45.
11. Ibid., 345.
12. Kwok Pui-lan, 'Unbinding Our Feet: Saving Brown Women and Feminist Religious Discourse,' in *Postcolonialism, Feminism, and Religious Discourse* (ed. Laura E. Donaldson and Kwok Pui-lan; London: Routledge, 2002), 76.
13. Ibid., 75.
14. Ibid., 71.
15. Meyda Yeğenoğlu, 'Sartorial Fabric-ations: Enlightenment and Western Feminism,' in *Postcolonialism, Feminism, and Religious Discourse* (ed. Laura E. Donaldson and Kwok Pui-lan; London: Routledge, 2002), 82–99.
16. Ibid., 84.
17. Ibid., 95–96.
18. Valerie Amos and Pratibha Parmar, 'Challenging Imperial Feminism,' *Feminist Review* 17 (1984): 3–19.
19. Ann Rosalind Jones, 'Writing the Body: Toward an Understanding of *L'Ecriture Feminine*,' *Feminist Studies* 7 (1981): 253–54.
20. Laura E. Donaldson, *Decolonizing Feminisms: Race, Gender, and Empire Building* (Chapel Hill and London: The University of North Carolina Press, 1992), 60–62.
21. Gandhi, *Postcolonial Theory*, 84. Emphasis in original.

22. Ania Loomba, *Colonialism/Postcolonialism* (London and New York: Routledge, 1998), 162.
23. Meyda Yeğenoğlu, *Colonial Fantasies: Towards a Feminist Reading of Orientalism* (Cambridge: Cambridge University Press, 1998), 28–29.
24. Ann Laura Stoler, *Carnal Knowledge and Imperial Power: Race and the Intimate in Colonial Rule* (Los Angeles and London: University of California Press, 2002), 44.
25. Valerie C. Cooper, 'Some Place to Cry: Jephthah's Daughter and the Double Dilemma of Black Women in America,' in *Pregnant Passion: Gender, Sex, and Violence in the Bible* (ed. Cheryl A. Kirk-Duggan; Atlanta: Society of Biblical Literature, 2003), 181–91.
26. Dube, *Postcolonial Feminist Interpretation*, 117.
27. Gandhi, *Postcolonial Theory*, 98. The emphasis is mine.
28. Schüssler Fiorenza, *The Power of the Word*, 6.
29. Ibid., 13–14; idem., 'Changing the Paradigms,' 296.
30. Schüssler Fiorenza, *The Power of the Word*, 47; 'Changing the Paradigms,' 289.
31. Schüssler Fiorenza, *The Power of the Word*, 120–21.
32. Ibid., 14. 'Wo/man' and 'wo/men' are Schüssler Fiorenza's lexemes for clarifying and unsettling the occlusive and domineering gestures of 'man' and 'men' as all-encompassing terms across genders (but not always) by reversing the direction of erasure (see pp. 6–7 n 21). The encounter, by her reckoning, is 'a good spiritual exercise for men' by forcing a double-think in ascertaining whether their sex is in reference, an experience familiar for women with respect to the traditional linguistic practice.
33. Ibid., 128; 'Changing the Paradigms,' 297–98.
34. Elizabeth Schüssler Fiorenza, 'Transforming the Margin—Claiming Common Ground: Charting a Different Paradigm of Biblical Studies,' in *Still at the Margins: Biblical Scholarship Fifteen Years after 'Voices from the Margin'* (ed. R.S. Sugirtharajah; London and New York: T & T Clark, 2008), 25.
35. Ibid., 25.
36. Schüssler Fiorenza, *The Power of the Word*, 128. Here, Schüssler Fiorenza quotes Edward Said's *Culture and Imperialism* (London: Chatto & Windus, 1993), 59. The emphasis is mine.
37. Schüssler Fiorenza, *The Power of the Word*, 125.
38. Ibid., 122; 'Transforming the Margin,' 24.
39. Denise Noble, 'Postcolonial Criticism, Transnational Identifications and the Hegemonies of Dancehall's Academic and Popular Performativities,' *Feminist Review* 90 (2008): 106–27.
40. Lena Sawyer, 'Engendering "Race" in Calls for Diasporic Community in Sweden,' *Feminist Review* 90 (2008): 87–105.

41. Zheng Wang and Ying Zhang, 'Global Concepts, Local Practices: Chinese Feminism since the Fourth UN Conference on Women,' *Feminist Studies* 36 (2010): 40–70.
42. David L. Eng, *Racial Castration: Managing Masculinity in Asian America* (Durham and London: Duke University Press, 2001).
43. For concise outlines of the status and duties of Israel's assembly, see Jeffrey H. Tigay, *Deuteronomy* (Philadelphia: Jewish Publication Society, 1996), 209–10; Jacob Milgrom, *Numbers* (Philadelphia: Jewish Publication Society, 1990), 335–36; idem., 'Priestly Terminology and the Political and Social Structure of Pre-Monarchic Israel,' *Jewish Quarterly Review* 69 (1978): 65–81. The litany of texts in example cover the initiatives of Israel's *qhl* and *'dh*, seemingly interchangeable terms variously rendered 'assembly' or 'congregation.' By Milgrom's assessment (Num, 335), *qhl* becomes the preferred term from the period of Israel's monarchy.
44. Tigay, *Deuteronomy*, 210.
45. Jack R. Lundbom, *Deuteronomy, A Commentary* (Grand Rapids, MI: Eerdmans, 2013), 651–52, connects this verbal aspect of the legislation to the later sequence on campsite purity (vv. 10–11). The nexus, in keeping with the analogical mind-set of the present project, facilitates the metonymic transfer/slippage between 'assembly' and 'camp.'
46. See, for example, John Van Seters, *The Yahwist: A Historian of Israelite Origins* (Winona Lake, IN: Eisenbrauns, 2013), 112–16; Angela R. Roskop, *The Wilderness Itineraries: Genre, Geography, and the Growth of Torah* (History, Archaeology, and Culture of the Levant 3; Winona Lake, IN: Eisenbrauns, 2011), 185–232; Tigay, *Deuteronomy*, 422–29; W.A. Sumner, 'Israel's Encounters with Edom, Moab, Ammon, Sihon, and Og According to the Deuteronomist,' *Vetus Testamentum* 18 (1968): 216–28.
47. Tigay, *Deuteronomy*, 425–27.
48. Ibid., 427.
49. Ibid., 425–26, 27.
50. Van Seters, *The Yahwist*, 112–14.
51. Roskop, *The Wilderness Itineraries*, 193–209.
52. Ibid., 208. The reference is to Roland Barthes, *The Pleasure of the Text* (trans. Richard Miller; New York: Hill and Wang, 1975).
53. Roskop, *The Wilderness Itineraries*, 191. The emphasis is original.
54. Ibid., 185.
55. Ibid., 208.
56. M. M. Bakhtin, *The Dialogic Imagination: Four Essays by M.M. Bakhtin* (ed. Michael Holquist; trans. Caryl Emerson and Michael Holquist; Austin, TX: University of Texas Press, 1981), 280–81.
57. Barthes, *The Pleasure of the Text*, 14.
58. Ibid., 20–21. Emphasis added.

59. Boer, 'Thus I cleansed Them,' 234–35. Emphasis added.
60. So Tigay, *Deuteronomy*, 211–12; Sumner, 'Israel's Encounters,' 216–28; S. R. Driver, *Deuteronomy* (International Classical Commentary; 3rd edn.; Edinburgh: T & T Clark, 1859), 261. Calum M. Carmichael's comment in *The Laws of Deuteronomy* (Ithaca and London: Cornell University Press, 1974), 175, is to the point. Following a survey of the uneven exposition on Ammon's and Moab's villainy, he surmises that 'D's ideological interests *create* or *erase* past events and actions' (my italics). The overriding intent of the legislation by its ambiguous motivation, then, 'is to prove that their [the Ammonites and the Moabites] generations at the time of the exodus *must have manifested the "fault" of their ancestry*' (my emphasis).
61. Loomba, *Colonialism/Postcolonialism*, 113.
62. Ibid., 113.
63. Stoler, *Carnal Knowledge*.
64. Ibid., 59.
65. Judith E. McKinlay, *Reframing Her: Biblical Women in Postcolonial Focus* (The Bible in the Modern World 1; Sheffield: Sheffield Phoenix Press, 2004), 20–21.
66. Regina M. Schwartz, *The Curse of Cain: The Violent Legacy of Monotheism* (Chicago and London: The University of Chicago Press, 1997), xi, 4–13, 77–83.
67. Ibid., 82–83.
68. See, among others, Duane L. Christiansen, *Deuteronomy 21:10–34:12* (Word Biblical Commentary 6b; Nashville: Thomas Nelson, 2002), 534; Carmichael, *The Laws*, 173. On the element of abundant offspring as a component of divine promise to Israel's patriarchs, see Gen 12:1–3; 15:4–5; 28:14.
69. Peter C. Craigie, *The Book of Deuteronomy* (Grand Rapids, MI: Eerdmans, 1976), 297. Helped by the subsequent reference to 'cultic prostitution' (vv. 17–18), Craigie surmises that voluntary genital mutilation born of the veneration of a deity is the specific issue in the view of Deuteronomy 23:1.
70. Randall C. Bailey, 'They're Nothing but Incestuous Bastards: The Polemical Use of Sex and Sexuality in Hebrew Canon Narratives,' in *Reading from this Place: Social Location and Biblical Interpretation in the United States* (ed. Fernando F. Segovia and Mary Ann Tolbert; Minneapolis: Fortress, 1995), 125–26.
71. McKinlay, *Reframing Her*, 26. McKinlay, on this point, cites Claudia V. Camp, *Wise, Strange and Holy: The Strange Woman and the Making of the Bible* (Journal for the Old Testament Supplement Series 320; Gender, Culture, Theory 9; Sheffield: Sheffield Academic Press, 2000), 17.
72. So Michael Fishbane, *Biblical Interpretation in Ancient Israel* (Oxford: Clarendon, 1985), 120. The connection to sexual impropriety (incest) is

inherent to the sequence, 'a contextual inference from the general to the particular.' The movement of mind is not lost in the interpretative gesture of Ezra 9:11–14 (see n 42 on the same page).

73. Such is the conclusion of Carmichael, *The Laws*, 175. Indeed, the insight from thematic abstraction across the legislation on admission to the assembly shows the reasoning for the exclusion of the Ammonites and the Moabites spurious. Quite conceivably, it is the imputed genetic heritage of the two groups that is the source of the issue.
74. The irony to this view, of course, is that it was the fear of *no* offspring—the precise concern of Lot's daughters (Gen 19:32)—that inspired the unconventional initiative.
75. Defecation is deemed *'rwt dbr*, an 'unseemly thing,' the very designation that renders the wife abhorrent to her husband in Deuteronomy 24:1. The connection is just one more node in the vast web of correlations that sustains the logic of exclusion across the laws in view.
76. Michael Riffaterre, *Semiotics of Poetry* (Bloomington: Indiana University Press, 1978), 19–22.
77. Ibid., 19.
78. Ibid.
79. Bakhtin, *The Dialogic Imagination*, 271–72.
80. Ibid., 272.
81. These components have been noted variously by, among others, Christiansen, *Deuteronomy 21:10–34:12*, 515; Carolyn Pressler, *The View of Women Found in the Deuteronomic Family Laws* (Beihefte zur Zeitschrift für die Alttestamentliche Wissenschaft 216; New York: Walter de Gruyter, 1993), 28; Driver, *Deuteronomy*, 258.
82. Driver, *Deuteronomy*, 259.
83. Deuteronomy 24:4 adds 'land' to the list.
84. Pressler, *The View of Women*, 21–43; Deborah L. Ellens, *Women in the Sex Texts of Leviticus and Numbers: A Comparative Conceptual Analysis* (The Library of Hebrew Bible/Old Testament Studies 458; London: T&T Clark, 2008), 189–234; Cheryl Kirk-Duggan, 'Precious Memories: Rule of Law in Deuteronomy as Catalyst for Domestic Violence,' in *Exodus and Deuteronomy* (ed. Athalya Brenner and Gale A. Yee; Minneapolis: Fortress, 2012), 258–88.
85. Ellens, *Women in the Sex Texts*, 190–93. See also Pressler, *The View of Women*, 43.
86. Ellens, *Women in the Sex Texts*, 193–204. See also Kirk-Duggan, 'Precious Memories,' 273–74.
87. Ellens, *Women in the Sex Texts*, 204–06.
88. Ibid., 209–11. See also Pressler, *The View of Women*, 31–32.

89. Ellens, *Women in the Sex Texts*, 213–14, 229–33. See also Kirk-Duggan, 'Precious Memories,' 277; Pressler, *The View of Women*, 30–31, 42–43.
90. Pressler, *The View of Women*, 24. The forcible nature to the sexual intercourse is the sense to the verb *tpś*: see discussion in Pressler, *The View of Women*, 37–38; Eve Levavi Feinstein, *Sexual Pollution in the Hebrew Bible* (Oxford and New York: Oxford University Press, 2014), 68–70, 78–81.
91. Ellens follows Raymond Westbrook's conclusion that the law curbs economic exploitation by stemming the financial gain for a first husband collecting on subsequent bridewealth payments: Ellens, *Women in the Sex Texts*, 235–48; Raymond Westbrook, 'The Prohibition on Restoration of Marriage in Deuteronomy 24:1–4,' in *Studies in Bible 1986* (ed. Sara Japhet; Scripta Hierosolymitana 31; Jerusalem: Magnes, 1986), 387–405. More common in the understanding of the law is a sense of sexual impropriety to the resumption of coital relations following a woman's sexual intercourse with another partner and/or a desire for a measure of decorum to matrimony: Feinstein, *Sexual Pollution*, 63–64; Lundbom, *Deuteronomy*, 675; Pressler, *The View of Women*, 46–51, 60–62; Patrick D. Miller, *Deuteronomy* (Interpretation: A Bible Commentary for Teaching and Preaching; Louisville, KY: John Knox, 1990), 164; Craigie, *The Book of Deuteronomy*, 305–06; Carmichael, *The Laws*, 206.
92. Schüssler Fiorenza, *The Power of the Word*, 14.
93. Laura E. Donaldson, 'The Breasts of Columbus: A Political Anatomy of Postcolonialism and Feminist Religious Discourse,' in *Postcolonialism, Feminism, and Religious Discourse* (ed. Laura E. Donaldson and Kwok Pui-lan; London: Routledge, 2002), 45. Europe's disparaging figurations of the colonized and the colonizable, of course, are part of the landscape of postcolonial studies. For comprehensive surveys, beyond those of interest here, see Loomba, *Colonialism/Postcolonialism*, 104–83; Ella Shohat and Robert Stamm, *Unthinking Eurocentrism: Multiculturalism and the Media* (London and New York: Routledge, 1994), 137–77.
94. Laura E. Donaldson, 'The Sign of Orpah: Reading Ruth through Native Eyes,' in *The Postcolonial Biblical Reader* (ed. R.S. Sugirtharajah; Oxford: Blackwell, 2006), 165–66.
95. The example of Anglo-colonial penmanship is given in Loomba, *Colonialism/Postcolonialism*, 114.
96. McKinlay, *Reframing Her*, 38.
97. Ibid., 38. 'Slept,' as McKinlay notes, is delectably ambiguous. The woman's name, Rahab ('broad' or 'bountiful' in the Hebrew), has the same sexual overtones, a nuance fortified in the naming of her profession (*zwnh*, perhaps a 'prostitute'). Further to her point, McKinlay recalls H. M. Barstad's unpublished paper (p. 38 n 5) that takes the name as an allusion to the generous dimensions of the woman's pudenda.

98. Dube, *Postcolonial Feminist Interpretation*, 77.
99. Ibid., 94–95.
100. Ibid., 95. See also McKinlay, *Reframing Her*, 40–41.
101. Steed Vernyl Davidson, 'Gazing (at) Native Women: Rahab and Jael in Imperializing and Postcolonial Discourses,' in *Postcolonialism and the Hebrew Bible: The Next Step* (ed. Roland Boer; Atlanta: Society of Biblical Literature, 2013), 72.
102. Ibid., 78.
103. Kwok, *Postcolonial Imagination*, 107. See also Judith E. McKinlay, 'A Son is Born to Naomi: A Harvest for Israel,' in *Ruth and Esther: A Feminist Companion to the Bible* (2nd Series; ed. Athalya Brenner; Sheffield: Sheffield Academic, 1999), 151–57. For a Marxist angle on Ruth's assimilation, see Athalya Brenner, 'Ruth as Foreign Worker and the Politics of Exogamy,' in *Ruth and Esther: A Feminist Companion to the Bible* (2nd Series; ed. Athalya Brenner; Sheffield: Sheffield Academic, 1999), 161–62.
104. Davidson, 'Gazing (at) Native Women,' 75–80.
105. Ibid., 78–79.
106. Loomba, *Colonialism/Postcolonialism*, 155–56.
107. Jenny Sharpe, 'The Unspeakable Limits of Rape: Colonial Violence and Counter-Insurgency,' in *Colonial Discourse and Post-Colonial Theory: A Reader* (ed. Patrick Williams and Laura Chrisman; New York: Columbia University Press, 1994), 221–43.
108. Ibid., 228–29.
109. Ibid., 231.
110. Ibid., 225.
111. Ibid., 230.
112. Anne McClintock, '"No Longer in a Future Heaven": Gender, Race and Nationalism,' in *Dangerous Liaisons: Gender, Nation and Postcolonial Perspectives* (ed. Anne McClintock, Aamir Mufti and Ella Shohat; Minneapolis and London: University of Minnesota Press, 1997), 89–112.
113. Ibid., 92. My emphasis.
114. Ibid., 100–01.
115. Ibid., 101.
116. Ibid., 89.
117. Stoler, *Carnal Knowledge*, 42–43.
118. Ibid., 55.
119. Ibid., 70–72.
120. Donaldson, *Decolonizing Feminisms*, 98.
121. Sharpe, 'The Unspeakable Limits of Rape,' 22.
122. Ibid., 226. Emphasis is mine.
123. Stoler, *Carnal Knowledge*, 60–61.
124. Sharpe, 'The Unspeakable Limits of Rape,' 225.

References

Amos, Valerie and Pratibha Parmar. 1984. 'Challenging Imperial Feminism.' *Feminist Review* 17: 3–19.

Bailey, Randall C. 1995. 'They're Nothing but Incestuous Bastards: The Polemical Use of Sex and Sexuality in Hebrew Canon Narratives.' In *Reading from this Place: Social Location and Biblical Interpretation in the United States*, ed. Fernando F. Segovia and Mary Ann Tolbert. Minneapolis: Fortress.

Bakhtin, M.M. 1981. *The Dialogic Imagination: Four Essays by M.M. Bakhtin*, ed. Michael Holquist, trans. Caryl Emerson and Michael Holquist. Austin, TX: University of Texas Press.

Barthes, Roland. 1975. *The Pleasure of the Text*, trans. Richard Miller. New York: Hill and Wang.

Boer, Roland. 2013. 'Thus I cleansed Them from Everything Foreign: The Search for Subjectivity in Ezra-Nehemiah.' In *Postcolonialism and the Hebrew Bible: The Next Step*, ed. Roland Boer. Atlanta: Society of Biblical Literature.

Brenner, Athalya. 1999. 'Ruth as Foreign Worker and the Politics of Exogamy.' In *Ruth and Esther: A Feminist Companion to the Bible*, ed. Athalya Brenner. 2nd Series; Sheffield: Sheffield Academic.

Camp, Claudia V. 2000. *Wise, Strange and Holy: The Strange Woman and the Making of the Bible*. Journal for the Old Testament Supplement Series 320; Gender, Culture, Theory 9; Sheffield: Sheffield Academic Press.

Carmichael, Calum M. 1974. *The Laws of Deuteronomy*. Ithaca and London: Cornell University Press.

Chia, Philip. 2006. 'On Naming the Subject.' In *The Postcolonial Biblical Reader*, ed. R.S. Sugirtharajah. Oxford and London: Blackwell.

Christiansen, Duane L. 2002. *Deuteronomy 21: 10–34:12*. Word Biblical Commentary 6b; Nashville: Thomas Nelson.

Cooper, Valerie C. 2003. 'Some Place to Cry: Jephthah's Daughter and the Double Dilemma of Black Women in America.' In *Pregnant Passion: Gender, Sex, and Violence in the Bible*, ed. Cheryl A. Kirk-Duggan. Atlanta: Society of Biblical Literature.

Craigie, Peter C. 1976. *The Book of Deuteronomy*. Grand Rapids, MI: Eerdmans.

Davidson, Steed Vernyl. 2013. 'Gazing (at) Native Women: Rahab and Jael in Imperializing and Postcolonial Discourses.' In *Postcolonialism and the Hebrew Bible: The Next Step*, ed. Roland Boer. Atlanta: Society of Biblical Literature.

Donaldson, Laura E. 1992. *Decolonizing Feminisms: Race, Gender, and Empire Building*. Chapel Hill and London: The University of North Carolina Press.

Donaldson, Laura E. 2002. 'The Breasts of Columbus: A Political Anatomy of Postcolonialism and Feminist Religious Discourse.' In *Postcolonialism, Feminism, and Religious Discourse*, ed. Laura E. Donaldson and Kwok Pui-lan. London: Routledge.

Donaldson, Laura E. 2006. 'The Sign of Orpah: Reading Ruth through Native Eyes.' In *The Postcolonial Biblical Reader*, ed. R.S. Sugirtharajah. Oxford: Blackwell.

Driver, S.R. 1859. *Deuteronomy*. International Classical Commentary; 3rd edn.; Edinburgh: T & T Clark.

Dube, Musa W. 2000. *Postcolonial Feminist Interpretation of the Bible*. St. Louis: Chalice.

Ellens, Deborah L. 2008. *Women in the Sex Texts of Leviticus and Numbers: A Comparative Conceptual Analysis*. The Library of Hebrew Bible/Old Testament Studies 458; London: T&T Clark.

Eng, David L. 2001. *Racial Castration: Managing Masculinity in Asian America*. Durham and London: Duke University Press.

Feinstein, Eve Levavi. 2014. *Sexual Pollution in the Hebrew Bible*. Oxford and New York: Oxford University Press.

Fishbane, Michael. 1985. *Biblical Interpretation in Ancient Israel*. Oxford: Clarendon.

Gandhi, Leela. 1998. *Postcolonial Theory: A Critical Introduction*. New York: Columbia University Press.

Grossberg, Lawrence. 1996. 'Identity and Cultural Studies: Is That All There Is?' In *Questions of Cultural Identity*, ed. Stuart Hall and Paul Du Gay. London: Sage Publications.

Hall, Stuart. 1996. 'Introduction: Who Needs "Identity"?' In *Questions of Cultural Identity*, ed. Stuart Hall and Paul Du Gay. London: Sage Publications.

Jones, Ann Rosalind. 1981. 'Writing the Body: Toward an Understanding of L'Ecriture Feminine.' *Feminist Studies* 7: 247–63.

Kirk-Duggan, Cheryl. 2012. 'Precious Memories: Rule of Law in Deuteronomy as Catalyst for Domestic Violence.' In *Exodus and Deuteronomy*, ed. Athalya Brenner and Gale A. Yee. Minneapolis: Fortress.

Kuan, Jeffrey Kah-Jin. 2000. 'Diasporic Reading of a Diasporic Text: Identity Politics and Race Relations and the Book of Esther.' In *The Bible and Postcolonialism*, 3, ed. Fernando F. Segovia. Sheffield: Sheffield Academic Press.

Kwok Pui-lan. 'Unbinding Our Feet: Saving Brown Women and Feminist Religious Discourse.' In *Postcolonialism, Feminism, and Religious Discourse*, ed. Laura E. Donaldson and Kwok Pui-lan. London: Routledge.

Kwok Pui-lan. 2005. *Postcolonial Imagination and Feminist Theology*. Louisville: Westminster John Knox.

Loomba, Ania. 1998. *Colonialism/Postcolonialism*. London and New York: Routledge.

Lundbom, Jack R. 2013. *Deuteronomy, A Commentary*. Grand Rapids, MI: Eerdmans.

McClintock, Anne. 1997. '"No Longer in a Future Heaven": Gender, Race and Nationalism.' In *Dangerous Liaisons: Gender, Nation and Postcolonial*

Perspectives, ed. Anne McClintock, Aamir Mufti and Ella Shohat; Minneapolis and London: University of Minnesota Press.

McKinlay, Judith E. 1999. 'A Son Is Born to Naomi: A Harvest for Israel.' In *Ruth and Esther: A Feminist Companion to the Bible*, ed. Athalya Brenner. 2nd Series; Sheffield: Sheffield Academic.

McKinlay, Judith E. 2004. *Reframing Her: Biblical Women in Postcolonial Focus*. The Bible in the Modern World 1; Sheffield: Sheffield Phoenix Press.

Milgrom, Jacob. 1978. 'Priestly Terminology and the Political and Social Structure of Pre-Monarchic Israel.' *Jewish Quarterly Review* 69: 65–81.

Milgrom, Jacob. 1990. *Numbers*. Philadelphia: Jewish Publication Society.

Miller, Patrick D. 1990. *Deuteronomy*. Interpretation: A Bible Commentary for Teaching and Preaching; Louisville, KY: John Knox.

Mohanty, Chandra Talpade. 1984. 'Under Western Eyes: Feminist Scholarship and Colonial Discourses.' *Boundary* 2: 333–58.

Muñoz, José Esteban. 1999. *Disidentifications: Queers of Color and the Performance of Politics*. Cultural Studies of the Americas 2; Minneapolis and London: University of Minnesota Press.

Noble, Denise. 2008. 'Postcolonial Criticism, Transnational Identifications and the Hegemonies of Dancehall's Academic and Popular Performativities.' *Feminist Review* 90: 106–27.

Pressler, Carolyn. 1993. *The View of Women Found in the Deuteronomic Family Laws*. Beihefte zur Zeitschrift für die Altestamentliche Wissenschaft 216; New York: Walter de Gruyter.

Riffaterre, Michael. 1978. *Semiotics of Poetry*. Bloomington: Indiana University Press.

Roskop, Angela R. 2011. *The Wilderness Itineraries: Genre, Geography, and the Growth of Torah*. History, Archaeology, and Culture of the Levant 3; Winona Lake, IN: Eisenbrauns.

Said, Edward. 1993. *Culture and Imperialism*. London: Chatto & Windus.

Sawyer, Lena. 2008. 'Engendering "Race" in Calls for Diasporic Community in Sweden.' *Feminist Review* 90: 87–105.

Fiorenza Schüssler, Elizabeth. 2007. *The Power of the Word: Scripture and the Rhetoric of Empire*. Minneapolis: Fortress.

Schüssler Fiorenza, Elizabeth. 2008. 'Transforming the Margin—Claiming Common Ground: Charting a Different Paradigm of Biblical Studies.' In *Still at the Margins: Biblical Scholarship Fifteen Years after 'Voices from the Margin,'* ed. R.S. Sugirtharajah. London and New York: T & T Clark.

Schüssler Fiorenza, Elizabeth. 2012. 'Changing the Paradigms: Toward a Feminist Future of the Biblical Past.' In *The Future of the Biblical Past: Envisioning Biblical Studies on a Global Key*, ed. Roland Boer and Fernando F. Segovia. Semeia Studies 66; Atlanta: Society of Biblical Literature.

Sharpe, Jenny. 1994. 'The Unspeakable Limits of Rape: Colonial Violence and Counter-Insurgency.' In *Colonial Discourse and Post-Colonial Theory: A Reader*, ed. Patrick Williams and Laura Chrisman. New York: Columbia University Press.
Shohat, Ella and Robert Stamm. 1994. *Unthinking Eurocentrism: Multiculturalism and the Media*. London and New York: Routledge.
Schwartz, Regina M. 1997. *The Curse of Cain: The Violent Legacy of Monotheism*. Chicago and London: The University of Chicago Press.
Spivak, Gayatri Chakravorty. 1999. *A Critique of Postcolonial Reason: Toward a History of the Vanishing Present*. Cambridge, Massachusetts: Harvard University Press.
Stoler, Ann Laura. 2002. *Carnal Knowledge and Imperial Power: Race and the Intimate in Colonial Rule*. Los Angeles and London: University of California Press.
Sugirtharajah, R.S. 2002. *Postcolonial Criticism and Biblical Interpretation*. Oxford: Oxford University Press.
Sumner, W.A. 1968. 'Israel's Encounters with Edom, Moab, Ammon, Sihon, and Og According to the Deuteronomist.' *Vetus Testamentum* 18: 216–28.
Tigay, Jeffrey H. 1996. *Deuteronomy*. Philadelphia: Jewish Publication Society.
Van Seters, John. 2013. *The Yahwist: A Historian of Israelite Origins*. Winona Lake, IN: Eisenbrauns.
Wang, Zheng and Ying Zhang. 2010. 'Global Concepts, Local Practices: Chinese Feminism Since the Fourth UN Conference on Women.' *Feminist Studies* 36: 40–70.
Westbrook, Raymond. 1986. 'The Prohibition on Restoration of Marriage in Deuteronomy 24: 1–4.' In *Studies in Bible 1986*, ed. Sara Japhet. Scripta Hierosolymitana 31; Jerusalem: Magnes.
Yeğenoğlu, Meyda. 1998. *Colonial Fantasies: Towards a Feminist Reading of Orientalism*. Cambridge: Cambridge University Press.
Yeğenoğlu, Meyda. 2002. 'Sartorial Fabric-actions: Enlightenment and Western Feminism.' In *Postcolonialism, Feminism, and Religious Discourse*, ed. Laura E. Donaldson and Kwok Pui-lan. London: Routledge.

CHAPTER 5

Coming Home: Through the Doors of Ephraim and Egypt

This chapter is a 'homecoming' in three senses. First, the principal text in focus, the story of the rape and dismemberment of the Levite's wife in Judges 19, touches upon the motif of 'coming home' at several points. The southbound Levite seeks to recover—to bring home—his wife, who had 'gone home' to her father's house. Alas, it is her lifeless body that he conveys indoors at the conclusion of the tale. Tarrying indoors in the homes of others, the father-in-law's house and that of an elder at Gibeah, is prominent also in the story. Thus 'coming home,' or at least going and staying *indoors*, is an integral part of the story of interest.

Secondly, the election of the prescribed Passover rituals (of Exod 11–13) as a literary horizon returns to the text of choice in this study's initial foray into biblical law and ritual. So, the book comes full circle. By the imputed connection between Judges 19 and Exodus 11–13, I persist in tracing the evolving contours of exclusion (and inclusion) inherent to acts of association across bodies of law and ritual that turn on thematic, ideational, and lexical correspondences—a mainstay of this study. On this trajectory, however, I breach the limits of the Pentateuch in drawing Judges 19 within the orbit of the expanding intertextual configuration of prescriptive discourses. As always, the literary influences I trace flow in multiple directions. A result in bringing these texts into conversation is the reconsideration of the rationale for violence and the demarcation of boundaries in the Passover tale. The account of the Passover reads *differently* in the shadow of the senseless violence the woman of Judges 19 suffers. An interest in keeping with the rest of this volume involves the exploitation of potentialities in texts and connections between texts by willful, tendentious readers. The 'tendency' in view remains within the genus of a counter-imperialistic animus: here the species is Asian American.

This brings me to my third reason for dubbing the chapter a homecoming. To the degree that acts of interpretation pursue connections of spurious authenticity between texts—if 'authenticity' be synonymous with the phenotypical traits of texts, the marks on a page, born of authorial intent—the particular quest of this chapter is the connections and significances in comportment with the specific interests gathered under the umbrella of 'Asian American biblical interpretation' and its attendant hermeneutical modes. As a transplant from Southeast Asia (Singapore), first to Canada then the United States, the sensibilities and postures inherent to an Asian American slant on Bible reading are familiar: an identity shaped by a cultural hybridity camped out on the fringes of American society, incessantly engaged in acts of translation in negotiations with a sometimes less-than-friendly metropolitan center, spawns a chameleonic perspective. Within the critical configuration of this chapter, I find myself in the unlikely position of being both 'anthropologist' and 'native informant,' the qualification 'unlikely' compounded by the fact that I am neither an anthropologist by training nor a native to North America. In this circumscribed manner, my odyssey through varied stances in reading with a terminus in Asian American hermeneutics is a homecoming of sorts. I trust that I'll fare better than the wretched woman of Judges 19.

And so, in these multifarious ways, I 'come home.' Let me begin with a brief description of an aspect to the critical position(ing)—a room in the house of Asian America—in viewing my chosen texts.

A Current in the Quest for an Asian American Hermeneutic

For quite a while now, Asian American biblical interpretation has invoked a spirit of alliance germane to the conception of a 'panethnic' Asian identity—albeit, one punctured with diversity—in engaging biblical texts. The task has been touted a dynamic posture of reading shaped by diverse energies in multilateral exchange, a pursuit of fresh vistas to texts and contexts in multiple directions. In his programmatic volume, *What is*

Asian American Biblical Hermeneutics? Tat-Siong Benny Liew calls for the recognition of an Asian America 'already entangled with multiple locations.'[1] 'Multiplicity,' 'elasticity,' and a penchant for invention, by Liew's estimation, are essential to honing a hermeneutic of engagement, one representative of the fusion, even diffusion, of voices within the alliance. All this, of course, is in line with the celebratory invocations of textual polyvalence of biblical criticism—drawing from the repertoire of poststructuralism—from sundry quarters of the academy's periphery. The sense of a coalition extends well beyond Asian America to encompass other voices from the fringes of American cultural discourse. Elsewhere, Liew stresses the kinship of minority scholars of the guild facing—here he quotes R. S. Sugirtharah—'a [common] hostile attitude towards the dominant culture' in response to their 'common experience of colonialism and neo-colonialism.'[2] The solidarity forged within the common experience of oppressive, hegemonic constraints yields an unwieldy federation. The result is an intellectual stance that postulates numerous points of departure in minority readings of the Bible, a range of views straddling multiple ethnicities and disciplines.

A consequence of this penchant and passion for pluralism—a point already touched on in the last chapter—is the divesture of a singular, overarching conceptual framework to the endeavor. Liew, with Randall Bailey and Fernando Segovia, speaks of 'rupturing the objective-universal optic' and of confronting the 'self-imputed scientific nakedness' that animates mainstream discourse in biblical studies.[3] Such 'traditional claims to social-cultural abstraction and ideological-political impartiality in scientific research' obscure the situated perspective of a largely monochromatic theoretical stance.[4] The task of minority criticism is anathema to such professions of neutrality. In its stead is an affinity for contextualized readings. Minority criticism, in espousing its interests, invokes

> the use of context as point of entry into the reading of a text. In this tactical procedure direct insight is drawn from the material matrix and/or discursive production in order to render the text, as the claim would have it, more comprehensible and more effective. This claim need not be totalizing in nature: it need not argue that without such contextualized light-shedding the meaning and impact of the text would remain altogether elusive. In fact, it is invariably *relativizing in tone*: it argues for distinctive and significant insight as a result of such contextualized light-shedding, *without excluding similar such insights from other locations and/or agendas*.[5]

The expansive and expanding parameters of minority criticism encompass a growing list of subjects and methods, casting in relief the constitution of others in interrogating the perspectives of some. The emergent optic is that of 'a highly convoluted scholarly discussion, immersed in differential relations and discursive frameworks of all sorts, yielding tensive and conflicting positions under a sense of critical engagement on and from all sides.'[6] The boon to multiplicity, as Liew puts it elsewhere in citing Kwok Pui-Lan, is akin to the 'anthropologist's argument that going overseas and encountering another culture might open one's horizon to see that one's own cultural way of doing something is not necessarily the only way or the best way.'[7] Multiple viewpoints and methods afford breadth to the enterprise, curbing mutually the excesses in all.

Asian American criticism's affinity for pluralism and polyvalence, as already hinted, almost certainly stems from its incessantly transgressive, polycultural existential angst. Thus, Sze-Kar Wan invokes the interstitial space of Asian Americans as a creative one that hinges on a hyphenated existence. The genesis of new visions in theologizing is born of an engagement of 'our both-and-ness with seriousness and realism.'[8] The hyphenated stance engenders 'a new, different world, so that persons at the margins stand not only between these two worlds and cultures but also *beyond* them.'[9] The title to Wan's piece, by his own indication (see p. 137), echoes one of Peter Phan's. Elsewhere, Phan mines the impressionableness and rootlessness—his terms—of the Vietnamese American identity in forging a theology that avoids the pitfall of parochialism.[10] He envisions a process of 'interculturation' that cycles through mutual criticism and borrowing to achieve a level of sophistication in theologizing through mutual enrichment: the exclusion of laity in the ecclesiology of one group (Vietnamese Catholics) is corrected even as the other (American Catholics) gains a heightened appreciation for the priestly vocation.[11] A rich and liberal vision attends Phan's theological exegesis. The same pluri-cultural vision obtains to Rita Nakashima Brock's sense of an inner cacophonous argument, an intercalation of identities 'claimed and denied.'[12] Her 'interstitial integrity' is a drawing from a grammar of Japanese culture and the sensibilities of US military academies, from Shinto ritual and the direct, no-nonsense stances of white southern discourse. Never peeling away the layers, she espouses the Korean American *nun chi* ability to render compassionate judgment out of 'a self-possessed awareness of living in multiple worlds.'[13]

Such generous sensibility, and its imputed benefits, is ubiquitous in Asian American biblical and theological/religious studies.[14] This affinity to Asian American hermeneutics spurs Liew to imagine a vision of 'referencing without referentiality' in surveying the contours of the subdiscipline.[15] Asian American biblical hermeneutics, by this view, is participation in the expanding intertextual matrix of contemporary Asian American biblical scholarship. Sustained critical engagement with the *already* established field, therefore, is the criterion for inclusion. Liew's postulate effectively sidesteps a static essentialism in defining the corpus. 'Asian America' is an elusive concept and being Asian American—or adopting its range of views—is a 'being-becoming,' a creative performance hinging upon evolving conditions.[16] The purchase of (re-)formation in the vision is a mobility that retains a radical and transformative edge. Eschewed is the stagnation of a fossilized optic under 'the tyranny of authenticity,' doomed forever to speaking a singular 'truth.' In the stead of 'truth' is a range of multitudinous 'centers' vying for a continuously displaced scholarly consciousness. Inescapably, the Asian American 'being-becoming' is an (r)evolutionary spiral interweaving sociocultural notes at times discordant.[17]

It is this conspicuous multivalence to the Asian American hermeneutic that grips my attention in reading. This should not be surprising, given the dynamism of Iser's 'wandering viewpoint' that inhabits my ideational faculties in interrogating the spaces between texts. The choice of a reading subject with a memory and imagination forged between cultures is apt in a volume that conceives reading as a dangling between multiple possibilities. Jeffrey Kah-Jin Kuan's diasporic Chinese American of Southeast Asian extract, a cultural hybrid freighted with southern Chinese, Malay, and Indian sympathies, all forged under the hegemonic umbrella of English, Dutch, or French colonial culture fits the projected readerly posture.[18] This *already* polychromatic imaginary gains complexity through intergenerational variance on the extent of assimilation and wavering degrees of allegiance to 'homeland' cultures.[19] R. S. Sugirtharajah's Sri Lankan vision as a 'highly contested site' caught between multiple cultures with nary a spot of sufficient comfort to call 'home'—an interpretive feeling reminiscent of Peter Phan's vision of a creative soul lodged in the 'betwixt and between'—springs to mind.[20] I think also of the tortured claims of Indian American youth in R. Radhakrishnan's narrative of how they live balanced between the comforts of a private ethnic enclave and the demands of a public, American (Euro-American, I assume) persona.[21] Foremost in my thinking too is Sze-Kar Wan's depiction of the split allegiance of the Asian American heart that is doubly rejected (neither 'Asian' nor 'American'), suspended over the chasm between camps.[22] Torn readers and polyvalent texts make good bedfellows.

But it isn't just the Janus subject that is of interest to me. It is the fact that the hegemonic culture (as the phrase clarifies) *is* dominant in the cognitive sweep of the subaltern gaze, and being so, commands the attention—benevolent or otherwise—of the periphery. Sang Hyun Lee puts it well in the claim that the marginalization of Asian America is a 'coerced liminality.' By an incessant litany of racist acts in discrimination— systemic and isolated, blatant, and subtle—the 'center' inflicts on Asian Americans an inferiority complex, an internalized distorted self-image, that blinds them to the fallacies of the mainstream.[23] The dominant aesthetic norms and mores are an imposition upon, its effects palpable within, the subaltern psyche. By Fernando Segovia's reckoning, a similar burden adheres to the Hispanic American condition. The intrusion takes the form of a recurring script that spews the qualifications 'lazy and unenterprising, carefree and sensual, undisciplined and violent, vulgar and unintelligent.' Segovia's conclusion, thus, is that Hispanic America's cultural hybridity 'is by no means the result of an irenic encounter but rather of a harsh and cruel tradition of colonialism and neocolonialism.'[24] The negativity of the view to the margins is but one side of the mainstream's triumph over the 'others.' The corollary perspective, in the parlance of postcolonial criticism, is that subalterns

> believe—and have been taught to believe—that the world of the colonizers is a superior world, where civilization, however conceived, has reached its zenith and now reaches out to the rest of the world. As a result, whatever is autochthonous or indigenous is regarded as ultimately inferior to what lies at the seat of the empire. This image has of course its counterpart among the colonizers: to lead and guide the inferior and the primitive to civilization, with contempt and derision going hand in hand with authoritarianism and paternalism.[25]

Hispanic American biculturalism, unfortunately, runs the risk of co-opting the disparaging demeanor of the center. The hyphenated existence of minorities, thus, tempers resistance with attraction, abhorrence with emulation. The place of protest is also that of embrace. The lure of the center and its attendant privileges is too great to ignore, even if the condescension proves appalling. Hegemony shapes its objects even as these slip the leash from time to time to undermine the gestures of oppression. Homi K. Bhabha's musings on colonial mimicry and hybridity, I think, capture well the ambivalence of the subaltern posture.

On 'Ambivalence' and 'Hybridity'

'Hybridity' is a slippery term in Bhabha's employ. As a condition of the colonized subject, the term denotes a projection and a product of the colonizer's quest for the genesis of a recognizable other, reformed in accordance with the aesthetic and cultural norms of hegemonic desire. Here, the thrust of colonial rhetoric is ambivalent, construing the colonized as foreign, yet familiar. Colonial propaganda, as Bhabha puts it,

> turns on the recognition and disavowal of racial/cultural/historical differences. Its predominant strategic function is the creation of a space for 'subject peoples' through the production of knowledges in terms of which surveillance is exercised and a complex form of pleasure/unpleasure is incited. It seeks authorization for its strategies by the production of knowledges of colonizer and colonized which are stereotypical but antithetically evaluated. The objective of colonial discourse is to construe the colonized as a population of degenerate types on the basis of racial origin, in order to justify conquest and to establish systems of administration and instruction.[26]

The colonial project of subjugation and exploitation thrives on the constitution of a class of cultural hybrids, the go-betweens in the economy of colonial governance. The prized desideratum is 'a subject of a difference that is almost the same, but not quite': 'the sign of a double articulation; a complex strategy of reform, regulation and discipline, which "appropriates" the Other as it visualizes power.'[27] The projected benefit to empire was the constitution of 'a class of interpreters' between colonizers and the governed, a coterie of mediators 'Indian in blood and colour, but English in tastes, in opinions, in morals and in intellect.'[28] The cultivation of such predilection for English manners so appropriate for service in the various departments of government was the province of the colonial mission school, with its purposes expressed in publications of educational policy.

Within the contours of colonial dispensations of power, in Bhabha's description, the 'ambivalence' and the hybrid vision of the colonized find their place. The subaltern articulations are double-voiced, mimic expressions of colonial demeanor from an inescapable indigenous ethos. Subalterns are a partial presence, the '*[a]lmost the same but not white*,' 'the effect of a flawed colonial mimesis, in which to be Anglicized is *emphatically* not to be English.'[29] They are the products of a rhetoric of disavowal, where—Bhabha puts it well—'the *reference* of discrimination is always to a process of splitting as the condition of subjection: a discrimination between the mother culture and its bastards, the self and its doubles, where the trace of what is disavowed is not repressed but repeated as something *different*—a mutation, a hybrid.'[30]

Understandably, the sundered optic of the colonized becomes the site of resistance. 'Hybridity,' by Bhabha's construal, 'represents that ambivalent "turn" of the discriminated subject into the terrifying, exorbitant object of paranoid classification—a disturbing questioning of the images and presences of authority.'[31] The subaltern gaze 'reverses the effects of colonialist disavowal (almost white but not quite), so that other "denied" knowledges enter upon the dominant discourse and estrange the basis of its authority—its rules of recognition.'[32] In a display of 'sly civility,' in the distance between cultures, the realm of colonial mimicry, as Stephen Moore puts it so well, 'the colonized heeds the colonizer's peremptory injunction to imitation, but in a manner that constantly threatens to teeter over into mockery.'[33]

'Teeter,' Moore's term of choice, is apt. The verb captures well the suspended, torn disposition of the subaltern identity in its reception of the dominant and dominating discourse—another aspect of the ambivalence of colonial mimicry. The subaltern stance is alloyed: a mixture of conformity and resistance, of aspiration and revulsion.[34] (Moore has in mind the view to Rome in Mark's gospel.) Unambiguous opposition is out of the question. The very ambiguity tempers Jesus's direction to give Caesar his due beyond that which is God's (Mark 12:17). The statement might be construed a call to deny empire its levies—understanding all to belong to God—or affirmation for Rome's legitimate claims. The obfuscation falls in line with Moore's perception, if tentative, of a Markan flirtation with a Lord 'merely mirroring Roman imperial ideology, deftly switching Jesus for Caesar.'[35] The anti-authoritarian slant to the gospel, thus, serves to displace Rome with the inception of a divine imperial order. The only disagreeable component to Roman imperialism is, well, Rome. The point to Moore's take on Mark is that empire's culture of hegemony is not entirely unattractive to the subaltern. It may become, in fact, an object of envy. The temptation is to tweak the order to better represent subaltern aspirations.

John Marshall's co-option of Bhabhan 'hybridity' in his analysis of Romans 13 presses the same point. Eschewing the simplistic dichotomies of the dialectics of imperial discourse—dominant/subaltern, collaboration/resistance, settler/native—Marshall charts a subject position to the colonial condition 'criss-crossed with discourses of both affiliation to colonial power and resistance to that same power.'[36] Paul's unfettered embrace of Rome's authority and his directive toward conformity, by Marshall's read, is shocking. The apostle's wielding of empire's rhetoric, 'of the divinely sanctioned rule of the powerful over the powerless,' is essential to the argument of Romans 13:1-7. The text is nothing short of affirmation for Caesar's order and an exhortation for his audience to conform to Roman political hierarchy. Power is sexy! Donning the colonizer's garb—decked out with the emblems of prestige—is, simply, a prospect too attractive.[37] And so, as Robert J.C. Young puts it in his reading of Bhabha, the ambivalence of the subaltern is 'continual fluctuation between wanting one thing and its opposite (also "simultaneous attraction toward and repulsion from an object, person or action")'—a mixture of conformity and resistance, a confusion of aspiration and abhorrence.[38] Such is the allure of the colonizer's lofty position that, again in Bhabha's words, 'the fantasy of the native is to occupy the master's place while keeping his [sic] place in the slave's *avenging* anger'[39]—a rage born of the 'slave's' dissembling demeanor too painfully aware of her/his inability 'to accept the colonizer's invitation to identity: "You're a doctor, a writer, a student, you're *different*, you're one of us."' [40] The subaltern, in this instance, knows better. The fantasy can go so far, no further.

Thus, the cleft orientation of the subaltern condition is split in more than one way. The cleavage extends beyond the hybridized sensibilities of the colonized to rest, also, between obsequious complicity and abhorrence. The draw of the privileged center ebbs and flows.

The Bhabhan conception of the subaltern gaze, I think, reflects well an Asian American imagination in attending to biblical texts. The hybridized, Asian American mind espouses a hermeneutic of reticence that ferrets out ambivalences and ambiguities in biblical interpretation. Such posture in interpretation, I submit, stems certainty, moral and epistemic, in character evaluations between Judges 19 and Exodus 11-13. The result is a disquieting perusal of said texts that reads as a map of Asian American anxiety born of a liminal and culturally hybridized condition. But enough with preliminaries and abstractions. Let's get reading.

The Tale of the Levite and His Wife

The grisly and macabre tale of the assault on the Levite's wife in Judges 19 tracks a course through episodes of romantic pursuit, hospitality, and convivial exchange over gastronomic delights. The violent and tragic turn of events that produces a dismembered corpse at the terminus of the narrative seems incongruous. At the tale's inception is the wife's desertion of her Levite husband for her father's home for reasons obscure. A desire for reconciliation brings the bereft husband to the father-in-law's domicile where he is received cordially. A cycle of feasting ensues. With the reconciliation presumably accomplished—the narrative passes over this point—the Levite departs for home with wife in tow. Due to a tardy departure and failing light, the party tarries at Gibeah of Benjamin. An old man returning from a day of labor offers hospitality to the travelers; drinking and eating, once again, follow. Here the tale goes awry. Pounding at the door disrupts the revelry. A mob of the local riffraff is bent on assaulting the Levite, sexually. The host seeks to divert the interest of the band with the timely offer of two women: the Levite's wife—a guest!—and the host's daughter. The rowdy fellows decline the two women, but are satisfied, strangely, when the Levite's wife alone is shoved out the door. Lustily partaking of the ransom set forth, the brutes satisfy their violent urges. The emaciated woman makes her way back to the house at dawn; she collapses at the door. When she fails to respond to her husband's summons upon his ghastly discovery at dawn, he saddles up, hauling her broken body homeward on a donkey. Upon arrival—mission accomplished, the woman is home—the Levite, with apparent nonchalance, hacks her body into 12 parts and distributes these to the tribes of Israel. In bloody parcels, the horrific deed is made known to all. But what, exactly, is this abominable act? Is it the rape of the woman or her dismemberment by the hand of her beloved? At what point in this repugnant series of action did the woman expire?[41]

There is a cadence to the narrative. Cycles of rising (*qwm*), going (*hlk*), arriving and/or entering (*bw'*), tarrying (*lyn*), and feasting (*'kl* and *šth*; 'eating' and 'drinking') bear the storyline. Numerous references to the passage of days and points in a day pockmark the narrative. For Weston Fields, the episodes of the narrative hinge on movements between light and darkness. The journey to Gibeah (vv. 8–14), for example, traces the passage of the sun from dawn to dusk. In reverse, the nightlong torment of the Levite's wife by the mob (vv. 25–26) terminates at dawn.[42] Dusk, by this chronological scheme, is the harbinger of peril and perversity. Jan P. Fokkelman perceives a plot framed by journeying and lodging. The tale moves through three segments of travel (vv. 3–4, 11–14, 27–28) and four of stay (vv. 5–7, 8–10, 15–21, 22–26).[43] Complications or quests—delays in departure, the encounter with the unruly mob, search for lodging—prolong episodes of stay. Nights, similar to Field's analysis, are periods of jeopardy.

Respecting motifs noted already by Fields and Fokkelman *inter alia*, I perceive three cycles in the unfolding of this disquieting story. Broadly conceived, the cycles trek through units of *transit*, *invitation* (at times bordering on compulsion) and *consumption* (see below). Each movement in the cycle is borne, usually, by select lexemes. The initiation of the first cycle (Cycle 1), as the précis above notes, is motivated by the woman's abandonment of her husband for her father's home (v. 2). The husband hits the road. The mapping of the postulated cycle of motifs to the tale is as follows:

	Transit	*Invitation/compulsion/seizure*	*Consumption*
Cycle 1	Levite and company travel to home of father-in-law (v. 3).	Father-in-law repeatedly prevails upon Levite to stay (vv. 4a, 5, 6b, 7).	They eat and drink (vv. 4b, 6a)
Cycle 2	Levite and company travel to Gibeah (vv. 9–15).	An old man persuades the Levite to tarry overnight at his home (vv. 16–20).	They eat and drink (v. 21).
Cycle 2b		Levite seizes his wife and shoves her out the door to face the mob (v. 25).	The mob assaults the woman (v. 25).
Cycle 3	Levite and company travel home to Ephraim (vv. 28–29a).	Levite seizes the woman's inert body (v. 29).	Levite partitions the woman's body (v. 29)

The idiomatic denotations of travel—'rising' (*qwm*) and 'going' (*hlk*)—signal the commencement of this first cycle. Similar verbs convey the storyline of the other cycles at their inception (see vv. 10, 28–29). The transit terminates with the conveyance (*bw'*) of the Levite indoors, into the house (*byt*; v. 4a). There, the father-in-law issues the invitation to stay. A curious component of the narrative at this point, indeed through all cycles, is a display of dominance: a flash of puissance in demeanor and deed. Thus, the father-in-law's initial invitation to tarry (v. 4a) is conveyed by *ḥzq*, a root (in verbal expression) with connotations of force, often carrying the sense of compulsion or seizure (see Gen 21:18; Exod 9:2; 12:33; Jer 20:7;

Ezek 3:14; Mic 4:9; Dan 11:21). Through the cycles of the narrative the affect shows up in diverse forms, in overtly persuasive discourse or brute force. In all cases, these displays of strength precede bouts of consumption. One imagines for v. 4 a stark, daunting display of rhetoric in heightened tones with wild gesticulations, pressing home the point that immediate departure is beyond good sense. The stark display of hospitality does the trick; the Levite stays the night. Indeed, this same initiative stands at the head of a series of inveiglements effective in postponing the Levite's homeward trek. The carousing goes on for days! The bouts of eating (*'kl*) and drinking (*šth*) place readers squarely in consumption's domain. This aspect to the initial cycle, indeed, is one shared with the second (v. 21). Even the butchery behind closed doors in the third cycle (v. 29)—more about this in a while—may be perceived as a consumption of sorts, but of course one void of gaiety.

The expected markers of travel as motif ('rising' and 'going'; vv. 9–15) initiate a second cycle (Cycle 2). While less strenuous by comparison to the previous cycle's invitation to tarry, the language of suasion remains evident in the words of the Ephraimite elder, host to the Levite and his traveling companions at Gibeah. The old man's response to the Levite's minimal request—no sustenance required—strikes a note of contrast between the surfeit of provisions in his household and the poverty of the town square: 'I will care for *all your wants*; only do not spend the night in the square' (v. 20, emphasis mine). The old man's choppy staccato lines signal exuberance and imply the absurdity of the alternative, remaining in the public square. Again the host (and the wine) wins the bout. The Levite tarries and, as the case of the first cycle, merriment fills the house, as food the empty bellies (v. 21–22). And so the paradigm holds in the second cycle: vigorous inducements to enter or remain in the house lead to rounds of eating and drinking.

A doublet of the nexus from invitation/compulsion to consumption is conceivable within the second cycle (Cycle 2b). The effect of the doublet is the enactment of a counterpart to the feasting indoors (v. 21) in the mob's 'devouring' of the woman on the other side of the threshold. This sinister twin to the action indoors rehearses in part the established sequence of motifs, beginning with the woman's seizure (v. 25), a stepped-up variant of *compulsion*. The reprisal of *ḥzq* ('to prevail upon')—recall its use in the father-in-law's prevalence over the Levite (v.4)—secures (partial) affinity with the cycle that would encode the rape as a trope of consumption. The overemphasis on consumption in the father-in-law's hospitality to the exclusion of the woman, according to Andrew Hock-Soon Ng, prefigures this act of 'cannibalism' in the Levite's house. 'Eating' becomes 'a powerful *leitwort* that foreshadows the meal-covenant that will serve to consolidate the homosocial hospitality... which entails the sacrifice of women.'[44] The woman's obscurity, for Ng, suggests that she is the object of the over-consumption in her father's house. In fact, her sustained trajectory toward obsolescence and objectification in the tale (a burial of sorts by Ng's construal), coupled with the alimentary dimension to male bonding, culminates in the dissection of her body to effect the mobilization of Israel's warriors (Judg 20:1, 11).[45] The effect is ironic: female dismemberment forges male solidarity.

The symmetrical optic to the event(s) at Gibeah construes the threshold a reflective surface between the two disparate spheres of consumption: indoors and out. There is no shortage of indices to the door as a boundary. The mob bangs *on the door*. To countenance their demands, the host must *go outside* (v. 23) where he offers to *bring out*, in the stead of the Levite, his daughter and the Levite's wife that the men might ravish them (v. 24). The narrative clearly enacts a boundary at the threshold quite beyond that of a mere portal to the home. 'Outside,' as Fields and Fokkelman point out, is the realm of danger. The gang's sinister demand juxtaposes the sites of hospitality and hazard, inside and outside: '*Bring out* the man who *came into your house*' (v. 22b; my italics in translations through this paragraph). The host's pleading with the rowdy rabble, in turn, underscores the sanctity of the house and the Levite's status as a preferred guest—'this man' (*h'yš hzzh*) who '*entered my house*' (*b'... byty*)—within its bounds. Acting as 'master of the house' (*b'l hbbyt*; v. 22), the old man counts the intended assault on his guest a severe contravention of acceptable custom, condemning it in the strongest of tones: the foul deed is nothing less than a *nblh* (a 'vile' or 'insensible affair')! At the point where negotiation breaks down, the woman's forced *exit from the house*—too bad that the sense of duty inherent to being 'master of the house' does not extend to her welfare here—satisfies the ravenous intentions of the mob. Her expulsion closes the door to chaos. (Did the feasting resume?) Reading with the sordid tale of Sodom's demise in mind (Genesis 19), Alice Bach goes further by conceiving the woman *as* the door. Lamenting the absence of a divine agent to convey the woman indoors out of danger, Bach deems the victim's body 'broken so that the final boundary, the door, could hold firm and protect the Levite against shame and death.'[46] In other words, the woman's body 'was the boundary that stopped the mob from committing rape–that is, rape of the Levite.' Bach's reading credits the Levite's deliverance to a substitution of victims: an exchange that sees the substitute going forth to preserve the security of the ransomed party indoors. So too, the parity to substitution—one for one—turns on the literary edifice of the threshold as boundary and reflective surface between the dichotomous zones of the tale. This semblance of a symmetry of sorts is borne out in Phyllis Trible's observation of a balance to the old man's attempt to dissuade the ruffians: the two prohibitive outbursts ('do not act so wickedly... do not do this vile thing'; v. 23) matches the two-part exhortation to pursue the alternative set forth ('ravish them... do whatever you want to them'; v. 24).[47] The old man's counter offer seeks to match the demand. The outside/inside, hazard/safety binary, thus, is central to the movements and the negotiations of the episode.

One final observation to this doublet of the second cycle: that exit from the house, and not entrance as expected (compare vv. 3–4, 21), precedes *consumption* marks the doublet's departure from the established movement in the sequence of motifs. The reversion of passage through the portal signals the vastly different brand of dining that is to occur—a frenzy of feeding void of goodwill. The anomaly, though a deviation from the norm, sustains the bipolar structure of space—with the door as boundary—as a constituent of the story. The threshold remains the locus of engagement with the tenebrous forces of the night.

The third cycle (Cycle 3), too, departs from the strict pattern of hospitable acts. The doublet of cycle two has prepared us for mutations of the alimentary motif. But the general paradigm remains. The cycle commences with the sequence of actions ('rising,' 'going') under the umbrella of *transit*. The Levite enters the house. Here, the expected element of an exercise of power takes the form of the grasping (once again, *ḥzq*) of the woman's inert body, readying its flesh for the mouth of the blade. 'Eating' occurs at the biting edge of 'the knife' (*hmm'klt*; from the root *'kl*, 'to eat') that slices clean into the woman's flesh. Again, the woman (or what remains of her) is the main course. The extravagance to the violence, in Mieke Bal's estimation, erases the woman's humanity.[48] The Levite's butchery—in keeping with the perception of this bit of the narrative as a doublet to the previous sequence—repeats the mob's 'mastery' over the woman's body, one more installment of a familiar pattern. In this morbid fashion, the *transit invitation/compulsion/seizure consumption* sequence holds steady through the third cycle.

If the third cycle shares with the rape of the Levite's wife a transmuted interpretation of 'eating,' it restores the normative direction of passage through the door—inward, as it was before the doublet of the second cycle—prior to *consumption*. This reversal, also, signals a return to the confines of the house as the sole locus of consumption, the way it was prior to the doublet to the second cycle. In other words, the second cycle contains in its doublet the sole departure from the paradigmatic sequence of motifs that end with meals in the interior. This restoration of 'normalcy,' of course, hardly signals a return to the salubrious social exchange indoors of earlier cycles. In effect, the butchery inside the Levite's home is an importation, to the interior, of the senseless violence of the exterior, hostile spaces. The latter cycles, thus, place the Levite's wife as victim—the object of consumption—on *both* sides of the threshold. Ironically, the path into the house—one to safety and refreshment for others in the story elsewhere—brings only mutilation in the final cycle.

In summary, the three narrative cycles structured by the repeated sequence of plot-level movements foster comparison across three acts of consumption within closed doors. The second cycle spawns a doublet that offers a sinister reflection of the meal inside the home of the host at Gibeah. This dark variant to the trope persists in the third cycle, this time breaching the threshold, bearing indoors the terror of the night.

THE SHADOW OF THE PASSOVER

The story of the Levite's wife is suffused with imagery, motifs, and lexemes evocative of the rites of the Passover. The ostensible index to that, the gesture that secures Exodus 11–13 as a literary horizon for the savage tale, is the Levite's goad to action in the closing lines of the chapter (v. 30): 'Has such a thing ever happened since *the day* that the Israelites came up from the land of Egypt until this day?'[49] The gist of the reference—Jan Fokkelman's assessment—is one of stark contrast to the glory of Israel's deliverance.[50] To be sure, the slaying of Egypt's firstborn is an event of prominence on 'the day the Israelites came up from Egypt.' The inception of the exodus, by the anonymous narrator's iteration, is that the people witnessed divine deliverance 'this day' (*hywm hzzh*; Exod 12:41, 51). By divine injunction, 'this day' (*hyywm hzzh*) Israel must recall in rituals (Exod 12:14; 13:3), in commemorative rites adorned with explanatory elaboration to ossify the significance of the spectacular deliverance (Exod 13:8). The celebrated event, commencing with the night of violence, marks the initiation of the year for Israel

(Exod 12:2). The prominence of the event—now the stuff of legend—effects nothing less than a reorientation of the people's sense of cyclical time. Egypt's humiliation, Jacob's vindication, is squarely in focus in the Levite's gesture to the foundational event of halcyon days in Israel's religious imagination.

In the shadow of Israel's celebrated exodus, the Judges tale yields its cache of correspondences to Exodus 11–13. The hermeneutical maneuver is an unambiguous allusion triggering the reader's imagination to seek additional affinities between the texts juxtaposed—the move is not unfamiliar from previous discussion. To the mind alerted to the connection similarities abound. The 'house' (*byt*), for starters, is a prop prominent across both passages. The lexeme appears 15 times in Exodus 11:1–13:16, and 14 times in Judges 19. In Exodus, the Israelite domicile is the realm of safety, the boundaries of which no one should breach lest the malevolent energies of the dark engulf her (Exod 12:22b). This same notion of a hazard-free zone attaches to the home of the host at Gibeah (Judg 19:22–26); the marauding ruffians and their nefarious deeds remain outside. 'Night,' too, is the time of danger in both the Judges and Exodus passages. In Egypt, the middle of the night is the designated time of slaughter, a deed calculated to incite anguish unprecedented and unsurpassed in magnitude (Exod 11:4–6): Israel, God cautions, must stay shut in *through the night* (Exod 12:22b). At Gibeah, the mob comes to the home of the Levite's host in Gibeah *at evening* (Judg 19:16–22). The violence desists at daybreak (Judg 19:25), the Levite emerging unscathed from the night's horrors (Judg 19:27). The difference across the doorways is night and day. Time and space are nodes of fabulation similarly inscribed across the texts.

The complement, in both texts, to the violence outdoors is communion around alimentary delights *indoors*. The nighttime interior spaces of the stories are for feasting. There are distinctions, of course, in the modes and moods to the 'eating.' The haste and earnestness of the Passover meal (Exod 12:11) is of an atmosphere distinct from the casual posture of revelry at Bethlehem and Gibeah. That the spirit of mirth so resplendent in the entertainment of the Levite is not common to the scene of the woman's postmortem dismemberment—'devouring' would be a term more appropriate—marks this morbid episode an odd and 'aberrant' member of the 'consumption' motif. But even in this strange intrusion on the alimentary motif there seems a plausible equivalence to the Passover meal in the common reference to the 'bone' (*ʿṣm*) or 'bones' (*tṣmym*). Yet, in this commonality there is contrast: the woman's dismemberment—the partitioning of her 'bones' (Judg 19:29)—stands opposed to the proscription of the severance of any bone in the Passover meal (Exod 12:46). If vivisection be cast the equivalent of the Passover feast, then surely the departure from the protocols of the rite is but one more marker of the story as a perverse construal of the festive event. Nevertheless, the grisly hack-job is, as it stands, one more exemplar of a feast behind closed doors. As an element in the series of cycles to the tragic story, the trope is an inflection of the harried scenes of Israel's final night under Egypt's thumb.

Indoors and outdoors, hostility and hospitality (with exception noted), the dichotomy seems clear. Both texts sustain a symmetrical opposition to the spaces across the threshold. There is a balance of sorts to the activities on both sides. This aspect to parts of the Judges narrative is in evidence from previous discussion. The Exodus text displays similar attention to the binary opposition in casting the slaughter of Egypt's offspring opposite the frenzied feeding within Hebrew households—a point made especially clear in the Mosaic utterances of Exodus 12:21–27. In both texts, also, the substitution of victims—a one-for-one exchange—underwrites the parity to the contrasting acts of 'consumption' taking place across the threshold. The woman is assaulted *in the place of* the Levite in Judges 19. In Exodus, in the institution of firstling offerings, the association of the ransom of a firstborn son (Exod 13:13–16) with the Passover event suggests that the Passover sacrifice is a substitutionary offering *in the stead of* the Hebrew child. The apotropaic rite of Exodus 12 is recast in a later divine prescription. The hunger of the bloodthirsty deity is sated by the slaughter of an animal, the evidence of the carnage posted *outside* on the bloodied doorposts of the home (Exod 12:22). As at Gibeah, violence without secures safety within. Equilibrium is maintained, across Exodus and Judges, by the offer of an *alternate* victim.

Beyond the point of transition between parallel zones (Judg 19:27; Exod 12:7, 22–23), the door is also the locus of expiration in both passages. In Exodus (12:22), the blood of the slain Passover animal pools at the threshold (or 'basin'; *hssp*), its application is to the external face of the portal. The threshold (*hssp*) in Judges (19:27), too, is the focus of the fading woman's grasping hands. The gesture of her (soon to be severed) limbs, perhaps, signaling her desire for inclusion in the security of the house. The conception of the doorway as the kill zone, by implication, is the location of the victim's expiration. If this inference is on the mark it follows, also, that a similar conveyance of the remains indoors occurs postmortem. Behind doors their remains are fed upon: the Passover beast by the Hebrew household; the woman's corpse by the edge of a blade. The victims, it appears, suffer violence on both sides of the door. From their perspective, passage indoors offers no guarantee of separation from the ravenous appetites of predators.

One final, perhaps minor, point of overlap with Exodus bears mention. An isolated detail in Judges 19 provokes perceptions of an air of ritual to a part of the harrowing tale of Judges, bringing the story ever closer in form to the confluence of ritual and narrative that is Exodus 11–13. Perhaps the first indication of this flavor to the narrative is the Levite's strange turn of phrase in signaling his intent to return to 'the house of YHWH' (v.18), an epithet not without cultic associations.[51] What seems to some a pious or supercilious tone to an incidental remark becomes, in light of later developments, the first of several slight invocations of a ritualistic air to the woman's dismemberment at the terminus of the sojourning. Several scholars, further along in the story, find in the incongruous inclusion of the definite article in '*the* knife,' the instrument of the woman's dissection, allusion to the implement of ritual slaughter such as the one wielded by Israel's patriarch of renown on Moriah. Just as Abraham took (*wyyqh*) '*the* knife' *hm'klt*; my emphasis) to slay his son, so the Levite takes hold of (*wyyqh*) '*the* blade' (*hmm'klt*; my emphasis) at the point of vivisection. Intimations of such connection lead Gale Yee to denounce the Levite's deed 'a grotesque antisacrifice that desecrates rather than consecrates.'[52] The woman's broken body, following Yee, is this story's version of the Passover sacrifice. Robert Boling, in agreement with Theodor Gaster, finds in the very act an attempt at ritual cleansing, a calculated move to forge healing in the aftermath of the senseless violence.[53] Along similar lines is Mieke Bal's take on the affair as a parody of sacrifice vis-à-vis Girardian conceptions of ritual slaughter.[54] The technical terms of ritualized performance effect an abjection of the defiled corpse leading *not* to purification, but to internecine strife—a twisted rite in a time of unbridled debauchery and hubris. The ma(r)kings of ritualization, to gauge by these responses to the narrative, are an undercurrent to the tale, and the Passover, in light of the Levite's index to that climactic moment of Israelite lore (in v. 30), is *the* rite in view.

To the point, common literary figurations and shared vocabulary afford comparison between the Passover rites of Exodus and the grotesque tale of Judges 19. The comparison yields a similar semblance of symmetry and opposition to the spaces on either side of the entrance to a house. In this respect, indeed, the several cycles of established motifs in the story play and replay the Passover account, each cycle a distinct figuration of the 'original.' Common across the passages too is the notion of a ransom for the intended victim in acts of violence/killing. Closer scrutiny reveals, furthermore, the fact that the woman of Judges 19, like the Passover beast, is the object of 'consumption' on both sides of the door. An air of ritual to the dismemberment of the corpse in Judges 19 is one more link to the ritual slaughter of the Passover story, fortifying the bolder nexi between the texts.

What is one to make of this overlaying of one text on another? What might the imaginative faculties of an Asian American hermeneutic bring to furnish the emerging gestalt that bridges these texts?

The Shadow of Asian American Hermeneutics

Two paths of Asian American engagement in the turns of the tale are discernible. The first, perhaps, is a tad more obvious to judge by currents in the field.

Exclusion and Marginalization

The boundaries of exclusion framing the torn and forlorn figure at the threshold permeate the Judges story, filling the entire fabric of its fabulation. From the outset, the woman's distinction from the other characters of the narrative is evident. She is a southerner of Judahite origin, from Bethlehem (v. 1), bent on returning to her father's house. The men in her life (husband and father), as Patrick S. Cheng observes, would have her move in the opposite direction, north to the boonies of Ephraim.[55] The woman's southward orientation is symptomatic of the ethnic/tribal distinction accorded her character, one that comes to the fore in the unpleasant affair at Gibeah. At Gibeah, she becomes the sole southerner (at heart) once the Levite signals to the Ephraimite elder his affinity for the north in declaring his final destination, his home: 'the remotest parts of the hill country of Ephraim, *from which I come*' (v.18, my emphasis). The Levite's contrived sense of belonging is ostensible, and the old man's generous reception, perhaps, is a reflex of a camaraderie by geography.[56] And so the satisfaction of the mob's demands at Gibeah sets the sole soul of southern extract *and* affinity beyond the safety of the house. Ephraim's lot stays indoors, shielded from Gibeah's rage. Why, after all, should an Ephraimite shield guard one who has turned her back on northern hospitality once before?

In the same scene, gender takes its place in the register of distinctions to the party expelled. The woman-for-a-man substitution, a surprising reduction of the initial offer of two women, underscores the masculine solidarity to the cavorting indoors.[57] This stark exclusion, of course, was building already in the finger-licking indulgence indoors at the home of the father-in-law. Nary a peep is heard from or about the woman after her escorting the Levite, her man, indoors. The elevation of spirits over alimentary delights is a masculine undertaking shared between the Levite and his father-in-law. En route to Gibeah the discussion about the optimal site to break journey, once again, is strictly a male conversation between the Levite and his servant (vv. 11–13). The exchange, by Karla Bohmbach's estimation, 'implies that conditions of gender are more of a hindrance to cooperation between individuals than is class.'[58] At Gibeah, in negotiations with the old man from Ephraim, the woman's obsolescence persists. The initial 'we' in the Levite's introduction of the party of travelers, as Trible notes, narrows to an 'I' that is headed home and in need of lodgings (v. 18).[59] The old man responds in kind, acknowledging only the Levite:

> 'Peace be to *you* (sg.). I will care for all *your* (sg.) wants; only do not *spend the night* (sg.) in the square.' (v. 20, my emphasis)

In the words of assurance, the bond is sealed. The exclusion merely intimated, alas, comes to prominence with the woman's expulsion into the night. Eve, alone, must face the absence of divine favor and fellowship beyond the garden.

But there is more in the spinning of the yarn to chart the woman's recession into oblivion. The qualifier of choice for the woman—a *pylgš*, a 'concubine' or 'secondary wife'—imbues her character with an ambiguity throughout the narrative. While the *pylgš* may demonstrate authority in some instances (2 Sam 15:16; 21:1-14; Esth 5:1-8 [compare 2:14]), she and her offspring may be objects of scorn (Gen 25:6). In other cases, the *pylgš* is associated with the servant class and distinguished from a 'wife' (Gen 35:22 [compare 30:4; 32:22]; 2 Sam 5:13; Song 6:8; Dan 5:3, 23). In Judges 19, to be sure, the *pylgš* suffers opprobrium and diminution in the eyes of the Levite and his Ephraimite host. But *pylgš* is not the sole epithet in use. The range of appellations include 'wife' (*'ššh*, v. 19), 'servant' ('*mlṣ*, v. 19) and, simply, 'girl' (*n'lh*; vv. 4, 3, 6). The array of labels, by the reckoning of several interpreters, opens up a distance between reader and character.[60] Who, or what, exactly, is this woman? Certainly, the Levite's mercurial temperament—romantic pursuit in one instance, throwing her to the wolves in another—offers no consistency on this matter. And the woman doesn't stick around long enough for clarity to emerge. She leaves the story in 12 bloody packages: fragmented in death and life.

Where the woman proves assertive moral ambivalence prevails. Her departure from her husband's house is couched in the parlance of sexual misadventure and idolatry: 'she played the whore' (*wttznh*) and departed for her father's house (v.2).[61] The daring move, glimpsed from the angle of a Gothic perspective on the tale by Ng's analysis, is a transgression of norms worthy of castigation in the strongest terms.[62] The concubine's gutsy venture outdoors alone, coupled with the derogatory epithet, signals 'the dereliction of patriarchy.'[63] The (imputed) pall of transgression to the woman's deportment extends beyond the Gothic lens. Whatever sympathy Christian commentary held for the woman evaporated in the sixteenth century on the heels of Nicholas of Lyra's rediscovery of the Hebrew text in the fourteenth century. (Most commentators from Late Antiquity on had worked with reference to the Old Greek which postulates anger, or a quarrel, as the cause for the woman's departure.)[64] The sentiments of Protestant commentators in the sixteenth century (Pellican, Brenz, Bucer, and Vermigli) are wholly those of moral outrage at the woman's behavior according to the Hebrew.[65] One word, *wttznh*, in this instance, effects an about-face in readerly sentiment. In the wake of the woman's gross violation of sociosexual norms, the violent denouement to the tale—in the estimation of these Protestant exegetes—is just desserts.

But outrageous sexual impropriety seems to many a modern reader ill fitted to the motivational logic of the plot. Danna Nolan Fewell and David Gunn point out that an infidelity of such scope would stifle any feeling of tenderness on the husband's part. Yet the Levite pursues the woman to 'speak tenderly to her and bring her back' (v. 3).[66] The woman's sudden arrival at her father's home, moreover, provokes no inquiry leading to denunciation; without protest, to our knowledge, the woman is received in her father's house. The details don't fit a construal of *wttznh* as sexual transgression in the common sense of the expression. And so 'playing the whore' in Judges 19, some surmise, must mean a dereliction of duty in the spirit of protest, a thumbing of the nose at patriarchal order.[67] Perhaps this is the sense to the woman's 'raging' at the point of departure according to the Greek. Even the Hebrew of the Massoretic strain is amenable to such interpretation if one accepts *znh* as a cognate of Akkadian *zenû*, a verb of such sense.[68]

But 'whoring' in the precisely sexual sense of the term, as Koala Jones-Warsaw alerts us, recalls the hypothetical errant daughter of the high priest and the class of woman inappropriate for marital union with priests in Leviticus 21:7, 14.[69] The woman's assertion of autonomy, in construing its place in the plot, earns her a berth on the do-not-take-as-wife train. Certainly, the Levite has not made her 'wife' (of a rank above *pylgš*) and, eventually, will show her the door. Suffice it to say at this point that 'she played the whore' (*wttnzh*) casts some aspersion, if only in the view of her husband, on the woman's character. The slur leaves an unsavory mark that mitigates any claim to moral superiority on the woman's part. She remains in the shadows. But what else could one expect of a *pylgš*?

The removal of the woman to the periphery is only emboldened by the connection with the Passover legend. The story of Israel's exodus is one in which divine purpose—by God's own confession—is a clear distinction between Israel and Egypt (Exod 11:7). That the Levite's woman 'played the whore' only aligns her more closely to Egypt, which joins the list of errant races guilty of 'playing the whore' with deities strange to Israel (Judg 2:17; 8:27). Those outside the secure precincts of the house—the Egyptians and the adulterous woman—are those that stand between Israel and the worship of their god (Exod 10:24–27; 11:10). The doors frame a view to slavery, oppression (Exod 13:3) and lascivious deportment that inspires a murderous rage (Exod 14:3–31). The woman's place at the periphery seems justified if she be associated with Egypt of the exodus.

But why stop at Exodus and a singular connection with Leviticus 21? Our imaginative (ad)ventures afford a network of possible equivalences and inferences across texts. As always, shared words and themes pave the path to a metonymic, overlapping view on entities of value and the things that threaten these. The intimations of sexual impropriety (Judg 19:2) place the Levite's wife with the sexual miscreants of concern in Deuteronomy 22:13–30, regulations for an aspect of behavior with the potential to ruin the nation's gene pool (Deut 23:1–7). As the desecrating sexual deviant of the priestly household (Lev 21:9)—a connection already mentioned—she must be consigned to the flames. The Levite's wife is the compromised, errant uterus that must be rendered defunct now by priestly ministration (Num 5:27). She is pushed out the door just as parties defiled or performing unclean acts must leave the camp (Num 5:1–4; Deut 23:9–14). We might think of her as the unsuitable payment of a votive offering—out of sums gleaned from unspeakable acts of sexual degeneracy (Deut 23:18). Certainly, she is unsuitable for a priest in marriage; desecration for the priest (Lev 21:9), as the Nazirite locks from corpse contamination (Num 6:9), would be inevitable. Like blemished beasts, the woman, her compromised womb, is wholly unacceptable to God (Lev 22:22–25). Animals offered to God, in contrast, must be pristine. The same strict requirement, a fault-free frame, applies to the choice of an animal for the Passover sacrifice (Exod 12:5). And so, our intertextual odyssey brings us back to the exodus myth.

The trot through the imagined textual tissue on the heels of a connection with the Passover only accelerates the woman's removal to the periphery. Easily, the analogical imaginary imbricates her body in the matrix of substances and practices quite abhorrent by Israel's religious imagination. The woman is positively toxic by this interpretive vein. She, as a misshapen adumbration of the Passover sacrifice, is an offering most unsuitable. The disquietude to the comparison—the woman's dismemberment to the Passover sacrifice—is exacerbated in the analogical logic that would find in her abjection, from house, from convivial discourse, a case of execration; her expulsion is nothing short of the discharge of 'contagion' and 'profanity.' In the (readerly) affirmation of the comparison(s) is a summon of the gravitas of Mosaic legitimacy to the rape of the woman and her humiliation, the reduction of her worth to a sign in 12 parts. To read the woman's dismissal against the battery of rites and rulings we entertain, and to do such *with sympathy* to the associations, is to be complicit in her erasure. It is, perhaps, to find solace and comfort, over and against the topsy-turvy tumult of Judges, that at least one thing has been set right. Oh, waste the wench, why not? Perhaps it is this unperturbed, cavalier progression of the narrative to its chilling conclusion that leads Trent Butler to consider the woman's ritualized dismemberment a repugnant affair 'in sharp contrast to the exodus event as its *polar opposite.*'[70] It is the nonchalance of the woman's ejection from the story, a stance facilitated by the ready-made range of negative associations through the intertexts, that abets the feeling of discomfiture in the comparison to the Passover. The horror of the Judges event exceeds its gore. How could such an act of egregious inhumanity, so casually parlayed, be an apt counterpart to Israel's deliverance from Egypt? That the convocation of the tribes is predicated on the presentation of the woman's broken body renders the muster of forces against Benjamin (Judg 20:8–11) an unholy alliance in a lawless time.[71] The nefarious deed, so forcefully denunciated by Butler, Keefe, and Yee (among others), darkens everything in its vicinity. Even readers, perhaps, are corrupted in the woman's erasure.

Erasure, hegemony's occluding gaze, is familiar to Asian American biblical and theological speculation. Perceptions of 'invisibility' and disempowerment find affinity with the plight of Asian Americans in the academic guild and society at broad, a fact laid bare in Patrick Cheng's reading of Judges 19 through the lens of queer Asian America.[72] Despite the emergence of several volumes of prominence, Asian American hermeneutics in biblical interpretation remains on the fringes. Queer Asian American biblical interpretation suffers the added indignity of marginalization, even rejection, *within* Asian American academic and religious discourse.[73] Of course, the obscurity of Asian American hermeneutics from the larger enterprise of biblical interpretation is a trait shared with other minority vantage points. Shocking, however, is the prevalence and perceived legitimacy of this obscurity as evidenced in Tat-Siong Benny Liew's account of several instances of brazen confession of ignorance and disinterest in the field at interviews for academic posts. The statements—all—are made, apparently, without expectation of a negative assessment for candidacy.[74] Asian American biblical scholarship, thus, knows something of the social dynamics that silences the woman in the course of the narrative, the prospect of being shown the door an ever-present possibility.

The racialization of Asian Americans, beyond the ivory tower, invokes 'nationality' as a marker of distinction. Accordingly, Gale Yee is drawn to a focus on the traits of narration and discourse in the book of Ruth that accentuate the perception of Ruth, the Moabite, as a 'perpetual foreigner.'[75] The blight of this qualification colors the hegemonic center's perception of Asian Americans with scant regard for the latter's duration of residence in the country, even with citizenship stretching back for generations.[76] The concomitant of perennial alien status is the exclusion and denigration of the 'foreigner' that is systemic (the Chinese Exclusion Act of 1882, the internment of Japanese Americans during World War II) and occasional (the racially motivated murder of Vincent Chin in Detroit, the suspicion accorded the Chinese American scientist Wen Ho Lee in the 1990s). Yee's reading of Ruth, thus, is infused with sensitivity to differentials in power and prestige that render perpetual foreigners vulnerable to oppression and abuse: the subordinate status of Ruth in the fields, her lack of access to the land, all of which leaves the Moabite open to exploitation by those seeking good, but more importantly, cheap labor. Looming in Yee's interpretive scheme are points in US history such as the opportunistic exploitation of Chinese labor in railway construction and their replacement of African Americans in plantations after emancipation, both examples cited by her.[77] Similar experiences of alienation and ostracization, corporate and individual, inform Frank M. Yamada's reading of Genesis 2–3, Jeffrey Kah-Jin Kuan's of Esther, and Liew's of Mark's gospel.[78]

Sang-Hyun Lee speaks of the persistence of such displays of exclusion and hostility in the present situation.[79] Lee distinguishes between 'cultural assimilation' (the assumption of mainstream America's customs and social mores) and 'structural assimilation' (the accordance of the opportunities and privileges of the mainstream to the newcomer).[80] While the former is within the grasp of Asian Americans, the latter eludes them until such time that (here, Lee cites Korean American sociologist Won Moo Hurh) 'the immutable independent, "race," becomes mutable through miscegenation or cognitive mutation of the WASP.'[81]

A chasm, informed by distinctions in physiognomy and pigmentation, separates Asian Americans from 'full membership' beyond citizenship.[82] As the woman of Judges 19, with arms stretched out at the door, wants in, so too Asian Americans. The bloody dismemberment of the Levite's wife indoors is evocative of this condition. Her longing to be received indoors—the presumed expression of her outstretched hands—is 'satisfied' by her removal into the Levite's house, only to be greeted by the edge of the blade. Alas, passage indoors for this transplant from the south brings none of the comforts of home. Asian Americans, to judge from the preceding views, might say the same of their lives in the United States. The tale of the woman's banishment to the margins reads as a narrative of Asian American anxiety.

'Ambivalence' and 'Hybridity'

A second, but related, vista to the story trades on Homi Bhabha's conceptions of 'ambivalence' and 'mimicry' as effects of a cultural hybridity germane to the colonial (and post-colonial) condition. Of particular interest is 'ambivalence' as the split vision of the subaltern gaze that is the locus of conformity *and* resistance to the rhetoric of colonization. The sundered colonized soul, in Bhabha's imagination, is a site for the dissolution of the colonial mission. It is the place where the evangelistic proclamation of an alleviation of the indigenous burden stumbles on the 'not quite white' rationale for segregation in the colonies, where racism mars the rhetoric of charitable dispensation. The transference of Bhabha's theoretical musings to the arena of Asian American biblical interpretation abets and informs a hermeneutic of suspicion and reticence with respect to any putative moral vantage point to a story. Contrary evaluations, to the degree that the subversive tones of colonized voices intersperse affirmations of conformity and subservience, effect disturbances to emergent, even dominant, statements of discursive evaluation.

If ambivalence as a posture of reading be of interest, one could scarce do better than a consideration of Jean-Jacques Rousseau's retelling of the biblical tale. This is Peggy Kamuf's feat, brilliantly accomplished.[83] Kamuf teases our ironizing eye to Judges, grooming our ears to hear in and through Rousseau's echo of the biblical story in four movements (chants) a potpourri of diffused voices. 'Le Lévité d'Ephraïm' was composed in 1762 under duress, in flight from an order for arrest by the *Parlement de Paris*. The occasion of the warrant for arrest was the publication of *Emile ou L'éducation*, a treatise on education deemed seditious of religious norms in the day. Immersed in turmoil, through moods vacillating between extremes, Rousseau composed a version of the story over two days as a distraction from his woes. From the outset, the quest to the task was the displacement of vengeance by charity for his persecutors. The result is a story quite inseparable from the author's vicissitudes and soul-searching in this tumultuous time.[84] Kamuf points to the encomium at the inception of Rousseau's narrative (Rousseau, 352–53) as one especially infused with ambivalence, with a tension between the condition the author sought to flee and the one desired.[85] This brief introit is a cacophony of voices inciting wrath and mercy *in the same breath*.[86] Is the wrathful muse here invoked for retribution, or muzzled for clemency's sake? For Kamuf, and perhaps Rousseau, it is neither, *or both*. Kamuf has Rousseau in this in-between space. And so the address 'at the outset of the *récit* speaks less of a fusion than of a confusion of voices, less of a single demand for justice than a difference in the notion of justice (is it forgiveness of sin or an eye for an eye?), and therefore of a possible reversal at the heart of the relation between judge and judged, accuser and accused, and so forth.'[87] Rousseau's ambivalence colors his perspective on the *prise de corps*. The legitimacy of the warrant for arrest is a contingency in the author's mind that rendered his work, in Kamuf's estimation, a medium *between* life and art in the sense that it inscribes the outer and inner frames of this preoccupied *rêverie, between a flight from vengeance and a complete submission to its demand.* The question thus becomes *how such a mixed inscription can ever sustain or prove the distance of one from the other.* Between real events and fictional story, between life and literature: this is the place of the signature. The question is also therefore the following: How is one to read Rousseau's signature on and in this text? Or rather, what signs 'Rousseau'?[88]

'Rousseau,' the signature to the work is already a contested space. If the 'signature' is that of a vengeful heart—this is the question that engrosses Kamuf—then it is one plagued with reticence as to the viability of the undertaking (the deflection of rage) and its object (who, exactly, is the victim or the victimizer?). The question of an escape from the wrath of Parisian society is an open one granted Rousseau's waffling on the ethical status of the act that inspired the order for his arrest.

Accordingly, Rousseau's reading/writing of the story, a reflection of his reverie, exploits tensions of plot that lay bare the ambivalence of its characters. The story cycles through repetitions of crimes that shuffles characters around in its portrayal of victimizers and victims. His work, preying on the silences of the biblical fable, is an orchestrated game of 'magical chairs' that unsettles any facile placement of a character in a singular role. In this endeavor, the biblical tale, in Rousseauian hands, is patient. The Levite's mutilation of the woman *repeats* the mob's violation of her body, an attack the Levite avoided by substituting the woman in his stead. The juxtaposition is pointed in Rousseau's retelling: the barbaric Levite (Rousseau dubs the man '*le barbare*') rends apart the woman's body (Rousseau, 359), just as the uncouth men of Gibeah—brutes (*Barbares*) they are!—had descended on her, a pack of wolves to tear her apart (*la déchire*; Rousseau, 358). The indirect victim of the sexual assault —the Levite—becomes the aggressor within the bounds of his home. And there is yet another doubling of violence. Benjamin's crime at Gibeah— drawing Judges 21 in the mix—is *twice* repeated *en masse*, at Jabesh Gilead and Shiloh (Judg 21:12, 23) to secure Benjamin's posterity. The quests for justice, for retribution and restoration, substitute offended parties for offenders. The orgy of violence is an escalation, the inflation of the crime from the rape of one to many. Israel, by Rousseau's embellishment at the conclusion of the third chant, seems to take this view in its communal lament that Heaven punishes by having good aims go astray by excess (Rousseau, 362). 'Retribution' is over the top, and no one is safe. As

Phyllis Trible puts it, through the twists and turns of the narrative (the Bible's *and* Rousseau's, I would add) crimes reenacted 'with vengeance' by men professing outrage for those same ignominious acts render the tale of 'justice' ironic.[89] The 'solutions' to the predicaments the story presents paint a portrait at once tragic and comedic, one in which predators and prey, in Kamuf's words, 'may have been serving all along as mask—or defense—for the other.'[90] The world in Rousseau's sights, a stage on which players neither void of malice nor free of victimization shuttle between roles, is the one Israel presents itself about this tumultuous time.

> Thus the guilty one will also be the avenger, the avenger will also be guilty; the victim will be made culpable and the criminal victimized. Everything is between brothers, in the circle of the same; everything passes by way of the voice of Israel which addresses a terrible message to itself from which there is no turning aside until it has found death over and over again.[91]

There are no heroes in this story.

Even the consistent victim of the tale, the Levite's wife, may not elude this schema of the reader's concoction. Already, Rousseau's pervasive stance on the narrative of 'a flight from vengeance *by* a submission to it'—Mieke Bal's insight here—conflates vengeance and guilt in the figure of the Levite's concubine.[92] The woman, under the burden of Rousseau's shaky ambivalent positioning, *becomes* guilt. Her expulsion from the house by her husband's hand is his submission to justice, the displacement of his shame.[93] But one hardly needs Rousseau's undecidedly guilt-ridden conscience to find fault with the woman. Koala Jones-Warsaw's reading of the biblical narrative imputes blame (to the woman) by a different path.[94] Her view to the text construes the entertainment of the Levite in Bethlehem a forced subordination to the authority of the father-in-law. The ignominy of the oppressive gesture extends to the daughter—the Levite's wife—by way of the postulated motive for the initiative: the purchase of an advantage to the daughter in what is evidently, already, a rocky relationship.[95] The woman is not innocent. The thrust to Jones-Warsaw's thesis—a point she makes against Trible's reading of the story—is, of course, an extension of the counter imperial vision to discern the broader, more complex, network of victimization across the story.[96] Jones-Warsaw's (and Rousseau's) thoughts in this vein come a touch closer to a readerly posture—one of three possible takes on the tale in David Penchansky's opinion—that finds a *just end* in the woman's demise.[97] To be sure, Jones-

Warsaw, and Rousseau, is a good distance from the unrestrainedly vitriolic interpretations of sixteenth-century Protestant interpreters. But a readerly disposition that would plumb the depths of human depravity will find no shortage of loose ends in the narrative to warrant such speculation. Notwithstanding the blatant cruelty to the woman's death, it does not tax the imagination to find an opportunistic aggressor in the Levite's wife. Certainly, there is nothing in the morass of intertextual associations framing the view to the woman (see above) that would stand in the way of a negative evaluation. Here, the negative nuances to that nebulous clause 'she played the whore' (v. 2) play a part, casting aspersion on the woman's good name. The story offers little resistance to the woman's damnation. Even Rousseau's twist on the tale that has the woman's *ennui* as the motive for her departure is hardly complimentary (Rousseau, 354). His narrative goes on to label her 'a woman of ill-faith' (*l'infidèle*), 'his [the Levite's] unfaithful spouse' (*sa volage épouser*), in a depiction of the Levite's forlorn misery (Rousseau, 354). The woman's reputation is tarnished for the inconsistency of her affections. Indeed, Rousseau's inflection of the story that would dilute any readerly vitriol toward the Levite by redeeming his character serves only to amplify any perception of fault on the woman's part. The Levite's protracted expressions of affection for his wife (Rousseau, 353–54), his collapse into her grave singing her praises (Rousseau, 359), his fastidious concern for her comfort in preparing her bed (Rousseau, 356)—all extra to the biblical version—accentuate the woman's dastardly deportment in deserting her man. Might we, following Rousseau's eye on the biblical story, construe the Levite her 'victim' in the story? Is the concubine the virulent 'contagion' and the agent of desecration so feared and unyieldingly circumscribed by biblical legislation. The biblical texts, it seems, conspire to calumny against the Levite's woman. Rousseau's embellishments, it may be said, follow a biblical lead.

By Kamuf's analysis, Rousseau's story fuses the horizons of biblical narrative and the author's interests, forging a tale symptomatic of emotional vectors in conflict attending the flight from Paris. Rousseau's tale, simply stated, is a troubled (and troubling) reading of the biblical narrative, one born of, and suited to, the machinations of a hybridized, conflicted imaginary. As the encomium to Rousseau's narrative, the split vision is unsettled and ill contained by a monochromatic frame of reference. This fidgety posture is but the reflex of the sequence of interchanging, conflicting points of view that would find victims and aggressors in *singular* figures.

The Southeast-Asian Chinese Diaspora in the United States, given its multihyphenated identity, is no stranger to Rousseau's dilemma in Jeffrey Kah-Jin Kuan's view. Infused with narratives of flight from hardship in southern China, forged in the multiracial post-colonial culture of English Malaya or the Dutch East Indies, the Straits-born Chinese enter upon the American scene *already* juggling multiple languages and competing narratives of origin. Endemic to the experience is the negotiation of different worlds, a liminal existence between cultures, forever engaged in translation. Accordingly, cultural identity—here Kuan cites Stuart Hall—is not a 'fixed essence':

> It is not some universal and transcendental spirit inside us on which history has made no fundamental mark...It is always constructed through memory, fantasy, narrative and myth. Cultural identities are the points of identification or suture, which are made, within the discourses of history and culture. Not an essence but a *positioning*.[98]

The business of incorporating the fresh slew of perspectives American, therefore, is not strange to a people already assiduously engaged in managing multiple 'identities.' The effect of this 'positioning' amid the interstices of cultures in negotiation is an imagination beset with 'uncertainty, ambiguity and caution.'[99] The cogency of any given optic, novel or staid, is susceptible to modification once cast within a pluralistic vision.

Such is the posture of suspicion Tat-Siong Benny Liew ascribes to his hermeneutic of reading through 'yin yang eyes.'[100] Eschewing mere assent and appreciation, Liew charts a course of disruption and discord through Mark's gospel. The approach of choice is crucial, if the voices that reinscribe imperialism are to be distanced from contrary trajectories within the book. 'Reading with yin yang eyes,' contends Liew, is to be cognizant 'that the very book used to oppose racial and cultural hybridity is itself highly hybridized with contradiction.'[101] The ambivalent stance—like Rousseau's on Judges 19—is a reflex of the reader's dissonant heart. Liew's hermeneutic of suspicion is essentially, by necessity, bidirectional in orientation: the text and its reception, the reader's context, are in focus. This aspect of the yin yang vision is of import since, in Liew's analysis, no culture is free of flaw; no group, nor book, is beyond the grasp of hegemonic desire. Perhaps an awareness of this fact is more urgent for Chinese Americans as their elevation to so-called 'model minority' status enhances the possibility of complicity in oppression. And so, elsewhere,

Liew exhorts Asian Americans so pigeonholed to identify, always, with the cause of the downtrodden. Why, one might ask, would Asian Americans do otherwise?

Eleazar S. Fernandez's assessment of the Filipino American condition throws light on this matter. In a brief essay, he unpacks the anatomy of Asian American motivation for seconding the value judgments of the dominant/dominating culture.[102] Bathed in lofty conceptions of the American (read: white) way, bolstered by years of colonial dominance, Filipinos arrive on American shores zealous for incorporation in the image of Euro-America—the very complicity to hegemony Liew fears. Shucking all things Filipino, their fervent quest is assimilation to the 'center.' Fernandez's words capture the vibe of the culture in explaining the absence of Filipinotowns.

> I do not imagine that there will be Filipinotowns in the near future either, not for Filipino Americans, who have been trained to believe that they are white America's 'little brown brothers,' even after years of being called 'brown monkeys.' There will be no Filipinotowns, because Filipino Americans are proud of their effort to blend, not with other people of color in America but with dominant white America... Filipino Americans have, in general, no aversion to 'Americanization,' because that is precisely what many aim for... Many Filipino-American youth, in an effort to be as American as possible, to be 'cool,' deny their culture and ethnic identity and, at times, even blame their parents for their physical features. They want to be just like any white youth, since that is the key to getting out of the hell of non-acceptance. Whites, in turn, often with the best of intentions, respond: 'We consider you to be just like us. You don't seem [Filipino].'[103]

Fernandez's scrutiny of the unenviable situation uncovers an internal logic of self-hatred that fuels a lust for acceptance and its concomitant deleterious effects. This aspect to the Asian American psyche is foregrounded in the haunting autobiographical quip of David Mura, the Japanese American author. The piece quoted below is part of a larger meditation on Asian American artistic creativity, a self-contemplation of the poet as artist.

> And I became a writer so I could sit in my room and write. So
> I didn't have to face an audience,
> So I could be alone, with my thought, my books, my poems,
> My words.

> So I could abandon myself to quietude and contemplation.
> So I could perceive and create beauty and complexity.
> So I could live the life of a superior being.
> Of course, this being had no color. Or sex.
> Of course, this being was a white male.
> Of course, I was a white male. (What does it mean to be a white male?)
> Of course, I tried very hard to forget this fact.
> Of course, I almost succeeded.
> Of course, I almost killed myself in succeeding.[104]

Fresh direction, the path out of the pit, as Mura states later, was a turn from a refusal to come to terms with his Japanese-American identity, his location in the US cultural landscape as a *sansei*. The avoidance of the issue became the very site of 'self-hatred and self-abuse, a long string of depression, promiscuity, and failed relationships.'[105] The experience, in Mura's view, is unique for visible minorities, for whom a reckoning with their phenotypical traits and the (assigned) social–economic significances is a daily affair. Mura's obliviousness to said distinctions, his path to perdition, was clear, if only in hindsight. In an ironic twist to Fernandez's 'hell of non-acceptance,' Mura's treatment of the matter sets himself up as both subject *and* patient in the act of exclusion. The uncritical acceptance and perpetuation in the Asian American imagination of Euro-American constructs of normalcy, in the poetic moment, fosters an abject depression. Suicide seems preferable to the existential angst. Fernandez's call to repentance, to an exorcism of the 'white god' in constructions of identity, seems all the more urgent in the light of Mura's grim trajectory to self-immolation.[106]

Self-loathing, however, may not be the sole deviant path. (A darker side to such attractions to the centers for the promulgation of cultural and aesthetic norms has already been touched upon with reference Liew's caution against Asian American complicity in oppression.) Jonathan Tran warns of another dangerous spin-off from such collusion with the (often unspoken) rhetoric of dominant cultures.[107] He speaks of a burgeoning tendency in the birthing of a multiethnic, Asian American identity for preying upon, first, the idiosyncratic traits of an earlier, immigrant generation (speech, deportment and dress) before training its ire on any group that manifests markers of a different cultural identity.[108] The manifestation of derogatory attitudes dressed in humor marks the initial move in this sinister direction. Tran's alarm stems from the correspondence of these tactics with practices inherent to white supremacy. The habits of conformity to the mainstream for immigrants of Eastern and Southern European extract in the sociocultural economy of twentieth-century America include a willingness to discard the markers of ethnic distinction (e.g., clothing, idiosyncratic patterns of speech) and a manifest disapproval of those who retain such distinctions.[109] The vehemence of disapproval and the zeal for integration, at times, spawned acts of violence. This penchant for validation by mockery extends to qualify the treatment of other groups (whites, blacks, Mexicans), paving the path to exploitative economic practices impacting with detriment the outsiders to the group.[110] Such pretentions to cultural ascendancy and their concomitant gestures of aggression, in Tran's view, are afoot already in Asian America. The Asian American psyche, thus, is not the sole victim in Asian American orientations toward the prejudices and practices of socioeconomic hegemony.

The ambivalence of the Judges story, as accentuated in Kamuf's analysis, reflects such intricate negotiations so essential to staking a place in the American social–ethnic landscape. The multifaceted personages of the tale resonate with the hybridized nature of Asian Americans. Here I speak not just of the intercultural engagements essential to geographical dislocation (though this is an important point) but also of the obfuscation—even a cloudy indeterminacy at times—in pegging the dynamics of power relations in interethnic strife. The twists and turns of the tale reflect the altering landscape in the tug-of-war between groups, a contest that turns on the Janus-mien to any group; the torn demeanor suspended between recovery and aggression, between the assuage of imperialistic oppression and its perpetuation. The sites of oppression vary as advantage passes from one to another. Every group, every person, is capable of meting out to another the pain it suffers. The fast-clipped tale, so perceived, is a microcosm of the larger, historicized experiences of ethnic/national groups in contention, with others and themselves. Tran's calculus, his fear, is that the marginalization of Asian America today is a step in its transformation into tomorrow's bully. The community's erroneous resolution, in Lisa Lowe's words, is nothing less than 'the simple assimilation to the dominant culture's roles and positions by the emergent group,' a 'caricature [of] the old colonialism.'[111]

Asian America, of course, need not go such way. And a hermeneutic of reticence and ambivalence bolsters a broader methodological repertoire to avert this malevolent path. The polyvisional, consistently revisionary, stance in reading, the fruit of the rapid succession of victims in the Judges story, casts a long shadow that renders plausible *and* problematic any judicial configuration that sanctions violence, even ones with divine sponsorship. Every character is a shade of gray, and the angle of vision determines the hue. Here a victim, there a predator, and in all a touch of both. Through such foggy lenses—the effect of reading with a view to the cavalier administration of 'justice' in the Judges story—the appeal of putative notions of legitimacy for blanket destruction across a swath of the Egyptian demography (Egypt's minors) wanes. The adumbration of blame for social ills—the now palpable unease to a singularly resolute and unyielding sense of pseudo-righteous wrath—should spur self-reflection. Am I, too, an agent of chaos? How have I been negligent and, thus, complicit in violence? Has the zeal for equity, the expectation for fair treatment, taken on a vindictive spirit, a force now blind to the arrogance and cruelty just so recently reprehensible? The excesses of the tale are infectious; its self-serving agenda of retribution egregious, casting in relief otherwise overlooked points of view in the divine program of deliverance (in Exodus). Dennis Olson's read on the exodus event, with no help from the grave injustices of Judges, finds the divine motives in the story questionable, to say the least.[112] The turns to sinister shades in constructions of divine motivation are occasioned, in part, by the perspectival plurality and the silences of texts. The view, like Rousseau's, is a kaleidoscopic vision affective of a labile position hardly satisfied by a single interpretation. The imaginary, the reader's, is insatiable. Such a position(ing) makes for perturbed readers.

A 'perturbed reader' is not an inappropriate qualification for the colonized, subaltern interpreter. The jaundiced view toward Exodus—through Judges—is not unlike the returning gaze of Bhabha's colonized subject, a stance not foreign to my methodological disposition throughout the chapter. The double-voiced articulation of colonial mimicry, through Bhabha's lens, is an act of 'sly civility,' an echo of the colonizer's rhetoric in an altered tone, a constant slipping between civil ascription to and a perversion of imperial prerogative.[113] Between colonizer and colonized views, the colonial subject flitters. Its gaze is a menace to the demands of colonial authority, a cloud of turbulence in the narcissistic airs of metropolitan self-congratulation. The subaltern's utterance of resistance is an ironized double to an initial iteration. Her parodic enunciations repeat, inflect and refigure empire's cadences, infusing its hegemonic expostulations with native animus. His is the emergent voice of the interstices, 'the overlap and displacement of domains of difference' where 'the intersubjective and collective experiences of *nationness*, community interest, or cultural value are negotiated.'[114] The ironized optic stems from the epistemological edges of the metropole, the realm of dissidence and dissonance, of revisionary histories.[115]

In such light, the mimesis of apotropaic ritual in Judges (as the inflection of the colonizer's talk of cultural ascendance in colonized mouths) is not a 'plenitudinous presence,' but a belated utterance, 'an image neither original—by virtue of the act of repetition that constructs it—nor "identical"—by virtue of the difference that defines it.'[116] The effusive violence of the tale, in counterhegemonic hands, strikes the beat of the Passover rite with a different drum. This familiar tune in a strange key is the narrative's mockery of Israel's triumphalist remembrance of deliverance. Its agonistic edge is 'a pressure, and a presence, that acts constantly, if unevenly, along the entire boundary of authorization.'[117] In cadences reminiscent of authority and prestige the narrative presses its subversive point. The embarrassment of the tale's excesses is a parrot's shrill and ludicrous rendition of its master's ramblings. The tale's imitation of the rite runs through several courses, rendering the performance a derisive stuttering, the inchoate mutterings of inebriation. The mimicry of Mosaic accents effects a 'strategic reversal of the process of domination through disavowal,' a disruption of 'the production of discriminatory identities that secure the "pure" and original identity of authority.'[118] In its spectacular and monstrous displays of depravity—an exuberant intemperance of carnivalesque proportions—the narcissistic demands of power (Israel's disposition by its rehearsal of divine election in the Exodus fable) are undone. The Levite's callousness disrupts and disturbs the felicity of a singular vision to an essential depravity—Egypt's. Imperialism's pretense to a civilizing mission, a strategy of justice and charity—save Benjamin, rape Shiloh; rescue Israel, gut Egypt—is shorn of its ardent glory. The echo of Exodus in Judges, thus, turns 'the gaze of the discriminated back upon the eye of power,' achieving nothing less than 'a re-cognition of the immediacy and articulacy of authority.'[119]

Rousseau and Bhabha, in their own ways, sound postmodernism's bell in signaling interpretation's contested spaces with their poly-angled, prismatic lenses on texts. Understandably, the discordant chimes are heard loudest in the quarters of the global village—Chela Sandoval puts it succinctly—plied by 'the scapegoated, marginalized, enslaved, and colonized of every community,' coteries *already* well experienced with 'this shattering, this splitting of signifieds from their signifiers.'[120] These are the communities of the cultural interstices where a 'schizophrenic' existence makes for 'modes of perceiving, making sense of, and acting upon reality that are the basis for effective forms of oppositional consciousness in the postmodern world.'[121] Bhabha's hybridized and ironized optic is, already, Asian America's habitus and, indeed, that of all those at the margins. The sensibility that espouses an affinity for *other* ways of seeing and being is the domain of Kuan, Liew, Tran, Phan, Lee, Yee, Kwok, and the other household names of Asian American biblical interpretation. Always re-visioning, always spying out fresh paths, the vision is relentless and suspicious of *truth*, of an overarching univocality that is domineering *and* seductive: a unicameral, monocultural sight to 'insight' that would inspire subaltern lust and its inevitable, subsequent despair.

In Summary: The Beginnings of a Way Forward

My dissonant, Rousseau-animated view to Judges 19 (with Exodus as backdrop) colludes with this project in shattering the singular vision to the characters of the narrative. The cast appears a menagerie of actors in an interstitial space suspended in a split existence, a positioning ever mindful of the breadth of human experience with its proclivities, benevolent and malevolent. The disturbed, ambivalent optic evinces a contrapuntal texture to the intertextual readerly maneuvers. The disposition (re-)presents well the burden of the Asian American split subject living under the enforced illusion of a benevolent equality, all the while aware, dimly, of his or her disenfranchisement, pressing for belonging *and* reform.[122] Tortured and torn is the Asian American psyche to which Judges 19 returns me. Healing, yet, is in the wings.

The balm of Bhabha's ambivalence is germane to Eleazer Fernandez's call for a comprehensive vision of the dynamic negotiations with power(s) in the North American landscape. In his summon is a heightened awareness of a heterogeneity to human proclivities that would avoid a skewed application of a monochromatic memory of an abominable deed for the victimization of another.[123] The error is the enshrinement of social constructs oblivious to the dynamic social locations and evolving power differentials between groups. What Fernandez advocates for Liberation Hermeneutics is the abandonment of an 'essentialization and romanticization of the poor' and, in its stead, the deployment of a 'power-knowledge nexus' capable of a 'historicization' of power dynamics.[124] The envisioned outcome is the demystification of hegemonic power and acute attention to 'the transformations, the shifting positions, and the power differentials diachronically and synchronically' capable of transporting Liberation Theology into a future that is ever critical 'of its own temptations and distortions.'[125]

Fernandez's stance is hand-in-glove with the psychic positioning of Sandoval's 'third form of subjectivity,' the emotional positioning of 'the scapegoated, marginalized, enslaved, and colonized of every community.'[126] (The hermeneutic should come easily to Asian Americans.) The purchase of such location is an 'oppositional consciousness,' a 'differential practice of "cognitive mapping"' resplendent with 'opportunities for re-cognition.'[127] The sensibility is that of 'a life lived metonymically from experience to experience,' a way of being 'demanded of those who hold out against conditions of hunger, deprivation, humiliation, colonization, and social subjection.'[128] The fossilized memory of Fernandez's fear and the monochromatic view to victimhood eschewed in Rousseau's reading of Judges 19 seem so far away from Sandoval's vision of oppositional consciousness.

In the same vein is Greer Anne Wenh-In Ng's longing for a discriminatory dexterity born of a cultural hybridity that checks excesses in cultural praxis.[129] The desired cultural sensibility is one infused with the flexibility of bamboo that resists, equally, Western hegemony and the detrimental aspects of neo-Confucian ethics. Ng's dream is of an Asian American identity for the amelioration of the lot of all races. Peter Phan seconds Ng in his clamoring for an ethic of *interculturation* between equals in Vietnamese American negotiations with the mainstream. Translation, mutual criticism and enrichment would foster a mutual borrowing of the strengths in each other, pushing back the Vietnamese American overemphasis on an institutional model for ecclesiology while sparking the mainstream's zeal for solidarity with the poor.[130] A similar salubrious, integrative and interactive, spirit invests R. Radhakrishnan's refusal to define an 'authentically Indian' identity that, by necessity, reinscribes the obligatory positionings of Indians in US society from the metropolitan perspective.[131] Instead, the Indian Diaspora should find the liberty to inhabit an intercultural space void of 'a paranoid reaction to the "naturalness" of dominant groups' and of a penchant for homogenization. Indian America, then, would be a locus of intercultural reciprocity, a place of openness to the greater good.

Rousseau's ambivalence and Bhabha's hybridity in the interrogation of Judges and Exodus, in the final analysis, brings me home to being Asian in America. Things are looking up.

Notes

1. Tat-Siong Benny Liew, *What is Asian American Biblical Hermeneutics? Reading the New Testament* (Honolulu: University of Hawai'i Press, 2008), 13. 'Panethnic' as a qualifier of Asian American identity, at once evocative of familial resemblance and cultural multiplicity, is a term invoked in Yen Le Espiritu, *Asian American Panethnicity: Bridging Institutions and Identities* (Philadelphia: Temple University Press, 1992). More concise and topic-focused treatments of Asian American thinking in biblical interpretation and/or theology are available in Mary F. Foskett and Jeffrey Kah-Jin Kuan (ed.), *Ways of Being, Ways of Reading: Asian American Biblical Interpretation* (St. Louis: Chalice, 2006); Fumitaka Matsuoka and Eleazar S. Fernandez (ed.), *Realizing the America of Our Hearts: Theological Voices of Asian Americans* (St. Louis: Chalice, 2003); Peter C. Phan and Jung Young Lee (ed.), *Journeys at the Margin: Toward an Autobiographical Theology in American-Asian Perspective* (Collegeville, MN: The Liturgical Press, 1999). Beyond the fray of biblical and theological studies is a growing volume of literature on Asian American studies. An excellent description of the current situation in Asian American experience, though drawn largely from West Coast perspectives, is Mia Tuan's *Forever Foreigners or Honorary Whites: The Asian Ethnic Experience Today* (New Brunswick and London: Rutgers University Press, 1998). For historical treatments of the same matter with inroads into the socioeconomic and political dimensions to the experience, see Ronald Takaki, *Strangers from a Different Shore: A History of Asian Americans* (New York and London: Little, Brown and Company, 1989). Also helpful on this front, with a focus on Chinese American experiences, are the essays in Arif Dirlik (ed.), *Chinese on the American Frontier* (Lanham: Rowman & Littlefield, 2001). David L. Eng, *Racial Castration: Managing Masculinity in Asian America* (Durham and London: Duke University Press, 2001) is a veritable entrée to the complexities of psychoanalytic theory, sexual orientation, and racial formation in casting Asian American masculine identity.
2. Tat-Siong Benny Liew, 'When Margins Become Common Ground: Questions of and for Biblical Studies,' in *Still at the Margins: Biblical Scholarship Fifteen Years after 'Voices from the Margin'* (ed. R. S. Sugirtharah; London; New York: T & T Clark, 2008), 48.

3. Randall C. Bailey, Tat-Siong Benny Liew and Fernando F. Segovia, 'Toward Minority Biblical Criticism: Framework, Contours, Dynamics,' in *They Were All Together in One Place? Toward Minority Biblical Criticism* (ed. Randall C. Bailey, Tat-Siong Benny Liew and Fernando F. Segovia; Semeia Studies 57; Atlanta: Society of Biblical Literature, 2009), 27. The call for contextualization and a broadening, cross-disciplinary view to minority biblical interpretation persists in Tat-Siong Benny Liew, 'What Has Been Done? What Can We Learn? Racial/Ethnic Minority Readings of the Bible in the United States,' in *The Future of the Biblical Past: Envisioning Biblical Studies on a Global Key* (ed. Roland Boer and Fernando F. Segovia; Semeia Studies 66; Atlanta: Society of Biblical Literature, 2012), 273–87.
4. Ibid., 26.
5. Ibid., 28. My emphasis.
6. Ibid., 31.
7. Tat-Siong Benny Liew, 'Colorful Readings: Racial/Ethnic Minority Readings of the New Testament in the United States,' in *Soundings in Cultural Criticism: Perspectives and Methods in Culture, Power, and Identity in the New Testament* (ed. Francisco Lozada Jr. and Greg Carey; Minneapolis: Fortress, 2013), 178. Liew's sentiments on the dynamic, intersectional perspectivism to Asian American biblical criticism reflect a consensus in the field and apply across the range of minoritized views in biblical and theological studies. See, for example, Uriah Yong-Hwan Kim, 'The *Realpolitik* of Liminality in Josiah's Kingdom and Asian America,' in *Ways of Being, Ways of Reading: Asian American Biblical Interpretation* (ed. Mary F. Foskett and Jeffrey Kah-Jin Kuan; St. Louis: Chalice, 2006), 84–98; Roy I. Sano, 'From Context to Context: Cognitive Dissonance,' in *Realizing the America of Our Hearts: Theological Voices of Asian Americans* (ed. Fumitaka Matsuoka and Eleazar S. Fernandez; St. Louis: Chalice, 2003), 115–28; Jeffrey Kah-Jin Kuan, 'Diasporic Reading of a Diasporic Text: Identity Politics and Race Relations and the Book of Esther,' in *The Bible and Postcolonialism, 3* (ed. Fernando F. Segovia; Sheffield: Sheffield Academic Press, 2000), 161–73; Sze-Kar Wan, 'Does Diaspora Identity Imply Some Sort of Universality? An Asian-American Reading of Galatians,' in *The Bible and Postcolonialism, 3* (ed. Fernando F. Segovia; Sheffield: Sheffield Academic Press, 2000), 107–31; Peter C. Phan, 'Betwixt and Between: Doing Theology with Memory and Imagination,' in *Journeys at the Margin: Toward an Autobiographical Theology in American-Asian Perspective* (ed. Peter C. Phan and Jung Young Lee; Collegeville, MN: Liturgical Press, 1999), 113–33; Fernando F. Segovia, 'Toward Intercultural Criticism: A Reading Strategy from the Diaspora,' in *Reading from this Place: Social Location and Biblical Interpretation in*

Global Perspective (ed. Fernando F. Segovia and Mary Ann Tolbert; Minneapolis: Fortress, 1995), 303–30.
8. Sze-Kar Wan, 'Betwixt and Between: Toward a Hermeneutic of Hyphenation,' in *Ways of Being, Ways of Reading: Asian American Biblical Interpretation* (ed. Mary F. Foskett and Jeffrey Kah-Jin Kuan; St. Louis: Chalice, 2006), 147.
9. Ibid., 146. The emphasis is original.
10. Peter C. Phan, 'The Dragon and the Eagle: Toward a Vietnamese American Theology,' in *Realizing the America of Our Hearts: Theological Voices of Asian Americans* (ed. Fumitaka Matsuoka and Eleazar S. Fernandez; St. Louis: Chalice, 2003), 165. The title to Wan's article echoes Phan, 'Betwixt and Between.'
11. Phan, 'The Dragon and the Eagle,' 169.
12. Rita Nakashima Brock, 'Cooking Without Recipes: Interstitial Integrity,' in *Off the Menu: Asian and Asian North American Women's Religion and Theology* (ed. Rita Nakashima Brock, Jung Ha Kim, Kwok Pui-Lan and Seung Ai Yang; Louisville and London: Westminster John Knox, 2007), 136.
13. Ibid., 136.
14. See above, n. 8.
15. Liew, *What is Asian American Biblical Hermeneutics?*, 2–9.
16. Ibid., 16.
17. For Lisa Lowe, *Critical Terrains: French and British Orientalisms* (Ithaca: Cornell University Press, 1991), 105, the poly-visional and dynamic disposition is necessary to countenance a discursive hegemony that is itself neither fixed nor monolithic, but always cast 'in the context of ongoing conflicts and pressures from a variety of locations.'
18. Kuan, 'Diasporic Reading,' 165–67.
19. On the heterogeneity of US Asian-origin collectivity in articulations of Asian American identity, see Lisa Lowe, *Immigrant Acts: On Asian American Cultural Politics* (Durham and London: Duke University Press, 1996), 60–83. A poignant meditation on the impact of intergenerational differences in Asian American encounters with the Bible is Frank M. Yamada, 'Constructing Hybridity and Heterogeneity: Asian American Biblical Interpretation from a Third-Generation Perspective,' in *Ways of Being, Ways of Reading: Asian American Biblical Interpretation* (ed. Mary F. Foskett and Jeffrey Kah-Jin Kuan; St. Louis: Chalice, 2006), 164–77.
20. R.S. Sugirtharajah, 'Orientalism, Ethnonationalism and Transnationalism: Shifting Identities and Biblical Interpretation,' in *Ethnicity and the Bible* (ed. Mark G. Brett; Biblical Interpretation Series 19; Leiden: Brill, 1996), 427.

21. R. Radhakrishnan, 'Is the Ethnic "Authentic" in the Diaspora?' in *The State of Asian America: Activism and Resistance in the 1990s* (ed. Karin Aguilar-San Juan; Boston: South End Press, 1994), 223.
22. Wan, 'Betwixt and Between,' 148–49.
23. Sang Hyun Lee, 'Marginality as Coerced Liminality: Toward an Understanding of the Context of Asian American Theology,' in *Realizing the America of Our Hearts: Theological Voices of Asian Americans* (ed. Fumitaka Matsuoka and Eleazar S. Fernandez; St. Louis: Chalice, 2003), 25–26.
24. Fernando F. Segovia, 'Toward a Hermeneutics of the Diaspora: A Hermeneutics of Otherness and Engagement,' in *Reading from this Place: Social Location and Biblical Interpretation in the United States* (ed. Fernando F. Segovia and Mary Ann Tolbert; Minneapolis: Fortress, 1995), 63, 66.
25. Ibid., 62 n.11.
26. Homi K. Bhabha, *The Location of Culture* (London: Routledge, 1994), 100–101.
27. Ibid., 122–23.
28. Ibid., 124–25.
29. Ibid., 128, 125. Emphasis original.
30. Ibid., 159
31. Ibid., 162.
32. Ibid., 162.
33. Stephen D. Moore, *Empire and Apocalypse: Postcolonialism and the New Testament* (Sheffield: Sheffield Phoenix Press, 2006), 90.
34. Ibid., 33.
35. Ibid., 37.
36. John W. Marshall, 'Hybridity and Reading Romans 13,' *Journal for the Study of the New Testament* 31 (2008): 169.
37. David Eng's critique of Lonny Kaneko's 'The Shoyu Kid' in his *Racial Castration*, 104–36, speaks of the psychic investment of subaltern subjects —the interned Japanese American lads of the tale in this instance—in the idealized imaginary of white America. The play of the boys at assimilation forges a frontier over and against the Japanese American experience of national disenfranchisement (pp. 118–19). Its momentary, ludic pretense to power shows itself ludicrous under the crushing gaze of a hegemonic vision that hails the subaltern ego as disparaged alien.
38. Robert J.C. Young, *Colonial Desire: Hybridity in Theory, Culture and Race* (London and New York: Routledge, 1995), 161.
39. Frantz Fanon (*The Wretched of the Earth* [trans. Richard Philcox; New York: Grove, 1963], 5) makes a similar point: 'The gaze that the colonized subject casts at the colonist's sector is a look of lust, a look of envy. Dreams of possession.

Every type of possession: of sitting at the colonist's table and sleeping in his bed, preferably with his wife. The colonized man is an envious man.'

40. Bhabha, *The Location of Culture*, 63–64. Emphasis in original.
41. Unlike the Hebrew, the Septuagint (to v. 28) places the woman's expiration at the door of the Ephraimite elder.
42. Weston W. Fields, 'The Motif "Night as Danger" Associated with Three Biblical Destruction Narratives,' in *'Sha'arei Talmon': Studies in the Bible, Qumran, and the Ancient Near East Presented to Shemaryahu Talmon* (ed. Michael Fishbane and Emanuel Tov; Winona Lake: Eisenbrauns, 1992), 23 n 16.
43. Jan P. Fokkelman, 'Structural Remarks on Judges 9 and 19,' in *'Sha'arei Talmon': Studies in the Bible, Qumran, and the Ancient Near East Presented to Shemaryahu Talmon* (ed. Michael Fishbane and Emanuel Tov; Winona Lake: Eisenbrauns, 1992), 41–45.
44. Andrew Hock-Soon Ng, 'Revisiting Judges 19: A Gothic Perspective,' *Journal for the Study of the Old Testament* 32 (2007): 207. See also Mieke Bal, *Death and Dissymmetry: The Politics of Coherence in the Book of Judges* (Chicago: University of Chicago Press, 1988), 123–24.
45. Ng, 'Revisiting Judges 19,' 203–13.
46. Alice Bach, 'Rereading the Body Politic: Women and Violence in Judges 21,' in *Women in the Hebrew Bible: A Reader* (ed. Alice Bach; New York: Routledge, 1999), 397.
47. Phyllis Trible, *Texts of Terror: Literary-Feminist Readings of Biblical Literature* (Philadelphia: Fortress, 1984), 74. See also Fokkelman, 'Structural Remarks,' 44.
48. Bal, *Death and Dissymmetry*, 126.
49. My emphasis. The NRSV's rendition here follows the Greek. The Hebrew text of the Massoretic variety places the note of astonishment—not a question—squarely in the mouths of the tribes receiving the dismembered portions.
50. Fokkelman, 'Structural Remarks,' 43. Trent C. Butler, *Judges* (Word Biblical Commentary 8; Nashville and Dallas: Thomas Nelson, 2009), 416, 428–29, cites Fokkelman with approval on this point.
51. Here, I follow the Hebrew text. On the imputed haughty, even deceptive, demeanor behind the quip, see Pamela Tamarkin Reis, 'The Levite's Concubine: New Light on a Dark Story,' *Scandinavian Journal of the Old Testament* 20 (2006):137; Jaqueline E. Lapsley, *Whispering the Word: Hearing Women's Stories in the Old Testament* (Louisville: Westminster John Knox, 2005), 43; Tammi J. Schneider, *Judges* (Collegeville, MN; Liturgical Press, 2000), 259. The recommendation of Robert G. Boling, *Judges* (Anchor Bible 6a; Garden City: Doubleday, 1975), 275, and J. Alberto Soggin, *Judges* (trans. J. S. Bowden; Old Testament Library;

Philadelphia: Westminster, 1981), 287, to follow the Septuagint at this point—'my house' instead of 'the house of YHWH'—responds to the oddity of the phrase. But of course, the incongruity of the Hebrew raises the visibility of the phrase as a pointer to another text.

52. Gale A. Yee, 'Ideological Criticism: Judges 17–21 and the Dismembered Body,' in *Judges and Method: New Approaches in Biblical Studies* (ed. Gale A. Yee; Minneapolis: Fortress, 1995), 165. See also Adele Reinhartz, '*Why Ask My Name?' Anonymity and Identity in Biblical Narrative* (Oxford and New York: Oxford University Press, 1998), 80.

53. Boling, *Judges*, 276–77. Ilse Müllner, 'Lethal Differences: Sexual Violence as Violence against Others in Judges 19,' in *Judges: A Feminist Companion to the Bible, 2nd Series* (ed. Athalya Brenner; Sheffield: Sheffield Academic Press, 1999), 140–41, takes this interpretive trend a touch further in finding the ritualized butchery an excorcism of the Levite's 'strangeness.' Camaraderie with Gibeah 'in the house,' therefore, is the ostensible accomplishment of the slaying. By contrast, Alice A. Keefe, 'Rapes of Women/Wars of Men,' *Semeia* 61 (1993): 85 n. 58, finds in the performance a signal of Israel's dissolution.

54. Bal, *Death and Dissymmetry*, 121, 127.

55. Patrick S. Cheng, 'Multiplicity and Judges 19: Constructing a Queer Asian Pacific American Biblical Hermeneutic,' *Semeia* 90–91 (2002): 121–22.

56. Müllner, 'Lethal Differences,' 136. The Levite's sense of belonging, as Müllner clarifies (pp. 135–36), is mitigated by Deuteronomy's inclusion of Levites with other vulnerable, landless parties (Deut 14: 27–29; 16:14). The gesture is, at best, a projection from an interstitial, liminal space. For a sustained treatment of the story that suspends the Levite between margin and center, see David Z. Moster, 'The Levite of Judges 19–21,' *Journal of Biblical Literature* 134 (2015): 721–30.

57. Michael Carden, 'Homophobia and Rape in Sodom and Gibeah: A Response to Ken Stone,' *Journal for the Study of the Old Testament* 82 (1999): 91–92, explains this oddity by understanding the Levite as the object of the mob's opprobrium, thus making sense of the offer of his wife, minus the host's daughter, as the sole victim.

58. Karla G. Bohmbach, 'Conventions/Contraventions: The Meaning of Public and Private for the Judges 19 Concubine,' *Journal for the Study of the Old Testament* 83 (1999): 88–89.

59. Trible, *Texts of Terror*, 72. Lapsley, *Whispering the Word*, 43, notes the contrasting statement by the narrator in verse 15 ('but no one took *them* in to spend the night'), which retains the plural pronominal reference for the party in need of a place to stay.

60. On the complexity to the appellation and the effect of the diversity of terms for the woman, see Cheng, 'Multiplicity,' 121–24; Schneider, *Judges*,

248–56; Susan Ackerman, *Warrior, Dancer, Seductress, Queen: Women in Judges and Biblical Israel* (New York and London: Doubleday, 1998), 236–37; J. Cheryl Exum, *Fragmented Women: Feminist (Sub)versions of Biblical Narratives* (Journal for the Study of the Old Testament Supplement Series 163; Sheffield: JSOT Press, 1993), 176. For a lucid survey of the patriarchal household, including the place of secondary wives, with reference to biblical sources and the cuneiform laws, see Tikva Frymer-Kensky's 'Patriarchal Family Relationships and Near Eastern Law' in her volume *Studies in Bible and Feminist Criticism* (Philadelphia: The Jewish Publication Society, 2006), 225–37. An overview of the category (*pylgš*) reaching back into Jewish commentary from Late Antiquity is available in Diane Kriger, 'A Re-Embracement of Judges 19: Challenging Public-Private Boundaries,' in *Vixens Disturbing Vineyards: Embarrassment and Embracement of Scripture. Festshrift in Honor of Harry Fox (lebeit Yoreh)* (ed. Tzemah Yoreh, Audrey Glazer and Justin Jaron Lewis; Boston: Academic Studies, 2010), 59–63.

61. Here I depart from the translation of the NRSV which follows the tradition in Greek. The semantic range to 'playing the whore'—sexual promiscuity, exogamy, a pining for strange gods—is a subject of interest in Chapter 2. On the nuances to the verb see also Naomi Koltun-Fromm, *Hermeneutics of Holiness: Ancient Jewish and Christian Notions of Sexuality and Religious Community* (Oxford and New York: Oxford University Press, 2010), 47–52; Randall C. Bailey, 'They're Nothing but Incestuous Bastards: The Polemical Use of Sex and Sexuality in Hebrew Canon Narratives,' in *Reading from this Place: Social Location and Biblical Interpretation in the United States* (ed. Fernando F. Segovia and Mary Ann Tolbert; Minneapolis: Fortress, 1995), 121–38; Phyllis Bird, '"To Play the Harlot": An Inquiry into an Old Testament Metaphor,' in *Gender and Difference in Ancient Israel* (ed. Peggy L. Day; Minneapolis: Fortress, 1989), 75–94.
62. Ng, 'Revisiting Judges 19,' 204–06.
63. Ibid., 206.
64. Wroth as the motive for the woman's hasty departure is the reading from one of the Greek texts (Septuagint[A]). An Aramaic Targum (Jonathan), the Vulgate and Josephus (*Jewish Antiquities* 5.2.8) follow suit. Modern interpreters who find this rendition plausible include Erik Eynikel 'Judges 19–21, An "Appendix:" Rape, Murder, War and Abduction,' *Communio Viatorum* 47 (2005): 104; Boling, *Judges*, 273–74; Daniel I. Block, *Judges, Ruth* (New American Commentary 6; Nashville: B & H, 1999), 523; Soggin, *Judges*, 284. Pamela Reis Tamarkin, in radical departure from interpretive currents, reads the Hebrew implicating the Levite as a pimp: 'She played the whore *on his account* (*'lyw*),' taking the preposition *'l* to indicate cause (Reis, 'The Levite's Concubine,' 129).

65. For a concise treatment of commentary on the passage in this period, see John L. Thompson, *Writing the Wrongs: Women of the Old Testament among Biblical Commentators from Philo through the Reformation* (Oxford New York: Oxford University Press, 2001), 208–14.
66. Danna Nolan Fewell and David M. Gunn, *Gender, Power and Promise: The Subject of the Bible's First Story* (Nashville: Abingdon, 1993), 133. See also Eynikel 'Judges 19–21,' 104; Bohmbach, 'Conventions/Contraventions,' 90; Lapsley, *Whispering the Word*, 37–38 n.12.
67. See also Lapsley, *Whispering the Word*, 38; Ng, 'Revisiting Judges,' 204–05 n. 6; Ken Stone, 'Gender and Homosexuality in Judges 19: Subject-Honor, Object-Shame?' *Journal for the Study of the Old Testament* 67 (1995): 91–92, 96; Exum, *Fragmented Women*, 179; Barry G. Webb, *The Book of Judges: An Integrated Reading* (Journal for the Study of the Old Testament Supplement Series 46; Sheffield: JSOT Press, 1987), 188.
68. See *DCH* 3: 123; *HALOT* 1: 275; BDB 276; *TDOT* 4: 99–104; *CAD* 21: 85; *AHw* 3: 1519–20.
69. Koala Jones-Warsaw, 'Toward a Womanist Hermeneutic: A Reading of Judges 19–21,' *Journal of the Interdenominational Theological Center* 22 (1994): 20–21. Jones-Warsaw spies also a connection to the case of the suspicion of a bride's pre-marital coitus in Deuteronomy 22:13–21, another text in the medley of rites and laws of our literary backdrop.
70. Butler, *Judges*, 416. My emphasis.
71. Such is the judgment of Keefe, 'Rapes of Women/Wars of Men,' 93–94. See also Yee, 'Ideological Criticism,' 165.
72. Cheng, 'Multiplicity and Judges 19,' 122–24.
73. Ibid., 124–25.
74. Liew, 'When Margins Become Common Ground,' 45.
75. Gale A. Yee, '"She Stood in Tears Amid the Alien Corn": Ruth, the Perpetual Foreigner and Model Minority,' in *They Were All Together in One Place? Toward Minority Biblical Criticism* (ed. Randall C. Bailey, Tat-siong Benny Liew and Fernando F. Segovia; Atlanta: Society of Biblical Literature, 2009), 119–40.
76. Ibid., 120.
77. Ibid., 121–22.
78. Frank M. Yamada, 'What Does Manzanar Have to Do with Eden? A Japanese American Interpretation of Genesis 2–3,' in *They Were All Together in One Place? Toward Minority Biblical Criticism* (ed. Randall C. Bailey, Tat-siong Benny Liew and Fernando F. Segovia; Atlanta: Society of Biblical Literature, 2009), 97–117; Kuan, 'Diasporic Reading,' 161–73; Liew, *What Is Asian American Biblical Hermeneutics?*, 18–33.
79. Lee, 'Marginality as Coerced Liminality,' 11–28.
80. Ibid., 23–24.

81. Ibid., 24.
82. The point comes across clearly in Bret Harte's popular poem 'The Heathen Chinee' (1870). The work expresses well Euro-American anxiety over cheap and abundant Chinese labor with a focus on perceived (negative) *essential* traits to the Chinese. For a contextualized analysis of the poem, see Ronald Takaki, *Iron Cages: Race and Culture in Nineteenth-Century America* (Oxford and New York: Oxford University Press, 1990), 222–29.
83. Peggy Kamuf, *Signature Pieces on the Institution of Authorship* (Ithaca and London: Cornell University Press, 1988), 79–99. Other critical and discursive forays into Rousseau's recasting of Judges 19–21 in varying scholarly milieux include Thomas M. Kavanagh, 'Rousseau's Lévite d'Ephraim: Dream, Text, and Synthesis,' *Eighteenth-Century Studies* 16 (1982–1983): 141–61; Mieke Bal, 'A Body of Writing: Judges 19,' *Continuum* 1 (1991): 110–26; Michael S. Kochin, 'Living with the Bible: Jean-Jacques Rousseau Reads Judges 19–21,' Hebraic Political Studies 3 (2007): 301–25. Bal's essay reads Kamuf's reading of Rousseau and Judges. Rousseau's paraphrase of the biblical story reworks the events of Judges 19–21. First published posthumously in 1781, the text, with critical notation, is available in Jean-Jacques Rousseau, *Oeuvres complètes* (ed. B. Gagnebin and M. Raymond; 4 vols.; Paris: Gallimard, 1959), 2:1205–1223. A translation in English is Jean-Jacques Rousseau, *Essay on the Origin of Languages and Writings Related to Music* (trans., ed. John T. Stott; *The Collected Writings of Rousseau* 7; Hanover and London: University Press of New England for Dartmouth College, 1998), 351–65. All subsequent references to Rousseau's composition (within parentheses) are to pages in this translation.
84. Kamuf, *Signature Pieces*, 80, 83; Kavanagh, 'Rousseau's Lévite d'Ephraim,' 145–46. Kavanagh makes the connection to the circumstances of the harried flight by his assessment that Rousseau's palpable outrage through the piece 'derives from the sublimation of a more profound, properly unconscious need to consolidate his status as *victim*' (p. 146; Kavanagh's emphasis). In the same vein is Kochin's judging the story 'a slice, or limb, from the body of text that is Rousseau's written self-preservation...that his readers are to reassemble according to his own directions in order to comprehend him' (p. 305). Rousseau's refashioning of the narrative, in Kochin's view, is autobiographical, a 'symbol-laden' story 'of unjust persecution.'
85. Kamuf, *Signature Pieces*, 86–87.
86. A specific tension in Kamuf's focus is between the exhortation to 'pardon the guilty' (*pardonner au coupable*) and, yet, several lines later, the admonishment for not punishing 'the crimes of your brethren' (*les crimes de vos frères*).
87. Kamuf, *Signature Pieces*, 87.
88. Ibid., 83. The emphasis is mine.

89. Trible, '*Texts of Terror*,' 83.
90. Kamuf, *Signature Pieces*, 86. Müllner, 'Lethal Differences,' 139, reaches the same conclusion, finding in the vile violations no delimitation 'to sexual violence by men as offenders or towards women as victims.' The story, thus, enacts a victimization in which 'strangeness [read: foreignness] and femininity overlap in the sexuality of violence' (p. 140).
91. Kamuf, *Signature Pieces*, 98. For a reading of Shakespeare's *The Tempest* that finds Caliban the subordinated 'native' other—under Prospero's thumb—turning imperialist and male chauvinist, see Laura E. Donaldson, *Decolonizing Feminisms: Race, Gender, and Empire Building* (Chapel Hill and London: University of North Carolina Press, 1992), 16–17. Relevant to our counter-hegemonic reading of Judges is Donaldson's view on Caliban's assault of Miranda as an 'overdetermined participation' in the imperialist project, both 'victim and victimizer' at once in the gendered and racialized power dynamics of the play.
92. Bal, 'A Body of Writing,' 118, 113. Emphasis in original.
93. Ibid., 115.
94. Jones-Warsaw, 'Toward a Womanist Hermeneutic,' 18–35.
95. Ibid., 21–22.
96. Ibid., 27.
97. David Penchansky, 'Staying the Night: Intertextuality in Genesis and Judges,' in *Reading between Texts: Intertextuality and the Hebrew Bible* (ed. Danna Nolan Fewell; Louisville: Westminster John Knox, 1992), 83.
98. Kuan, 'Diasporic Reading,' 165–66. Emphasis original.
99. Ibid., 167.
100. Liew, *What is Asian American Biblical Hermeneutics?*, 26–28.
101. Ibid., 27.
102. Eleazar S. Fernandez, 'Exodus-toward-Egypt: Filipino-Americans' Struggle to Realize the Promised Land in America,' in *Voices from the Margin: Interpreting the Bible in the Third World* (ed. R. S. Sugirtharajah; 3rd edn.; Maryknoll, NY: Orbis, 1970), 242–57.
103. Ibid., 248–49.
104. David Mura, 'A Shift in Power, a Sea Change in the Arts: Asian American Constructions,' in *The State of Asian America: Activism and Resistance in the 1990s* (ed. Karin Aguilar-San Juan; Boston: South End Press, 1994), 184–85.
105. Ibid., 187.
106. Such bouts of self-degradation as a concomitant of an attraction for the cultural metropole are common in Asian American musings on their interstitial existence. See, for example, Brock, 'Cooking without Recipes,' 131–33; Tuan, *Forever Foreigners*, 147–51; Jung-Young Lee, *Marginality: The Key to Multicultural Theology* (Minneapolis: Fortress, 1995), 42–47. A

poignant expression of the sentiment is Nelli Wong, 'When I was Growing Up,' in *This Bridge Called my Back: Writings by Radical Women of Color* (ed. Cherríe Moraga and Gloria Anzaldúa; New York: Women of Color Press, 1981), 7–8. For Elizabeth Schüssler Fiorenza, *The Power of the Word: Scripture and the Rhetoric of Empire* (Minneapolis: Fortress, 2007), 38, the condition is an effect of cultural and political domination leading to an 'internalized oppression, which cannot be reduced to low self-esteem of individuals but creates a public mentality that accepts such negative labeling and practices of injustice as "naturally given" and "common sense."' The corollary is a 'horizontal violence, contempt and internal conflict among the minoritized and oppressed' that causes them 'to act against their own interests and to search for individual solutions rather than to name systemic domination.'
107. Jonathan Tran, 'Why Asian American Christianity Has No Future: The Over Against, Leaving Behind, and Separation from of Asian American Christian Identity,' *SANACS Journal* 2 (2010): 13–56.
108. Ibid., 19–21.
109. Ibid., 19.
110. Ibid., 20. For similar assessments of current conditions, see Lai Ling Elizabeth Ngan, 'Bitter Melon, Bitter Delight: Reading Jeremiah Reading Me,' in *Off the Menu: Asian and Asian North American Women's Religion and Theology* (ed. Rita Nakashima Brock, Jung Ha Kim, Kwok Pui-Lan and Seung Ai Yang; Louisville and London: Westminster John Knox, 2007), 178; Tuan, *Forever Foreigners*, 147–51.
111. Lowe, *Immigrant Acts*, 72.
112. Dennis T. Olson, 'Literary and Rhetorical Criticism,' in *Methods for Exodus* (ed. Thomas B. Dozeman; Cambridge: Cambridge University Press, 2010), 27–29. Olson's deconstructive take on the tale builds on a review of arguments by Edward Greenstein ('The Firstborn Plague and the Reading Process,' in *Pomegranates and Golden Bells: Studies in Biblical, Jewish, and Near Eastern Ritual, Law and Literature in Honor of Jacob Milgrom* [ed. David P. Wright, *et al.*; Winona Lake, IN: Eisenbrauns, 1995], 555–68). See, also, Robert Allen Warrior, 'A Native American Perspective: Canaanites, Cowboys, and Indians,' in *Voices from the Margin: Interpreting the Bible in the Third World* (ed. R.S. Sugirtharajah; Maryknoll, NY: Orbis, 1970), 235–41.
113. Bhabha, *The Location of Culture*, 126, 141.
114. Ibid., 2. Text in italics is Bhabha's.
115. Ibid., 6.
116. Ibid., 153.
117. Ibid., 156.
118. Ibid., 159–60.

119. Ibid., 160.
120. Chela Sandoval, *Methodology of the Oppressed* (Theory out of Bounds 18; Minneapolis and London: University of Minnesota Press, 2000), 34.
121. Ibid., 34.
122. Eng, *Racial Castration*, 22.
123. Eleazar S. Fernandez, 'Multiple Locations-Belongings and Power Differentials: Lenses for a Liberating Biblical Hermeneutic,' in *Soundings in Cultural Criticism: Perspectives and Methods in Culture, Power, and Identity in the New Testament* (ed. Francisco Lozada Jr. and Greg Cary; Minneapolis: Fortress, 2013), 146–47.
124. Ibid., 147.
125. Ibid., 147.
126. Sandoval, *Methodology of the Oppressed*, 33–34.
127. Ibid., 34, 35.
128. Ibid., 27.
129. Greer Anne Wenh-In Ng, 'Land of Maple and Lands of Bamboo,' in *Realizing the America of Our Hearts: Theological Voices of Asian Americans* (ed. Fumitaka Matsuoka and Eleazar S. Fernandez; St. Louis: Chalice, 2003), 104.
130. Phan, 'The Dragon and the Eagle,'168–69.
131. Radhakrishnan, 'Is the Ethnic "Authentic" in the Diaspora?,' 228–29.

References

Ackerman, Susan. 1998. *Warrior, Dancer, Seductress, Queen: Women in Judges and Biblical Israel*. New York and London: Doubleday.
Bach, Alice. 1999. 'Rereading the Body Politic: Women and Violence in Judges 21.' In *Women in the Hebrew Bible: A Reader*, ed. Alice Bach. New York: Routledge.
Bailey, Randall C. 1995. 'They're Nothing but Incestuous Bastards: The Polemical Use of Sex and Sexuality in Hebrew Canon Narratives.' In *Reading from this Place: Social Location and Biblical Interpretation in the United States*, ed. Fernando F. Segovia and Mary Ann Tolbert. Minneapolis: Fortress.
Bailey, Randall C., Tat-Siong Benny Liew and Fernando F. Segovia. 2009. 'Toward Minority Biblical Criticism: Framework, Contours, Dynamics.' In *They Were All Together in One Place? Toward Minority Biblical Criticism*, ed. Randall C. Bailey, Tat-Siong Benny Liew and Fernando F. Segovia. Semeia Studies 57; Atlanta: Society of Biblical Literature.
Bal, Mieke. 1988. *Death and Dissymmetry: The Politics of Coherence in the Book of Judges*. Chicago: University of Chicago Press.
Bal, Mieke. 1991. 'A Body of Writing: Judges 19.' *Continuum* 1: 110–26.

Bhabha, Homi K. 1994. *The Location of Culture*. London: Routledge.
Bird, Phyllis. 1989. '"To Play the Harlot": An Inquiry into an Old Testament Metaphor.' In *Gender and Difference in Ancient Israel*, ed. Peggy L. Day; Minneapolis: Fortress.
Block, Daniel I. 1999. *Judges, Ruth*. New American Commentary 6; Nashville: B & H.
Bohmbach, Karla G. 1999. 'Conventions/Contraventions: The Meaning of Public and Private for the Judges 19 Concubine.' *Journal for the Study of the Old Testament* 83: 83–98.
Boling, Robert G. 1975. *Judges*. Anchor Bible 6a; Garden City: Doubleday.
Butler, Trent C. 2009. *Judges*. Word Biblical Commentary 8; Nashville and Dallas: Thomas Nelson.
Carden, Michael. 1999. 'Homophobia and Rape in Sodom and Gibeah: A Response to Ken Stone.' *Journal for the Study of the Old Testament* 82: 83–96.
Cheng, Patrick S. 2002. 'Multiplicity and Judges 19: Constructing a Queer Asian Pacific American Biblical Hermeneutic.' *Semeia* 90–91: 119–33.
Dirlik, Arif, ed. 2001. *Chinese on the American Frontier*. Lanham: Rowman & Littlefield.
Donaldson, Laura E. 1992. *Decolonizing Feminisms: Race, Gender, and Empire Building*. Chapel Hill and London: University of North Carolina Press.
Eng, David L. 2001. *Racial Castration: Managing Masculinity in Asian America*. Durham and London: Duke University Press.
Espiritu, Yen Le. 1992. *Asian American Panethnicity: Bridging Institutions and Identities*. Philadelphia: Temple University Press.
Exum, J. Cheryl. 1993. *Fragmented Women: Feminist (Sub)versions of Biblical Narratives*. Journal for the Study of the Old Testament Supplement Series 163; Sheffield: JSOT Press.
Eynikel, Erik. 2005. 'Judges 19–21, An "Appendix:" Rape, Murder, War and Abduction.' *Communio Viatorum* 47: 101–15.
Fanon, Frantz. 1963. *The Wretched of the Earth*, trans. Richard Philcox. New York: Grove.
Fernandez, Eleazar S. 1970. 'Exodus-toward-Egypt: Filipino-Americans' Struggle to Realize the Promised Land in America.' In *Voices from the Margin: Interpreting the Bible in the Third World*, ed. R. S. Sugirtharajah. 3rd edn.; Maryknoll, NY: Orbis.
Fernandez, Eleazar S. 2013. 'Multiple Locations-Belongings and Power Differentials: Lenses for a Liberating Biblical Hermeneutic.' In *Soundings in Cultural Criticism: Perspectives and Methods in Culture, Power, and Identity in the New Testament*, ed. Francisco Lozada Jr. and Greg Cary. Minneapolis: Fortress.
Fewell, Danna Nolan and David M. Gunn. 1993. *Gender, Power and Promise: The Subject of the Bible's First Story*. Nashville: Abingdon.

Fields, Weston W. 1992. 'The Motif "Night as Danger" Associated with Three Biblical Destruction Narratives.' In *'Sha'arei Talmon': Studies in the Bible, Qumran, and the Ancient Near East Presented to Shemaryahu Talmon*, ed. Michael Fishbane and Emanuel Tov. Winona Lake: Eisenbrauns.

Fokkelman, Jan P. 1992. 'Structural Remarks on Judges 9 and 19.' In *'Sha'arei Talmon': Studies in the Bible, Qumran, and the Ancient Near East Presented to Shemaryahu Talmon*, ed. Michael Fishbane and Emanuel Tov. Winona Lake: Eisenbrauns.

Foskett, Mary F. and Jeffrey Kah-Jin Kuan, ed. 2006. *Ways of Being, Ways of Reading: Asian American Biblical Interpretation*. St. Louis: Chalice.

Frymer-Kensky, Tikva. 2006. *Studies in Bible and Feminist Criticism*. Philadelphia: The Jewish Publication Society.

Greenstein, Edward L. 1995. 'The Firstborn Plague and the Reading Process.' In *Pomegranates and Golden Bells:* Studies in *Biblical, Jewish, and Near Eastern Ritual, Law and Literature in Honor of Jacob Milgrom*, ed. David P. Wright, David Noel Freedman and Avi Hurvitz. Winona Lake, IN: Eisenbrauns.

Jones-Warsaw, Koala. 1994. 'Toward a Womanist Hermeneutic: A Reading of Judges 19–21.' *Journal of the Interdenominational Theological Center* 22: 18–35.

Kamuf, Peggy. 1988. *Signature Pieces on the Institution of Authorship*. Ithaca and London: Cornell University Press.

Kavanagh, Thomas M. 1982–1983. 'Rousseau's Lévite d'Ephraim: Dream, Text, and Synthesis.' *Eighteenth-Century Studies* 16: 141–61.

Keefe, Alice A. 1993. 'Rapes of Women/Wars of Men.' *Semeia* 61: 79–97.

Kim, Uriah Yong-Hwan. 2006. 'The *Realpolitik* of Liminality in Josiah's Kingdom and Asian America.' In *Ways of Being, Ways of Reading: Asian American Biblical Interpretation*, ed. Mary F. Foskett and Jeffrey Kah-Jin Kuan. St. Louis: Chalice.

Kochin, Michael S. 2007. 'Living with the Bible: Jean-Jacques Rousseau Reads Judges 19–21.' Hebraic Political Studies 3: 301–25.

Koltun-Fromm, Naomi. 2010. *Hermeneutics of Holiness: Ancient Jewish and Christian Notions of Sexuality and Religious Community*. Oxford and New York: Oxford University Press.

Kriger, Diane. 2010. 'A Re-Embracement of Judges 19: Challenging Public-Private Boundaries.' In *Vixens Disturbing Vineyards: Embarrassment and Embracement of Scripture. Festshrift in Honor of* Harry Fox *(lebeit Yoreh)*, ed. Tzemah Yoreh, Audrey Glazer and Justin Jaron Lewis; Boston: Academic Studies.

Kuan, Jeffrey Kah-Jin. 2000. 'Diasporic Reading of a Diasporic Text: Identity Politics and Race Relations and the Book of Esther.' In *The Bible and Postcolonialism*, 3, ed. Fernando F. Segovia. Sheffield: Sheffield Academic Press.

Lapsley, Jaqueline E. 2005. *Whispering the Word: Hearing Women's Stories in the Old Testament*. Louisville: Westminster John Knox.

Lee, Jung-Young. 1995. *Marginality: The Key to Multicultural Theology*. Minneapolis: Fortress.

Lee, Sang Hyun. 2003. 'Marginality as Coerced Liminality: Toward an Understanding of the Context of Asian American Theology.' In *Realizing the America of Our Hearts: Theological Voices of Asian Americans*, ed. Fumitaka Matsuoka and Eleazar S. Fernandez. St. Louis: Chalice.

Liew, Tat-Siong Benny. 2008. *What Is Asian American Biblical Hermeneutics? Reading the New Testament*. Honolulu: University of Hawai'i Press.

Liew, Tat-Siong Benny. 2008. 'When Margins Become Common Ground: Questions of and for Biblical Studies.' In *Still at the Margins: Biblical Scholarship Fifteen Years after 'Voices from the Margin,'* ed. R. S. Sugirtharah. London; New York: T & T Clark.

R. S. Sugirtharah. 2012. 'What Has Been Done? What Can We Learn? Racial/Ethnic Minority Readings of the Bible in the United States.' In *The Future of the Biblical Past: Envisioning Biblical Studies on a Global Key*, ed. Roland Boer and Fernando F. Segovia. Semeia Studies 66; Atlanta: Society of Biblical Literature.

Roland Boer. 2013. 'Colorful Readings: Racial/Ethnic Minority Readings of the New Testament in the United States.' In *Soundings in Cultural Criticism: Perspectives and Methods in Culture, Power, and Identity in the New Testament*, ed. Francisco Lozada Jr. and Greg Carey. Minneapolis: Fortress.

Lowe, Lisa. 1991. *Critical Terrains: French and British Orientalisms*. Ithaca: Cornell University Press.

Lowe, Lisa. 1996. *Immigrant Acts: On Asian American Cultural Politics*. Durham and London: Duke University Press.

Marshall, John W. 2008. 'Hybridity and Reading Romans 13.' *Journal for the Study of the New Testament* 31: 157–78.

Matsuoka, Fumitaka and Eleazar S. Fernandez, ed. 2003. *Realizing the America of Our Hearts: Theological Voices of Asian Americans*. St. Louis: Chalice.

Moore, Stephen D. 2006. *Empire and Apocalypse: Postcolonialism and the New Testament*. Sheffield: Sheffield Phoenix Press.

Moster, David Z. 2015. 'The Levite of Judges 19–21.' *Journal of Biblical Literature* 134: 721–30.

Müllner, Ilse. 1999. 'Lethal Differences: Sexual Violence as Violence against Others in Judges 19.' In *Judges: A Feminist Companion to the Bible, 2nd Series*, ed. Athalya Brenner. Sheffield: Sheffield Academic Press.

Mura, David. 1994. 'A Shift in Power, a Sea Change in the Arts: Asian American Constructions.' In *The State of Asian America: Activism and Resistance in the 1990s*, ed. Karin Aguilar-San Juan. Boston: South End Press.

Nakashima Brock, Rita. 2007. 'Cooking without Recipes: Interstitial Integrity.' In *Off the Menu: Asian and Asian North American Women's Religion and Theology*, ed. Rita Nakashima Brock, Jung Ha Kim, Kwok Pui-Lan and Seung Ai Yang. Louisville and London: Westminster John Knox.

Ng, Andrew Hock-Soon. 2007. 'Revisiting Judges 19: A Gothic Perspective.' *Journal for the Study of the Old Testament* 32: 199–215.

Ng, Greer Anne Wenh-In. 2003. 'Land of Maple and Lands of Bamboo.' In *Realizing the America of Our Hearts: Theological Voices of Asian Americans*, ed. Fumitaka Matsuoka and Eleazar S. Fernandez. St. Louis: Chalice.

Ngan, Lai Ling Elizabeth. 2007. 'Bitter Melon, Bitter Delight: Reading Jeremiah Reading Me.' In *Off the Menu: Asian and Asian North American Women's Religion and Theology*, ed. Rita Nakashima Brock, Jung Ha Kim, Kwok Pui-Lan and Seung Ai Yang. Louisville and London: Westminster John Knox.

Olson, Dennis T. 2010. 'Literary and Rhetorical Criticism.' In *Methods for Exodus*, ed. Thomas B. Dozeman. Cambridge: Cambridge University Press.

Penchansky, David. 1992. 'Staying the Night: Intertextuality in Genesis and Judges.' In *Reading between Texts: Intertextuality and the Hebrew Bible*, ed. Danna Nolan Fewell. Louisville: Westminster John Knox.

Phan, Peter C. 1999. 'Betwixt and Between: Doing Theology with Memory and Imagination.' In *Journeys at the Margin: Toward an Autobiographical Theology in American-Asian Perspective*, ed. Peter C. Phan and Jung Young Lee. Collegeville, MN: Liturgical Press.

Phan, Peter C. 2003. 'The Dragon and the Eagle: Toward a Vietnamese American Theology.' In *Realizing the America of Our Hearts: Theological Voices of Asian Americans*, ed. Fumitaka Matsuoka and Eleazar S. Fernandez. St. Louis: Chalice.

Phan, Peter C. and Jung Young Lee, ed. 1999. *Journeys at the Margin: Toward an Autobiographical Theology in American-Asian Perspective*. Collegeville, MN: The Liturgical Press.

Radhakrishnan, R. 1994. 'Is the Ethnic "Authentic" in the Diaspora?' In *The State of Asian America: Activism and Resistance in the 1990s*, ed. Karin Aguilar-San Juan. Boston: South End Press, 1994.

Reinhartz, Adele. 1998. *'Why Ask My Name?' Anonymity and Identity in Biblical Narrative*. Oxford and New York: Oxford University Press.

Reis, Pamela Tamarkin. 2006. 'The Levite's Concubine: New Light on a Dark Story.' *Scandinavian Journal of the Old Testament* 20: 125–46.

Rousseau, Jean-Jacques. 1959. *Oeuvres complètes*, ed. B. Gagnebin and M. Raymond. 4 vols.; Paris: Gallimard.

Rousseau, Jean-Jacques. 1998. *Essay on the Origin of Languages and Writings Related to Music*, trans., ed. John T. Stott. *The Collected Writings of Rousseau* 7; Hanover and London: University Press of New England for Dartmouth College.

Sandoval, Chela. 2000. *Methodology of the Oppressed*. Theory out of Bounds 18; Minneapolis and London: University of Minnesota Press.
Sano, Roy I. 2003. 'From Context to Context: Cognitive Dissonance.' In *Realizing the America of Our Hearts: Theological Voices of Asian Americans*, ed. Fumitaka Matsuoka and Eleazar S. Fernandez. St. Louis: Chalice.
Schneider, Tammi J. 2000. *Judges*. Collegeville, MN: Liturgical Press.
Schüssler Fiorenza, Elizabeth. 2007. *The Power of the Word: Scripture and the Rhetoric of Empire*. Minneapolis: Fortress.
Segovia, Fernando F. 1995. 'Toward a Hermeneutics of the Diaspora: A Hermeneutics of Otherness and Engagement.' In *Reading from this Place: Social Location and Biblical Interpretation in the United States*, ed. Fernando F. Segovia and Mary Ann Tolbert. Minneapolis: Fortress.
Segovia, Fernando F. 1995. 'Toward Intercultural Criticism: A Reading Strategy from the Diaspora.' in *Reading from this Place: Social Location and Biblical Interpretation in Global Perspective*, ed. Fernando F. Segovia and Mary Ann Tolbert. Minneapolis: Fortress.
Soggin, J. Alberto. 1981. *Judges*, trans. J. S. Bowden. Old Testament Library; Philadelphia: Westminster.
Stone, Ken. 1995. 'Gender and Homosexuality in Judges 19: Subject-Honor, Object-Shame?' *Journal for the Study of the Old Testament* 67: 87–107.
Sugirtharajah, R.S. 1996. 'Orientalism, Ethnonationalism and Transnationalism: Shifting Identities and Biblical Interpretation.' In *Ethnicity and the Bible*, ed. Mark G. Brett. Biblical Interpretation Series 19; Leiden: Brill, 427.
Thompson, John L. 2001. *Writing the Wrongs: Women of the Old Testament among Biblical Commentators from Philo through the Reformation*. Oxford New York: Oxford University Press.
Takaki, Ronald. 1989. *Strangers from a Different Shore: A History of Asian Americans*. New York and London: Little, Brown and Company.
Takaki, Ronald. 1990. *Iron Cages: Race and Culture in Nineteenth-Century America*. Oxford and New York: Oxford University Press.
Tran, Jonathan. 2010. 'Why Asian American Christianity has no Future: The Over Against, Leaving Behind, and Separation From of Asian American Christian Identity.' *SANACS Journal* 2: 13–56.
Trible, Phyllis. 1984. *Texts of Terror: Literary-Feminist Readings of Biblical Literature*. Philadelphia: Fortress.
Tuan, Mia. 1998. *Forever Foreigners or Honorary Whites: The Asian Ethnic Experience Today*. New Brunswick and London: Rutgers University Press.
Wan, Sze-Kar. 2000. 'Does Diaspora Identity Imply Some Sort of Universality? An Asian-American Reading of Galatians.' In *The Bible and Postcolonialism*, 3, ed. Fernando F. Segovia. Sheffield: Sheffield Academic Press.
Wan, Sze-Kar. 2006. 'Betwixt and Between: Toward a Hermeneutic of Hyphenation.' In *Ways of Being, Ways of Reading: Asian American Biblical*

Interpretation, ed. Mary F. Foskett and Jeffrey Kah-Jin Kuan. St. Louis: Chalice.

Warrior, Allen. 1970. 'A Native American Perspective: Canaanites, Cowboys, and Indians.' In *Voices from the Margin: Interpreting the Bible in the Third World*, ed. R.S. Sugirtharajah. Maryknoll, NY: Orbis.

Webb, Barry G. 1987. *The Book of Judges: An Integrated Reading*. Journal for the Study of the Old Testament Supplement Series 46; Sheffield: JSOT Press.

Wong, Nelli. 1981. 'When I was Growing Up.' In *This Bridge Called my Back: Writings by Radical Women of Color*, ed. Cherríe Moraga and Gloria Anzaldúa. New York: Women of Color Press.

Yamada, Frank M. 2006. 'Constructing Hybridity and Heterogeneity: Asian American Biblical Interpretation from a Third-Generation Perspective.' In *Ways of Being, Ways of Reading: Asian American Biblical Interpretation*, ed. Mary F. Foskett and Jeffrey Kah-Jin Kuan. St. Louis: Chalice.

Yamada, Frank M. 2009. 'What Does Manzanar Have to Do with Eden? A Japanese American Interpretation of Genesis 2–3.' In *They Were All Together in One Place? Toward Minority Biblical Criticism*, ed. Randall C. Bailey, Tat-Siong Benny Liew and Fernando F. Segovia; Atlanta: Society of Biblical Literature.

Yee, Gale A. 1995. 'Ideological Criticism: Judges 17–21 and the Dismembered Body.' In *Judges and Method: New Approaches in Biblical Studies*, ed. Gale A. Yee. Minneapolis: Fortress.

Yee, Gale A. 2009. '"She Stood in Tears Amid the Alien Corn": Ruth, the Perpetual Foreigner and Model Minority.' In *They Were All Together in One Place? Toward Minority Biblical Criticism*, ed. Randall C. Bailey, Tat-Siong Benny Liew and Fernando F. Segovia. Atlanta: Society of Biblical Literature.

Young, Robert J.C. 1995. *Colonial Desire: Hybridity in Theory, Culture and Race*. London and New York: Routledge.

CHAPTER 6

Epilogue: Scenes from Afar

So I was ready to imagine that the world in which I found myself in London was something less than the perfect world I had striven towards. As a child in Trinidad I had put this world at a far distance, in London perhaps. In London now I was able to put this perfect world at another time, an earlier time. The mental and emotional processes were the same.

V.S. Naipaul

There was an arrestive quality to the voice, a throaty gurgling. Its reverberations in the room could rouse a pupil from the languor of the stifling afternoon heat. No lackluster performance would escape M's eye or that back-stiffening tone so effective in turning the tide of sloth. Practical Criticism was her domain at our mission school. I learned well, early on, to have at hand adequate, if clumsy, definitions for the technical terms of the craft, at least the ones assigned for the week. The spur to my discipline was the indelible memory of a previous humiliation: my stuttered attempt at an excuse, the strained containment of a full-blown blub, the posture of submission by a form already overburdened by adolescence and the burgeoning awareness of an insipid sexuality. M's displeasure was unyielding, her piercing stare unavoidable. A loosening of the skin on the outer sides of her eyes and a deepening of the creases there was the slight signal of her pleasure, her halting approval. Under her surveillance, my hands searched for the recognizable gestures of contrition. Groveling, no matter the circumstance, was appropriate. I was careful to not betray

---

V. S. Naipaul, *The Enigma of Arrival* (New York: Vintage Books, 1987), 131.

the semblance of insolence. Relief came only with the deflection of her attention, the reflex of a perceived lapse of attention in another part of the room perhaps.

The taut fabric across her bust was a contrast to her pursed lips. The latter feature was regrettable. It didn't quite rise to a smile, but had rather the misfortune of a contrived congeniality missing its mark. A rhythmic rising of the left shoulder in her stride brought a single fold to the front of her pristine blouse. Her craggy neck shifted ever so gently with the lifting of the shoulder. The force of the gait was a scowl. Was it self-assurance or the seriousness of an evangelistic zeal teetering on disdain? It all smacked of smugness in our tropical eyes, a confidence glaringly absent in us, in me. But why was she here in steamy Singapore? Why this second-rate, backwater island that fancied itself a nation? There were rumors of a 'poor fit' in British schools, tales of a debonair presumption unbendable to the still patriarchal spirit of the guild. Maybe it was her gray steely mien, so off-putting to a burly principal's eye for an underling pliable to an unfolding agenda for self-congratulation and advancement, the head's. Or, maybe, it was a scandal, a misplaced affection for the husband of the wrong woman. The injury might have sparked weavings of insidious tawdry tales, worming their way into the corridors and staffrooms. The excitement of a fresh start, an adventure in the Orient, the chance to break free of the clutches of a stodgy, man-serving order—was this what she thought? Why would she leave the salubrious sophistication of the West? Why remove oneself to the edges of a recently resplendent empire? In any case, here she was in sweltering Singapore, on Churchill's erstwhile bastion of military might in the East, Albion's pride in the South China Sea, schooling us in the cadences of civility.

Her Scottish brogue barked in our tanned pallid faces the aesthetic merits of double entendre, of Inscape in Hopkins, of dramatic irony in Shakespeare. Her tartan tongue unfurled Oldham's—our school's founder—vision of 'a beacon of truth and light.' In the timbre of her tone was the melancholy of the pipes of the Boy's Brigade at Founder's Day parades. In her silences rang the familiar, still now dulcet, sounds of Scotland the Brave. The kilts danced to the rhythms of the march. Her lessons were a reminder of the euphony of our blessed inheritance, the English language with its precisions and its glorious rhythms freighted with the sempiternal principles to guide us into wholeness. It, she, was our hope, my lifeline out of the vast smallness of Asia.

Thursday afternoons were sometimes islands of respite from our lessons. For reasons still obscure to me, M would steal half an hour, on occasion, to regale us with tales of her youth. There might have been a story of an encounter with an inebriated stationmaster or of excursions beyond curfew at a boarding school. The details escape me. These were never my concern. The narratives were but scaffolding on which to project the imagined rhythms of English life, material gleaned from Enid Blyton and Agatha Christie. My palimpsestic eye invented, *rewrote* her narratives, with mundane (yet veritably sublime in my estimation) episodes of playful exchange on the storied 'commons' of Blyton's making. The football games of these settings were culled from the fictive sequences of Michael Hardcastle. The stuff of the stories, mine and M's, was from afar, lodged in the pages of books about things I knew nothing of. It was a country in abstract. Like the comics at the local stands on the five-foot way, the tales were the issue of a land quite beyond my ken. In dribs and drabs, they kindled in me a longing, a sense of the loss of something never possessed. The absence filled my thoughts. The words, the forms of the sequences, were vehicles for the projections of malcontent. They were my private escape from my shadowed existence, the inescapable sense that things were happening *elsewhere*.

Beyond M's oasis was another world, mine by heritage and presence. It was a place teeming with the raucous commerce of Smith Street, full with sweaty bodies plying the stalls for the week's provisions. Keong Saik Road was my corner in this world of Singapore's Chinatown. Saturdays meant a visit with *a gong*—maternal grandfather—to my aunt's store across the road from his home. The shelves were dusty, sparsely stocked with sundry household items: hair cream, toothpaste, ear picks. I couldn't see, in hindsight, how she made a living. I don't recall witnessing a purchase. There were no customers, just visitors, incessant loud Cantonese dribble: the exchange of gossip. Two doors down, hugging the inner side of the recessed walkway typical of the prewar urban scape, was the newsstand we'd frequent on the way back to *a gong*'s place. The rows of candied offerings had a selection of sweetened preserved foods: arbutus, tamarind, cuttlefish, dried plums, sugared nutmeg. Dangling on pegs above these were comic books, folded sheets of a brownish hue that left a musky smell on our moist fingers. These were the *Dandy*s and the *Beano*s, now to my mind seemingly misplaced reminders of our taste for empire. A packet of dried arbutus and a cowboy's revolver with belt, buckle, and holster—my choice of a toy for the week—would be my haul. Then it was back to *a gong*'s for an hour on his knee at the window surveying the traffic below. Such were the small pleasures of the morning.

The afternoon would have in store the throng of Temple Street, Chinatown's wet market several blocks away. In my mother's tow, we'd make the familiar stops. There was often a reminder to work hard at school as we glimpsed the fishmonger's raw blistered hands tearing at the scales. Inevitably, mother's disparaging remarks about the quality of the goods would accompany the transaction. Similar exchanges would precede purchases at the greengrocer. 'Is the *gai lan* fresh?' 'Why so expensive this week?' 'Surely you're bluffing me.' The brand of Confucian social protocol I knew didn't carry the self-deprecating niceties of familial exchange into haggling with street vendors, certainly not on Temple Street. Perhaps it was the stench of the exposed innards of slaughtered beasts or the moisture between the toes of our sandaled feet that signaled our place in the subculture of the street market. The place seemed a mixture of life and decay, of consumption and refuse, of sumptuous dining and bloody slaughter. There was none of the clean lines of New Criticism, of M's sessions. Tidiness was abhorrent to this world. Beside putridness were bowls of fragrant noodles with sides of glistening barbequed pork. Rice with mixed meats fresh and preserved cooked in clay pots by drains cluttered with the cast-offs of frenzied trading.

The way back to *a gong's* took us past the death houses of Smith Street. These were shops stocked with the desirables of the departed. Currency, cars, houses, appliances, and the trappings of wealth were available in wood and paper, ready for the flames that would send them to the other side. The colors were the shades of prosperity, of red and pink. Acquisitions in that other place, of course, would come only through a relative's contributions from this side. The scent in the air was of incense. The heavy sweetish odor made the mood somber, yet strangely festive. Death lacked the grimness, the finality it bore elsewhere. Grief, at the wakes I'd been at, was reserved for the viewing of the casket, for the procession to the grave, for the lowering of the box. Beyond these times, in the makeshift tents for guests, was spirited gambling and drinking. Children's play wound its way around adult gaming. In the midst of death were the lusts of the living.

Years removed, from the wintry sterility of Minnesota, the incongruity of the two spaces seems clearer, larger. Hindsight, as they say, has the clarity of an invented neatness. Its sights, however, are masturbatory, the splatter of remembered forms. The sensation of a pining for a greater being remains. It is the sense of myself, even now, as a *displacement* from glory, perhaps the one of M's world. The hunger seeks a plenitude, an escape from parochialism, from a mantle of shame, of vapidity. Such is the wicked restlessness of the hybrid heart, a soul not *in* the in-between space but shuttling back and forth across the chasm. The heart tarries on the side of one, but always with a feeling of the loss of the other, always ashamed for the occlusion of the other, always only *almost* here or there at any one time. The cleavage remains. I think across the disparate paths. There is no other way, no fleeing the resonance of one in the tones of the other. Oscillating, hesitating, always, I *see* no other way. This little book has been my confession.

Index

A
Abjection, 19, 27, 76, 87, 90, 124, 126–128, 172, 177
Achenbach, Reinhard, 17, 92n10
Aesthetic object, 8, 9, 14–16, 26, 141
Ambivalence, 20, 90, 119, 161, 162–163, 175, 179–181, 187, 190
Ammonites, 118, 125, 128–129
Analogical imagination, 5, 89, 107
Anderson, Cheryl B., 1, 2, 12
Apostasy, 84, 85, 89, 125
Asian American hermeneutics, 3, 4, 156, 159, 173, 178
Assembly (of Israel), 20, 109, 117–119, 122, 127, 135, 140

B
Bach, Alice, 81, 99n56, 167–168
Baden, Joel S., 47n7
Bailey, Randall C., 125, 128, 157, 193n3, 198n60
Bakhtin, Mikhail, 8, 46n6, 121, 128
Bal, Mieke, 168, 172, 182, 200n82
Bar-On, Shimon, 48n12, 50n24
Barthes, Roland, 8, 14, 90n1, 94n17
Bhabha, Homi, 7, 20, 113, 161–163, 179–180, 188, 189, 190, 192
Biculturalism, 160
Binary opposition, 90, 111, 171
Bird, Phyllis, 101n78, 198n60
Blanks, 12–16
  See also Gaps
Blemish, 74–76, 127, 177
Bloom, Harold, 87
Boer, Roland, 99n56, 102n81, 121–122, 137, 142n1
Bohmbach, Karla G., 174
Boyarin, Daniel, 4, 21n5
Brenner, Athalya, 97n45
Brooke, George J., 45n1, 45n2, 46n3
Burnt offering, 74

C
Carmichael, Calum, 91n3, 100n72
Cheng, Patrick S., 173, 178
Chia, Philip, 142n1
Chief priest, 60, 71–73, 77, 79, 82, 85, 86, 87
Childs, Brevard, 40, 41, 46n7
Clitoridectomy, 112
Consistency building, 11, 12, 13, 16
Corpse contamination, 65, 72, 77, 78, 79, 177

D

Davidson, Steed Vernyl, 134
D (Deuteronomic source), 135
Decolonization/colonization, 3, 179, 191
Defilement, 62–66, 68, 76–77, 80, 81, 87, 89
Déjà lu, 61
Desecration, 63–66, 73, 76, 79, 83, 85, 87, 95, 177, 183
Destroyer, the, 35, 36, 38, 48n17, 88
Diaspora, 7, 184, 191, 193
Divorce, 82, 107, 115, 117, 124, 131–132
Donaldson, Laura E., 113, 132, 138, 148n93
Douglas, Mary, 5, 61
Dube, Musa, 114, 133

E

Edomites, 118, 119
E (Elohistic source), 27
Egyptians, 40, 51, 128, 176
Ellens, Deborah, 99n56, 130–131
Empire, 114, 129, 133, 134, 140, 141, 160, 161, 162, 163, 188, 212, 213
Endogamy, 82, 89, 123
Eng, David L., 116, 192n1
Espiritu, Yen Le, 192n1
Essentialism, 159
Exum, J. Cheryl, 99n56, 198n59

F

Fanon, Frantz, 112, 113
Feinstein, Eve Levavi, 100n64, 101n77
Feminism, 108–114, 116
Feminist criticism, 3, 4, 19, 107, 108, 109, 110, 115, 133

Fernandez, Eleazar, 185, 186, 190, 191, 192n1, 193n7
Fields, Weston W., 164, 165
Firstlings, 40, 41, 58, 88
Fishbane, Michael, 98n56
Fokkelman, Jan P., 165, 167, 169
Footbinding, 112
Foucault, Michel, 94n21
Frymer-Kensky, Tikva, 98n56, 198n59

G

Gandhi, Leela, 113, 114
Gaps, 6, 8, 12–13, 16, 55, 67, 77, 89
  See also Blanks
Genital discharges, 64, 77, 87
Gestalt, 11–13, 16, 67, 90, 120, 129, 142, 173
Green, Barbara, 46n6
Guilt offering, 64–68, 76, 85

H

Haberman, Bonna Devorah, 82, 99
Halakhic Letter from Qumran (Dead Sea Scrolls), 66
Hall, Stuart, 108, 142n2, 184
Harlotry, 84
Hegemony, 7, 20, 110, 132, 134, 140, 142, 161, 162, 178, 185, 187, 191
Hermeneutic code, 90n1
Heteroglossia, 128
H (Holiness Legislation), 17, 101n77
Homogeneity, 112
Houtman, Cornelis, 47n9, 48n14, 50n26
Hybridity, 7, 20, 156, 160–163, 179, 184, 191–192

I

Ideation, 6, 12, 15, 16, 69
Imperialism, 20, 21, 110, 113, 114, 115, 116, 123–124, 132–135, 139–142, 162, 184, 189
Incest, 119, 125–128
Inner-biblical allusion, 60
Interculturation, 158, 191
Intertextuality, 21n5
Iser, Wolfgang, 2, 8–13, 15, 16, 19, 26, 27, 58, 63, 90n1

J

Jeremiah Apocrypha (Dead Sea Scrolls), 45n2
Jewish Antiquities (Josephus), 198n63
J (Yahwistic source), 47n10, 120

K

Kamuf, Peggy, 180–183, 187, 200n82
Keefe, Alice A., 178, 197n52
Kermode, Frank, 13
Kirk-Duggan, Cheryl, 130
Knohl, Israel, 17, 49n19, 92n10, 94n22
Koltun-Fromm, Naomi, 101n78
Kuan, Jeffrey Kah-Jin, 142n1, 159, 179, 184, 190, 192n1, 193n7
Kwok Pui-lan, 112, 134, 143n4, 148n93, 158
Kyriarchy, 114, 132

L

Lacan, Jacques, 113
Levine, Baruch, 91n6, 95n28
Levinson, Bernard M., 17, 50n26, 92n10
Levites, 3, 5, 6, 13, 19, 56–60, 62, 87, 88, 89, 100n64, 197n55
Liew, Tat-Siong Benny, 157–159, 178, 179, 184–186, 190, 192n1, 193n3, 193n7
Liminality, 160, 193n7
Lipka, Hilary, 72–73, 101n77
Loomba, Ania, 113, 122, 123, 124
Lowe, Lisa, 187, 194n19

M

Malfeasance, 63, 64, 65, 67, 68, 83, 85, 86, 95n28, 98n53, 126
Marginalization, 90, 114, 160, 173, 178, 187
McClintock, Anne, 132, 136, 137, 139
McKinlay, Judith E., 124, 125, 133
Metonymy, 94n22
Milgrom, Jacob, 66, 72, 80, 91n3, 94n22, 95n27, 95n28, 98n53, 101n77
Mimicry, 7, 41, 161, 162, 179, 188, 189
Minority criticism, 157, 158
Miscegenation, 82, 123, 179
Moabites, 118, 125, 128–129, 141
Mohanty, Chandra Talpade, 110, 111, 112
Moore, Stephen D., 162
Müllner, Ilse, 197n52, 197n55
Mura, David, 185, 186

N

Najman, Hindy, 45n1, 45n2, 46n3
Nazirite, 5, 56, 60, 62–68, 71–79, 86–89, 94n22, 96n42, 127, 177
Ngan, Lai Ling Elizabeth, 202n109
Nicholas of Lyra, 175
Nihan, Christophe, 92n10, 96n40, 101n77
Noble, Denise, 116
Noth, Martin, 47n7, 47n11, 56–57, 59, 90n2, 91n3, 91n6, 95n28, 96n42

O

Oaths, 60, 67
 See also Vows
Offspring, 31, 41, 44, 80, 82, 119, 123, 125, 126, 127, 130, 171, 174
 See also Semen; Seed
Orientalism, 194n17, 194n20
Othering, 90, 115, 122
Others, 2, 5, 44, 56, 58, 59, 61, 69, 76, 112, 127, 130, 133, 142, 155, 158, 160, 169, 178, 182, 185, 187
Otto, Eckart, 92n10

P

Passover, 3, 19, 20, 26, 27, 30, 31, 32, 33, 34, 36–44, 47n10, 48n17, 49n19, 49n22, 50n24, 50n26, 89, 155, 169–173, 176–177, 189
Phan, Peter C., 158, 159, 190, 191, 192n1, 193n7
Polygamy, 112
Polyphony, 46n6, 128
Postcolonialism, 109, 115, 142n1, 148n93, 193
Postcolonial theory, 3, 109, 115
P (Priestly source), 50n24, 91n9
Pressler, Caroline, 130, 131, 148n91
Proairetic code, 90n1
Pseudo-Ezekiel (Dead Sea Scrolls), 45n2

R

Race, 3, 89, 111, 114, 116, 118, 123–126, 132, 135, 137–140, 142, 176, 179, 191, 193
Radhakrishnan, R., 159, 191
Rahab, 102n81, 133–134, 141
Ram of expiation, 65
Readerly pleasures, 120, 121, 128
Register (of reading), 20
Repertoire, 13, 14, 16, 86, 89, 90, 108, 123, 132, 134, 135, 138, 157, 187
Reticence, hermeneutic of, 21, 163, 180, 187
Riffaterre, Michael, 127, 128
Römer, Thomas, 56, 59, 91n3, 92n10
Roskop, Angela, 120, 121
Rousseau, Jean-Jacques, 20, 180–184, 188–192, 200n82

S

Said, Edward, 115
Sandoval, Chela, 189, 191
Sati, 112
Schectman, Sarah, 100n64
Schleiermacher, Friedrich, 16
Schmid, Konrad, 92n10
Schüssler Fiorenza, Elizabeth, 114–116, 132, 143n4, 202n105
Schwartz, Regina M., 92n10, 124
Seed, 63, 80, 81–83, 85, 89, 126, 127, 130, 135, 139
 See also Semen; Offspring
Segovia, Fernando, 142n1, 157, 160, 193n3, 193n7, 198n60
Segregation, 60, 138, 142, 180
Semen, 63, 64, 80, 81, 82, 88, 100n64
 See also Seed; Offspring
Sharpe, Jenny, 135, 136, 138, 139
Ska, Jean-Louis, 47n7, 91n3
Skin disorders, 77, 80, 87
Sly civility, 162, 188
Stoler, Ann Laura, 114, 123, 124, 137, 139

Subaltern, 7, 20, 116, 122, 129, 140, 141, 142, 160–163, 179, 188, 190
Subjectivity, 90, 108, 121, 122, 131, 142n1, 191
Subject (of reading), 10, 14, 61, 85, 107, 108, 120, 121, 159
Sugirtharajah, R.S., 142n1, 143n4, 159

T
Third World Woman, 110
Tran, Jonathan, 186, 202n106
Trible, Phyllis, 174, 182
Tuan, Mia, 201n105

U
Unleavened bread, 32–34, 36, 39, 40, 43, 49n19, 49n22
Uterus, 3, 63, 82, 83, 85, 88, 90, 127, 130, 134, 141, 176
See also Womb

V
Vacancies, 15

Van Seters, John, 47n10, 48n16, 50n24, 120
Veil, 112
Vows, 3, 5, 19, 20, 60, 67, 87, 107, 109, 117, 127
See also Oaths

W
Wandering viewpoint, 2, 3, 4, 9, 10, 11, 13–16, 19, 20, 26, 27, 58, 69, 88, 108, 159
Wave offering, 89
Well-being offering, 60, 75, 76
Westbrook, Raymond, 148n91
Womb, 63, 80, 81, 86, 88, 100n64, 118, 127, 130, 134, 135, 139, 141, 177
See also Uterus
Wright, David P., 97n51, 202n111
Writerly pleasures, 120

Y
Yee, Gale, 172, 178, 190
Yeğenoğlu, Meyda, 113
Young, Robert J.C., 163

CPSIA information can be obtained
at www.ICGtesting.com
Printed in the USA
BVOW06*1046250617
487781BV00004B/17/P